The Virgin Homeowner

Also by Janice Papolos

The Performing Artist's Handbook
Overcoming Depression (with Demitri Papolos, M.D.)

The
Virgin Homeowner

The Essential Guide
to Owning,
Maintaining,
and Surviving
Your First Home

Janice Papolos

New York   W. W. Norton & Company   London

For information about permission to reproduce selections from this book,
write to Permissions, W. W. Norton & Company, Inc., 500 Fifth Avenue,
New York, NY 10110.

The text of this book is composed in Linotype Centennial
Composition and Manufacturing by The Haddon Craftsmen, Inc.
Book design and illustrations by Poulin & Morris Design Consultants

Library of Congress Cataloging-in-Publication Data
Papolos, Janice.
    The virgin homeowner : the essential guide to owning, maintaining,
and surviving your first home / Janice Papolos.
        p.   cm.
    Includes bibliographical references (p.   ) and index.
    ISBN 0-393-04035-6
    1. Home ownership.   I. Title
HD7267.8.PS6   1997
643'.1—dc20   96-31304
                                                        CIP

W. W. Norton & Company, Inc., 500 Fifth Avenue, New York, N.Y. 10110
http://www.wwnorton.com

W. W. Norton & Company Ltd., 10 Coptic Street, London, WC1A 1PU

3 4 5 6 7 8 9 0

For Demitri, Alex, and Jordy, my allies on the homefront

Contents

Appendices

Preface

In 1993, after the birth of our second child, and after living in New York City apartments for over twenty years, my husband and I joined the grown-up world and bought a house. While every now and then funny and disastrous scenes from *The Money Pit, Mr. Blandings Builds His Dream House,* and *Baby Boom* would surface to conscious levels, we tamped them down with assurances to ourselves that these were merely Hollywood's comedic exaggerations. We were so busy figuring out how to finance the house and negotiate this major move—physically and emotionally—we had little energy left to figure out the mysterious workings of a house and what our part would be in maintaining it. As I look back now, I am stunned that I didn't know what a new homeowner was supposed to do, not only to keep the house comfortable and running economically, but to keep disaster from coming in from every crack and crevice! I guess I thought it would all sort itself out gradually while we found our sea legs and got more comfortable in our new surroundings.

Not likely! There is no honeymoon with a house. There are things we should have been learning and doing right from the time of the inspection that would have resulted in fewer mishaps and panic-filled moments.

Part of the problem was that I had a mystified awe of the house. I swear, there were times (thankfully rare) when I viewed it as more intelligent and more powerful than we were. And while I'm in a confessional mode, there was a time or two in which I felt the house was being downright vindictive. (If you own your own home, you may understand this paranoid fantasy.)

Little by little, though, we began to learn from the plumber, the electrician, and the oil burner service men. And our friends. I kept bumping up against new vocabulary and concepts like "flashing," "creosote," and "ventilation." Since I thought flashing had something to do with elderly gentlemen in raincoats, and I'm still a little unsure as to why my furnace is not breathing enough oxygen, I'm afraid we rather amused our house "doctors."

One day, while sitting in front of the fireplace I had fortunately found out I was supposed to have cleaned (see Chapter 5, "Creosote Is a Dirty Word"), I sighed and said to my husband, Demitri: "Somebody should write a book for the virgin homeowner." He laughed and pointed a finger my way.

All right, I thought. Let me look into it. Gingerly, I broached the subject with friends and family. They were enthusiastic and proceeded immediately to tell me all the funny and perilous situations they had encountered—and survived—as first-time homeowners. It turns out that none of us are very enlightened. And we're all so very anxious.

So that's what these pages are all about: helping new homeowners level the playing field, so to speak, and become knowledgeable about and comfortable with their new habitat. Even if you aren't lucky enough to have inherited the Bob Vila gene for home repair, I think I can prove to you that taking care of a house does indeed fall under the category of "totally doable." (After all, this is coming from a woman whose greatest victory on the mechanical front prior to owning a home was the successful changing of a halogen lightbulb!)

How to Use This Book

In the best of all possible worlds, readers would come across this book just *before* they began house hunting. Starting with "Ground Zero," they could read it straight through and tour all potential homes with an informed and educated eye. Then, when the right house appeared, they could choose the right home inspector and do a bang-up job at the home inspection. Weeks later, and after the moving van departed, they would be comfortable with the systems of a house and clued in to its maintenance routines.

But life doesn't work like that. Many of you will pick this book up in the hectic days just before the move, or some months into your adventures on the domestic frontier. The ungodly time crunch of this settling-in period may not allow your reading every word from beginning to end, in one or two sittings. So let me highlight some of the important safety issues you need to take care of first.

Before you spend a night (or another night) in your new home, make sure you have *working* smoke detectors in all the right places and an emergency plan for escape in the event of a fire (read pages 378–88) and install two carbon monoxide detectors (see page 309). If your chimney doesn't have a chimney cap, call a chimney sweep and have one made for it without delay (see page 164). Have the chimney checked and cleaned at the same time. Then make sure all heating equipment is tuned up and checked before the start of the heating season (read about this on pages 306–7). If you have municipal water and didn't have your water tested for lead during the home inspection, run a test according to the directions in Chapter 9, "The Healthy House," and while you're open to that section, scan the elements of a healthy, nontoxic home so that you make informed decisions when choosing paints and any new furnishings. And by all means, if you've got a toddler or two, read Chapter 11,

"The Age of Innocence," and secure windows and stairways, check the automatic garage doors, and order any necessary safety paraphernalia before you even think of letting your little road runners loose in their new and unfamiliar environment. (And while you're checking doors and windows, make sure that they're providing the appropriate level of physical security as discussed in the first half of Chapter 8, "The Uninvited Guest, Part II.")

Once you're all relatively safe and sound, familiarize yourself with the major systems of your house by reading Chapters 2, 3, and 4. Then if the circuit breaker trips or a fuse blows or a leak develops, there'll be no cause for panic. You'll also understand what a delicate flower your septic system is and how best to keep it healthy.

And if—when all the chaos subsides—you get hit with a bit of "post-parting depression" and keenly miss your friends and former lifestyle, I hope that the last chapter, "Finally Home," is heartening as well as helpful as you go through the emotional experience of turning a house into a home and carving out a niche for yourself in a new community.

So sit down on your packing boxes, or in a corner of your probably underfurnished new home, and delve into this volume. Then get ready to appreciate what a marvelous facility a house is. Think of it. Physics and chemistry and electricity combine to give you and your loved ones shelter, warmth, comfort, and convenience. A house is a goodly thing. You keep the house; the house will keep you.

Acknowledgments

This book could not have been written without the help of the twenty experts who guided me through every system of a house as well as the many safety and environmental issues facing a homeowner today. Each individual spent hours dissecting his or her subject, dispensing advice, and supplying me with written material. And each did so with the teaching abilities of a master, and always with a gracious and good-natured humor. I am proud to be associated with and deeply indebted to Deputy Fire Marshal Fred S. Baker, Detective Michael Barrett, Charles Bassman, Neal Carley, Dennis Devlin, Gregg Gilbertson, Steve Gladstone, Larry Janesky, John Krozer, Mark LaLiberte, Steve Oldham, Susan Pedersen, Paul Peterson, Dan Quinlan, James Rossetti, Charles Schwartz, Gary Stone, Ken Swain, Dan Wilder, and Frank Wright.

I would also like to acknowledge the other professionals who responded generously to my requests for information and assistance. They are Salvatore Albicocco, Raymond Alexander, Susan and Jeffrey Baril, Robert Byrne, James Calabrese, Richard Conner, Kevin Cook, Patrick Coughlin, Jack Deal, Tim Farrelly, Michael Greenberg, Betsy Gillespie, Steve Griffin, William Hall, Daniel Hare, Joe Harrison, Don Holohan, Pat Huelman, Ken Kinsley, Gregg Malanga, Kurt Mankell, Kevin McNamara, Richard Morris, Joanne Nanavaty, Kevin O'Malley, Arthur O'Neill, Mike Poniatowski, John Prizio, King Rogers, Mary Jo Scanlon, Dwight Shackelford, Keith

Stadler, Maggie Swed, Edward Tomasulo, Peter Truss, Dianne Walsh, and Michael Vinnick.

A special thank-you to our Realtor, Jill Bregy, C.R.S, G.R.I., of Prudential Connecticut Realty, who patiently explained the inner workings of the real estate business and supplied me with extremely valuable contacts and resources.

Carol Cohen of HarperCollins Interactive was the first to validate the idea of this book when I broached it timidly over the telephone one snowy January evening, and it was her enthusiasm that jump-started the proposal process. My superb literary agent, Pam Bernstein, used her expertise to shape the proposal and steer it to Gerald Howard at Norton. His astute ideas and suggestions greatly enhanced the manuscript, and I understand completely why he is held in such esteem in the literary world. He was always supportive and sensitive, and it was a privilege to work with him. Additionally, I am grateful to copy editor extraordinaire Ted Johnson. I was lucky to have a master of English as well as a maven on houses scrutinize these pages. Three other Norton professionals deserve my thanks: Sean Desmond, Andy Marasia, and Deborah Morton Hoyt.

My new neighbors in Westport shared their war stories, introduced me to professionals, and offered encouragement and advice. Thank you to Laurie Nelson Austin, Karen and Rusty Ford, Helen Garten, Marina and Ward Leo, Elizabeth Lewin, Mitsuyo and Richard Pactor, Jeanette Linsey, Dewey and Susan Loselle, Lynn and Jason Miller, Roselle Shubin, and Ruth and Alan Winnick.

I would also like to publicly acknowledge my husband, Demitri, without whose insistence we'd still be apartment-bound. I owe him my subject as well as my gratitude for all his support, love, and assistance throughout the writing of this book.

And finally, the following people deserve special mention for their unique and very personal contributions. With all my heart I thank Rose Belfiore Albicocco, Beatrice Cohen, Rob Cohen, Elin Defrin, Deborah Falcone, Mary Fiedorek, Scott Franz, Cheryl Gallan, Dianna Mitzner, Mervyn M. Peskin, M.D., J. Mark Rubenstein, Victoria Secunda, Shel Secunda, Denise Shekerjian, Karin Smaat, Elsa Thomas, Harriet White, and especially Barbara L. Sand.

But First, a Word About Money . . .

Before we begin, let me say a few words about the eye-popping estimates for home repairs you're going to see scattered throughout this text. They may be a bit on the high side, because many of them are quotes from a metropolitan area, but house repairs are not cheap, not in Arizona, not in Alabama. As my friend David Wright from the tiny town of Edenton, North Carolina, likes to say, "My house accepts contributions only in hundred-dollar bills."

So, accepting that home repairs are expensive and that they're a fact of life, we need to ask ourselves two questions: How much money do we need to have in reserve to pay for annual repairs and maintenance, and—here's the biggie—where is all this money coming from?

Much depends, of course, on how old and needy the house is when you move in. If you know the roof is going to have to be replaced in five years and the quote was $5,000 for the job, you've got some serious saving to do. If the old oil tank has to be excavated and a new one installed in your basement, start scanning the horizon for that $3,000 now. Beyond the imminent projects you already know about are the miscellaneous repairs that crop up all the time. They may always be different, but you can count on them to occur. As my mother is fond of saying, "Once you own a house, you'll never have to wonder where your next nickel is going."

I spoke with Elizabeth Lewin, author of *Your Personal Finan-*

cial Fitness Program (Facts On File), and she told me that, depending on the age and location of the house, a homeowner should annually budget between 1 and 2 percent of the value of the house for major home repairs (a new roof, a driveway repaving, the curing of a leaky basement, the outdoor paint job, falling trees that don't hit the insured roof and so the homeowners pay for their removal themselves, and other big jobs). Ouch! This easily translates to a couple of thousand dollars a year, and with mortgages, monthly bills, 401(K) contributions, college savings plans, and crooked little teeth to straighten, what is a homeowner to do, besides pray avidly?

Elizabeth suggests a more rational approach. She advises that a homeowner set up a savings account marked "House Reserve" and make a fairly frequent, routinized deposit into it. For example, when you pay your mortgage, make a deposit in the house account. A money market account or short-term-bond fund could be another way to save. Both are available through mutual fund companies that can arrange automatic transfers of funds from your checking account into the fund of your choice. Eventually you'll build up a nice little nest egg for your nest egg.

Elizabeth Lewin made a point to say that very new homeowners (she laughed and called them "extra virgin" homeowners) will probably not establish this savings account in the first months or year of homeownership. There are just too many set-up costs to allow much saving to take place.

Somehow we all manage, and you won't be the exception, but there's definitely a period of adjustment while you figure out where to spend less money in some areas because you have a big, new, superhungry category called "The House." Try to strike a balance where you don't deprive yourself, but you don't get caught out by a total lack of planning. You know, sometimes the house serves as a goad or a motivator, even, and you just might find more economic opportunities coming your way because you are more focused and you simply *have* to create them in order to feed your house.

Once you adjust your thinking and begin to enjoy your home, the pride of ownership will make taking care of it more of a tonic and less of a bitter pill. This is your corner of the world now. Tend it well. And remember, the house and its maintenance and repairs and improvement are just a transferring of assets. What you give out *will* come back to you.

The
Virgin Homeowner

1. Ground Zero; or What I Should Have Learned from the Home Inspection

Early one cool, misty morning in April, we took the elevator to the lobby of our New York City apartment building to meet our contractor and one of our good friends. We had found "The House" the week before and we were scheduled to meet the home inspector and Realtor up in Connecticut for the home inspection. After gulping down a cardboard cup of deli coffee, I handed out directions and we all piled into cars and drove off.

Something momentous was about to happen. After six dispiriting months of house-hunting, Demitri and I had come across the best house we were going to find in our price range and had raced to put a binder on it. Immediately the action turned fast and furious. We had ten days to find an inspector, get a report, and ascertain the house's true physical condition. But we were so fixated on the mortgage approval, the loss of our urban lifestyle, and the complexity of the actual move that we barely registered the importance of the home inspection. It was simply one more thing to get through.

As I look back now, I see that our particular home inspection was like the overture to a great musical-theater piece. All the themes we'd soon be experiencing on the set of the home front were announced, and if we had been listening closely we would have begun to understand the tone of the piece, its inner workings, its unique and even quirky elements.

Instead, I might as well have been tone-deaf, because this is how I handled our home inspection:

The Janice Papolos Method of Participating in a Home Inspection

1. Shake hands warmly with the home inspector.
2. Get busy discussing floor plans and furniture placement with your friend who's got a great eye for interior design.
3. Experience great relief when your partner goes downstairs with the home inspector to get educated about all that pipe and furnace stuff.
4. Wave warmly out the window to the septic people, who are inspecting the septic system, but don't cut short your conversation about fabric and throw rugs to go out and get their card or learn anything about the system. However, when the Realtor brings back the news that the "leaching fields are good," think to yourself: "Wow, I've learned a new phrase, 'leaching fields.' "
5. Take orders for lunch.
6. Shake hands warmly with the home inspector at the conclusion of the inspection.
7. Return to your New York City apartment feeling it was a very productive day.

If Only I Could Turn the Clock Back

I know you've all heard of buyer's remorse. But here's a new one. I've got home inspection remorse, and I've got it in spades.

If I had stopped flitting around like the hostess with the mostest, and if I'd known what questions to ask, I could have gotten an education that would have spared me a year's worth of panic, gnawing doubt, and general hysteria. The home inspection is a once-in-a-lifetime learning experience. Here's a better way to participate:

The Smart Homebuyer's Method of Participating in a Home Inspection

1.   Make sure you book a home inspector who is sympathetic to your plight as a virgin homeowner and has a penchant for teaching. (The next few pages are designed to help you make the right choice.)

2.   If you're reading this book *before* your home inspection, take a careful look at Chapters 2, 3, 4, 9, and 10 to familiarize yourself with all the systems of a house as well as with the many environmental issues about to come your way.

3.   Get a loose-leaf binder that you've separated with dividers and mark the dividers with the titles of the components and structural elements of the house. For example: "Heating System," "Electrical Service," "Water Heater," "Septic System," "Fireplaces," "Foundation," "Roof," "Deck," "Environmental Concerns," "Air-Conditioning," "Pool and Jacuzzi," "Interior and Exterior," "General Maintenance," etc. Then you can make notes in the appropriate sections at the inspection and better assimilate the information in an organized fashion afterward.

4.   Make a list of questions. All of them will be answered during

the inspection and you can place the answers in the tabbed
sections.

5. While you're at the stationery store buying the binder, pur-
    chase at least three brightly colored tags with strings. Ask the
    home inspector to use them to tag the main water, hot water,
    and outdoor garden spigot turnoff valves.

6. If you have young children, book a baby-sitter, because you are
    not bringing them along. Nor your parents, your contractor,
    your designer, your landscape designer, your architect, or any
    of your friends. You are there to concentrate on the condition
    of your house.

The home inspection usually takes place after a Purchase and
Sale contract is signed, and after you have placed a deposit in an
escrow account. There are two major contingencies (or avenues of
exit from the agreement) written into most Purchase and Sale contracts. The first is a financial contingency: If you can't obtain a
mortgage, you will not be expected to go through with the purchase
of the house. The second is the inspection contingency: If you have
a structural inspection of the property as well as a pest inspection
and the reports indicate serious problems, you have the right to
back out of the deal.

You normally have about a week to ten days to have the home
inspected, get the results, and decide whether the house is truly
sound and worth moving into, so you have to move quickly to settle on an inspector and schedule the inspection.

How to Find Your Ideal Inspector/Teacher

Your real estate attorney who has done many closings and seen
copies of home inspection reports, should be able to recommend a
good home inspector, or a friend in the area may be able to do the

same. A trusted Realtor can no doubt give you three names and advise you to interview them all and see whom you like and wish to book. No matter who gives you the recommendation, however, this decision is so important that it is worth the half a day or so it may take for you to talk to several potential inspectors.

Here's one important clue to finding the ideal inspector: Although there are very good inspectors out there who are not members of the American Society of Home Inspectors (ASHI), the inspector who is an ASHI member is certain to be highly qualified.

It's a difficult credential to obtain: a candidate applying for ASHI membership has to submit proof that he or she has already conducted 250 paid inspections. A difficult eight-hour exam must be passed, and a peer review board combs through a sample of the inspection reports to ensure that ASHI criteria are met. In addition, ASHI members must earn forty education credits every two years and follow a standard of practice in inspection and report, as well as a code of ethics.

ASHI membership means the home inspector is not working in a vacuum: members attend seminars and conferences, and there is a bulletin board on the Internet so ASHI inspectors all over the country can log on and talk over individual problems or issues of concern in the field.

The organization is very consumer-oriented. If you call ASHI at 800-743-2744, it will fax you a list of ASHI-certified inspectors in the area you're moving to, free of charge—within minutes. (I tried the number at 6:00 A.M., and at 6:02 I had a list climbing up my fax machine.) If you look in the Yellow Pages under "Building and Land Inspection Service," you can see which inspectors display the ASHI logo.

Several home inspectors in my area recommended I call Steve Gladstone, the owner of Stonehollow, Inc. and the president of the

Southern New England Chapter of the American Society of Home Inspectors. They all felt that he is an extremely knowledgeable and experienced inspector as well as a dedicated teacher.

We met at his office in Stamford, Connecticut, and initially, we talked about the vetting process a new homeowner should conduct when deciding which inspector to hire.

Steve suggested that you call an inspector, introduce yourself, and say: "I'm buying a house in ——. Do you inspect in this area?" Tell the inspector the age, size, and location of the house and say: "I need someone who will do a thorough inspection of the house and educate me at the same time."

You'll also want to ask if the inspector has experience with the type of house you're thinking of buying. For example, has the home inspector had a lot of experience with 1790 farmhouses, as well as spanking-new contemporaries?

Now you want to learn what the inspection will consist of and what services will be offered. According to Steve Gladstone, you want to hear that the inspection of a typical three- or four-bedroom house takes approximately two and a half hours on site, that the written report will be sent in two days and will be about sixteen or eighteen pages long, and that it will be in "user-friendly" language. (Restrain yourself from asking prices at this point.)

If you like the answers you're getting and the inspector is giving the impression that he or she will patiently explain everything to a virgin homeowner who is in dire need of an education, continue the interview.

You might next want to ask the inspector if he's going up on the roof and down into the crawl space. If he answers: "I definitely get down into the crawl space, and like to go up on the roof, but will not if it's snowy and icy, though I will use binoculars and will look more closely at the sheathing and spend more time in the attic looking for water stains and perhaps go back after the snow melts," you are talking with someone credible. (A level-headed person does not climb up on an icy roof.) If you are buying in winter and the roof surface is not clearly visible, it may be a good idea to have your attorney write a contingency into the contract that specifies that a roof inspection will take place when the roofing is clear of snow and ice.

The inspector will then go on to describe the environmental services that are offered as part of the home inspection, with their own separate price list. And here we enter increasingly complicated and confusing territory.

You must have a termite inspection (see Chapter 7, "The Uninvited Guest, Part I"). If there's a septic system on the property, it must be probed, pumped, and inspected (see Chapter 4, "To Rid-X or Not to Rid-X"). Your bank may require you to test for a soil gas called radon—on the lowest living level of the house as well as in the well water (see Chapter 9, "The Healthy House"). The question of an aged and possibly leaking buried oil tank has to be discussed; you may need special testing (a thorny issue I'll also discuss in Chapter 9).

In addition, if there's a well on the premises, a full potability (this means drinkability) and mineralization test must be conducted. Finally, you have the option of testing for lead paint indoors and out. (This is a very serious subject, and I advise you to read pages 283–89 with a very attentive eye and mind, especially if children under the age of six will be living in the house, or you or your partner is pregnant or planning on becoming pregnant).

At this point, you're going to get hit with the prices. And they're going to incite more than a little anxiety, because all you've been hearing for days is points, insurance fees, tallies from the bankers and lawyers, and now you're about to receive yet another charming price list from yet another voice on the other end of the phone. It's overwhelming. So let's put this in perspective.

You're about to spend more money than probably you've ever spent in your life, and the home inspection is the best insurance policy that the house you're buying is sound and that something will not rise up and bite you in a few years (or if it does, you'll be expecting it and will have budgeted for it).

If there's any further negotiating to be done with the home seller, it arises from the findings of the home inspection (this will be discussed in detail later in this chapter). You enter the home inspection with little knowledge and with your eyes closed, and, unlike me, you can leave with a lot of knowledge and your eyes opened.

However, Steve Gladstone feels many people misunderstand the responsibilities and functions of home inspectors. The home inspector is not Superman—he does not have X-ray vision; he does not see through walls. You can hope for a smart Clark Kent. This is a *visual* inspection done within a three-hour window, and it is a check, not a warranty. The inspector is not looking at cracked switch plates, and he will not check every sash cord in the house. He will, however, look at the structure of the house and the roof, check all the major mechanical systems, and look at the system components to establish their condition at the time of the inspection. "Basically, the home inspector is looking for items that will cost you $500 or more to repair or replace, as well as checking for possible environmental contaminants or hazards" says Steve Gladstone.

Steve also told me, "Defects will be uncovered in almost every home, no matter how expensive or magnificent. Our job is to distinguish between less significant deficiencies and major flaws and to help put the findings in perspective for our clients."

So, you like the sounds of the answers you're getting on the phone, the inspector seems to relish the idea of you as an apt and eager pupil, and the two of you seem simpatico. Now you're going to hear about the prices.

In 1996, going rates for an inspection of a typical three- or four-bedroom house and the environmental testing in southern Connecticut and in Houston, Texas, were as follows:

	Connecticut	Texas
Home inspection and report	$ 300	$ 250
Termite inspection	80	70
Radon (2-location, EPA protocol test)	125	85
Radon in water	100	radon no problem
Septic system inspection	425	300
Water testing (full potability and mineralization)	110	75
Lead in water	60	125
Oil tank testing	400	Gas or electric used

When you call a few home inspectors in your area, you'll quickly learn what the going rates are, but the above should give you some idea of what to expect.

Remember, if you have city water and are hooked up to a city sewer system, or if your house was built after 1978 when lead paint was banned, or if your heating system is electric or gas, then much of this testing does not apply to you. Most people will want to test for termites, for lead in the water supply, and for radon, however.

Not only is every house a different proposition, but different regions of the country need home inspections customized to that particular area. For instance, in California and other frequent-quake locales, the home inspectors look closely at a raised foundation to ensure that the frame is bolted securely to the foundation. They will also check to see that a gas water heater has seismic straps so that it couldn't pull away from the wall in the event of an earthquake and start a fire. Inspectors in Florida and other areas that face frequent hurricanes check to see that a house's construction is as hurricane-resistant as possible. Your real estate agent and the home inspector you choose will inform you of the region's specific safety codes and advise you how a house can be brought up to code.

The Written Report

One way to assess an inspector is to ask for a copy of a previous report that the inspector has done for another client so you can determine how useful a comparable report would be for you.

"The report you receive should be a narrative report, not a checklist," cautions Neal Carley, a home inspector in Fairfield, Connecticut, who's been in the business for thirty-five years and had a previous career as a builder. "It should be chock-full of details that really clue you in to the state of the structural or electromechanical components. Maintenance and repair advice should be spelled out, and the faults of the house should be noted in a nonalarmist way, with a plan of action to remedy them."

Andrew Kleeman, a home inspector in Pennsylvania, was singled out in an August 1994 *Smart Money* article on home inspections for the details of his report. In one section, he writes about a few displaced tiles above a bathtub spout. "Use of the fixture will allow seepage behind the tiles," he states. He then goes on to recommend that the tiles be repaired. "The estimated cost to reset the affected tiles onto the existing backerboard is $100. If tile removal reveals currently unanticipated backerboard damage, full retiling of this section of the bathing enclosure will be warranted—total costs would probably range from $250 to $500."

Peter Seirup, the president of Home Directions in Ridgefield,

Connecticut, instructs his clients about service contracts and insurance policies via his report. For instance, in one report Mr. Seirup wrote: "Annual servicing of an oil burner maximizes combustion efficiency and reliability. Service contracts are offered by most local fuel companies at a cost of just over $100 a year. Such contracts usually cover the annual burner tune-up, as well as any other necessary repairs to the oil burner during the year at no additional charge." Also: "Buried oil tanks have become an issue, since older ones often eventually leak. This tank is new enough so that the risk of leaking is low. Nevertheless, I suggest you get oil tank protection plan from the fuel service company."

As you can see, good teaching and good reporting also give new homeowners an idea about maintenance and repair budgeting. We become so fixated on affording the initial down payment and the monthly nut that we tend to dismiss the fact that we might need to earmark money for service contracts, oil tank insurance, and routine and not so routine repair bills. The home inspection can bring clarity and reality about such budgeting into your consciousness.

An Actual Inspection: Minute-by-Minute

Steve Gladstone called me about a week after our interview and asked if I'd like to attend a home inspection he was slated to do in Westport. (Talk about a corrective experience! I'd finally get to walk through a house with an expert and pay proper attention to the procedure.) A couple named Richard and Mitsuyo were considering buying a house here, and their real estate agent had given them the names of three local inspectors. In the interviewing process they'd chosen Steve, and when he told them about this book, they were gracious enough to let me walk through the inspection with them.

As I drove up to the house at 8:30 A.M. on a beautiful Saturday morning in May, I was amused to find that I was experiencing the same kind of nervousness and excitement I'd felt when anticipating the inspection of our own home.

I spotted Steve up on the roof, checking the shingles, the skylights, and the condition of the chimneys, and two men near a truck that read Stright Septic Company walking the side lawn with long measuring tapes. Richard and Mitsuyo and their Realtor, Julia, arrived shortly after.

After all the introductions, Steve explained how we were to spend the next few hours. He said: "We're going to establish the condition of the house. We are looking for indications of problems—things that might be unprofessionally installed, cracks, bulges, or stains. As we go, I'll give you information about maintenance and machinery, and keep a careful eye on safety items for children, adults, and pets, as well as on security elements." Richard then signed a paper requesting a radon test, a lead in water test, a termite inspection, and the complete septic inspection. He intended to unearth the buried oil tank and put a new one in a storage shed, so he didn't circle the oil tank test. He did, however, make sure that the tank insurance was to be transferred into his name on the date of closing so that he was covered in the case of any contaminating spills (see page 290).

Out of the corner of my eye, I was watching the septic company men, Bob Aillery and Theodore (TC) Cooper, prodding the earth with long metal poles, looking for the access opening to the tank. I was wondering if it would be as tough to find as ours was, and if they would have to use the sewer rat—the radio transmitter—to find it (see Chapter 4). Meantime, we continued to circle and learn about the house. The asphalt driveway and the deck were in perfect condition, and it was obvious that the couple who had owned the house had put it on the market in beautiful condition. (The real

estate agent explained that they had wisely hired an inspector before listing the house and had gone through the report and made
every repair indicated.)

Every wire was pointed out, every projection from the house
was identified, every gutter and leader was examined. Steve advised
Richard to remove the mulch and leaves resting too close to the
wood siding, as they retain water and give insects a step-up into the
house. He examined the cracks in the foundation, declared them
meaningless, and suggested that Richard and Mitsuyo photograph
them and paste them into the home inspection report. Then when
they go to sell the house someday, they can prove that the cracks
don't portend any major problem with the structure of the house.
He also advised them to have the electrical service lines raised and
warned Richard to be careful placing a ladder anywhere near the
area where they enter the house.

Inside this very light and airy, totally renovated house, we
started in the kitchen. Every appliance was turned on to verify its
working condition, and Steve opened every cabinet door, tested the
ice maker of the refrigerator, and heated some water in the microwave. Both fireplaces were examined. In the laundry room, he
told Richard and Mitsuyo to turn off the water valves supplying the
washing machine before they went away for any length of time so
that a rubber hose couldn't break and damage the house with water.

But Steve really hit his stride when we went down to the furnace room. Patiently, he explained how the oil burner worked and
why it might not go on and how to reset it if it wouldn't start. He
pointed out the main water valve and showed them how to reset the
circuit breakers in the service panel. (If there's such a thing as inspection envy, I was beginning to experience it as I thought about
all the panic I'd suffered merely because I'd removed myself from
my own home inspection.)

Except for one popped shingle, a little frost-heave movement on the stairway outside the basement door, a few loose tiles in one of the bathrooms, and a pool gate that needed some attention, the house was simply gorgeous. Julia and I both commented that our houses couldn't pass such scrutiny, and I made up my mind right then and there that I'd never move. (But if I do, I'm having Steve do a prelisting inspection.) Part II of the inspection—the attic walk-through, the air-conditioning and Jacuzzi check—seemed like pro forma stuff.

A small wave of Bob Aillery's hand summoned us all to the side lawn, and everything that had come before became the prelude to *Gone with the Wind.* The septic system was in complete failure.

There was no device on the tank—a baffle—to prevent solids from going into the leaching pits, and these pits were practically sealed off. The supplementary tank that satisfied the board of health's code wasn't even connected to the primary tank. Everyone froze.

Richard eventually cleared his throat and asked Bob what the cost to repair or replace the system would be. Bob was reluctant to quote a figure right then, but depending on the soil conditions, a new system in this area could run between $10,000 and $20,000.

Apparently, the people who'd owned the house before the present sellers had contracted for the system update and paid for it. The man who had put it in was dead, and the company doing the annual pumping had missed a great deal when they failed to note that missing baffle. None of this was the seller's fault, but certainly Richard and Mitsuyo weren't anxious to inherit a $20,000 problem. Everyone seemed so deflated. Hard negotiations lay ahead, and no one knew what the outcome would be.

Steve completed the inspection and hung four radon testers (two in the basement level's family room and two in the living room of the main level), and we closed up the house.

If the News Isn't Good: Post-inspection Negotiations

As soon as Richard and Mitsuyo and Julia left, I asked Steve what was going to happen. The tension of the last few hours had been horrible. It was very hard to keep it all in perspective. It was a house. A good house—with a problem. A problem that could be fixed. But who was going to fix it? Or maybe the better question was: could someone afford to fix it? If the sellers couldn't afford a $20,000 hit as well as the cost of building the new house they were moving into, they'd be forced to take the house off the market and use their building fund to ready the property for sale again down the road. Richard and Mitsuyo would be back to square one.

This is a good time to discuss the negotiation procedures that in many cases follow the home inspection. The dynamics of the situation are dicey and difficult. Neither side really knows if the other is serious or just posturing, or what the true bottom line for the other is. There can be misunderstandings and angry feelings.

I wanted to speak with Dan Wilder of Fairfield Residential Realty about the post-inspection negotiating conundrums. Dan is a buyer's broker—his only loyalty is to the buyer. Therefore he has no conflict of interest when he offers the buyer advice.

"You negotiate for as strong a settlement as you can," he told me. "Now, your negotiating strength is based on how you negotiated the price of the house initially. You would try to go for the entire amount, but sometimes the buyer and seller split the cost, sometimes the buyer pays a third and the seller pays two-thirds, and sometimes the buyer pays the whole thing. If there's a backup offer in the wings, the seller can stand firm and be quite happy for you to back out of the deal.

"You have to ask yourself: 'What's the total cost to put the house in A-one shape? Is it still a value to me compared to the other houses I've seen?' If a house is priced at $270,000 and it needs a septic system and thus costs you some money, but this house is comparable to a $350,000 house, you're better off buying it and fixing the septic system. A new septic system in an older house adds to the marketability of the house."

Dan then reminded me that no house is perfect, and beyond the price of the house, a homeowner normally invests many thousands of dollars to customize the house to his or her lifestyle, taste, and security and comfort level. (When I think of the money we spent on new Andersen windows, doors and deadbolt locks, the electronic security system, the outdoor lighting, the new propane water heater, the gas stove, the two walls we knocked down . . . it does add up to many thousands of dollars.) He concluded, "If you have a house in perfect condition except for this septic problem, you might want to pay a share, because then you have a new septic and a house in perfect condition. A real value."

I also asked Dan Wilder if you negotiate a lot of little things that tally up, but he seemed opposed to nitpicking and advised that a buyer concentrate on just those systems that are basic to running the house—the plumbing, the septic system, the heating system, the well, the electrical service—and possible environmental problems such as radon. Buyers always request that these things be brought up to snuff. If the roof needs replacement in a year, you would negotiate it; if the roof could go for another five years, you wouldn't.

Dan also advises his clients to negotiate for money instead of seller-contracted repairs. He feels a buyer should not leave a major repair up to a certainly harried and possibly disgruntled seller, whose thoughts and efforts are now all concentrated on his or her next move in life, not this house and its problems.

I'm a sucker for happy endings, and I found out that Richard and Mitsuyo will be our new neighbors. The sellers agreed to pay the entire amount of the costs of the new septic system. Apparently they were also anxious to get on with the next phase of their lives and were able to absorb the expense at that time.

Richard and Mitsuyo closed on their new home in September.

Steve Gladstone showed me the Closing Checklist he gives to all his clients with the inspection report folder. He advises them to use this in the final walk-through of the house which takes place directly before you show up at the bank to sign those endless papers and receive the keys to your new house. He has given me permission to reproduce it in these pages; it comes at the end of this chapter.

Buying from a Builder

Lest you think I have tunnel vision and only think about people buying existing houses, I want to address the following pages to people buying directly from a builder. You have your homework cut out for you also, and you need to understand the components of a well-built, energy-efficient house way before you even talk to or settle on a builder.

First, I recommend you read several books. *House* by Tracy Kidder and *The Well-Built House* by Jim Locke (the builder profiled in the Kidder book) take you through the process and teach a lot about the builder's point of view, the decisions made during the actual building, and the interaction between client and builder.

Norm Abrams Builds His New House is another must-read. Norm Abrams, the host of the TV series *This Old House,* chronicles the story of the house he and his wife, Laura, built in the Boston area, and it's an eye-opening account of the process, with lots of details, photos, and diagrams.

The Health House Workbook is an essential also. Recently published by the American Lung Association, Minneapolis Affiliate, it is a three-ring-binder workbook/monograph which teaches and talks you through the building process with an emphasis on building houses that are healthy and efficient. Some of the topics include selecting a site, interviewing a builder, understanding a house as a system, and choosing low-toxicity building products for a better indoor environment. It costs $24.00 plus $5 for shipping and handling and is available from the American Lung Association, 4220 Old Shakopee Road, Suite 101, Minneapolis, MN 55437 (612-885-0338; fax: 612-885-0133).

Interesting things seem to be going on in Minneapolis. That city harbors not only the above book, but also a great company named Shelter Supply (you'll read about the company and one of its owners, Mark LaLiberte, in Chapter 9). From Shelter Supply you can purchase a wonderful videotape produced by the Cold Climate Institute of the University of Minnesota, entitled *Shopping for a Performance-Built House: Test Drive Before You Buy.* (Call Shelter Supply at 1-800-762-8399 to order this and other videos and books.)

After you view this tape, you'll understand the dynamics of air and moisture that are always at play inside and outside a house, as well as the proper building techniques that allow for these constantly changing dynamics and make sure the house performs well and is durable, efficient, and healthy. You'll also know what clues to look for and what questions to ask to ensure that you don't purchase a "lemon," as they put it so aptly on the tape.

After you've done the essential homework (pun intended), ask for references from people who actually live in a prospective builder's houses. Call these references and ask the following questions: Is the house comfortable? Have they had any problems with the house? Are their heating and electric bills reasonable? Are there any moisture problems? Would they buy another home from this builder?

If the answers coming back to you are positive and enthusiastic, you need to sit down with the builder and discuss building techniques. You want a builder who sees a house as a dynamic system whose components are connected and interact.

If you do decide to buy a brand-new home from a builder, you should definitely hire a home inspector to do a two- and possibly a three-stage inspection—even if the builder offers you a one-year warranty, as most do, and even though the building inspector will be signing off on different systems of the house at different times. Remember, even a good builder is not always on the site every day during construction, and building inspectors are looking for code *violations.* Their job is to note *minimum* construction standards, not necessarily the level of quality and workmanship. This is where you want the professional experience of a home inspector hired by you and working for you.

I asked Steve Gladstone what a new house inspection would consist of, and he said he typically does a two-part inspection. "I go in before the Sheetrock goes up, and I check the structural framing, the plumbing, the electrical wiring and duct installations, the siding, the roof, and the exterior grading. I also check the insulation in the attic. Then I write up a short progress report and talk with my client over the telephone and report all my findings. He or she can then talk things over with the builder and see that any deficiencies are taken care of."

He continued: "Just before the pre-settlement walk-through, I do a complete inspection and bring the clients with me so that I can teach them about the house and its systems. I talk to them about their heating system, I demonstrate how to shut off the water and electricity, and I talk a lot about general maintenance details. At this point I do a complete report and a punch list of things that may not have been finished properly, so that the builder can take care of these things. I suggest that they make note of any systems that deteriorate during that twelve-month warranty period and notify the builder."

I asked Steve what he charges for this two-part inspection, and he said that the first inspection is somewhere between $200 and $250, and the final inspection with the complete report is approximately $300, depending on the size of the house. (This fee does not include environmental testing.) Clients who want a third walk-through before the twelve-month warranty runs out to ensure that everything has been finished correctly typically pay an additional $250.

I wondered if this arrangement made for a certain friction between the buyer and the builder, but Steve said that good builders shouldn't object to an inspector coming in, as long as he is fair and not unrealistically picky.

The day after our talk, Steve faxed me an article written by Katherine Salant for the *Washington Post*. Not only did the article extol the idea of an inspector coming in on behalf of the new-home buyer, but the writer interviewed the sales and marketing heads of seven home-building firms in the Washington area to see how they felt about a buyer's hiring an inspector. It seems these firms were very amenable to the idea, but they said that "as yet, few buyers had done so." Linda Towns, marketing chief of K. Hovnanian, one of the largest home construction companies on the East Coast, was quoted as saying: "If hiring a home inspector makes a customer feel more comfortable, we'd welcome the idea."

In my opinion, the hiring of a home inspector should be standard operating procedure in the purchase of a home from a builder. I seriously recommend your considering it.

The 6-6-6 Decoding Report

We received our report about two days after the inspection, and after attempting to read it through, we got the impression that all was well with the house, and I packed it away somewhere. I remember reading that the roof was on the newish side and there were—apparently—no termites, so I went on with my packing and my crying and the millions of other preparations one attends to in a move.

A few months after we moved in I came across the home inspection report and gave it another furrowed-brow read-through. (What do New Yorkers know from caulking and grading and gutters?)

Recalling my inability to get a toehold amid all the unfamiliar details, I thought it might be a good idea to organize the information in a chronological time frame. What should I do in the first six days in the new home? What projects need to be attended to in the first six months? And what should I schedule in the first 600 days (or approximately two years) of home ownership? In our case, based on the report we received, our list would have looked like this:

6 days:

- Purchase smoke detectors and at least two carbon monoxide detectors and at least three fire extinguishers; purchase emergency medical kit and stock house with Tylenol, aspirin, ipecac syrup, etc.
- Arrange fuel company and insurance for underground oil tank.
- Have furnace cleaned, inspected, and tuned up for heating season.
- Get deadbolts on back and side doors.

60 days:

- Replace untempered glass on back door.
- Have fireplace cleaned [we moved in in August and were not using it right away].
- Have gutters cleaned.
- Have front section of house regraded so that rain water flows away from house.
- Recaulk bath tiles.
- Put vent in furnace room and increase amount of combustion air.

600 days (or sometime in the first two years)

- Have oil tank removed and a new tank put in basement.
- Put ventilating fan in downstairs bathroom.
- Replace windows in office for energy efficiency.
- Replace electric water heater with a new one that runs off the boiler in order to save $150 a month on the electric bill.

Take your home inspection report and transfer the advice and suggestions of repair onto your own sheet below. It organizes the overwhelming amount of information and focuses you as to the priorities. If you have any questions about any of the advice or information in the report, do not hesitate to call your inspector for more specific explanations.

6 days:

....

....

....

....

....

60 days

....
....
....
....

600 days (or within two years)

....
....
....
....

Annual Maintenance Suggestions (add to calendar on page 411):

....
....
....
....
....
....

The Closing Walk-Through Checklist

As I mentioned on page 41, Steve Gladstone gives all his clients a checklist to bring to the final walk-through of the house. This takes place after the previous owners have moved out and before you go to the bank to sign your life away. Steve prefaces his checklist: "We recommend that on the day before or the morning of your closing you take our original report and this form and perform a careful evaluation of the conditions of your new home. Make sure that items and conditions listed in the report are still consistent with the report, and that no additional damage or problems have occurred."

The checklist, reprinted by permission of Stonehollow, Inc., is as follows:

- **Lighting.** Exterior and interior, where possible. Test fixtures, make sure track lights, dimmers, fans, and specialty lighting which was included in the sale still remain, and function properly.

- **Flooring.** Make sure floors have not been scratched or damaged by removal of furniture. Check tile floors or carpeting for damages. If the washer and dryer have been removed, check for damages in areas not previously visible. In the basement areas, check for water stains or mildew stains not previously viewed (due to stored items).

- **Windows.** Look for cracked or broken windows. Check all screens and storms. Make sure locks work, and make sure that you have keys for any window or door locks. Open sashes and raise and lower them for proper operation.

- **Plumbing.** Run all sink fixtures, showers, tubs, and toilets individually to assure good operation and no leakage evidence, especially under sinks. If the refrigerator has been removed and there was an ice-maker connection, be sure not to turn this on until the new unit is connected. We recommend new hoses be installed for the clothes washer. These should be changed every few years. In homes with wells and/or water treatment equipment, make sure there are no leaks or obvious problems with the equipment. Call service companies to let them know when you've moved in.

- **Heating system.** Raise the thermostats and test to make sure the heating system responds with heat. Be sure to replace filters on forced-air systems monthly and follow recommendations that were made in the original report. (We recommend a heating/air conditioning expert test efficiency of equipment before the closing.) PURCHASE CARBON MONOXIDE DETECTORS.

- **Air-conditioning.** Do not test these if the temperature is below 60 degrees, as damage can result. If it is warm enough to test, allow the heating system about ten minutes to equalize before turning on the cooling system. Cleaning filters and vacuuming radiators will often improve the efficiency of these systems.

- **Appliances.** Test all appliances and make sure they are in working order whenever possible.

- **Doors.** Check all doors to ensure proper closure. Be sure to obtain all keys to exterior doors and garage. Obtain garage door operators and keys to window locks, accessory sheds, etc. from owner.

- **Exterior.** Test exterior water spigots (if possible) to assure no leakage/drips. Walk the exterior perimeter of home and view roofing, gutters, driveway, siding, trim, exterior doors/windows, deck/patio/porch, landscape to assure no changes have occurred.

Be sure any repairs agreed to in the contract have been made and the included fixtures agreed to in the contract have remained. If items were to be removed or debris carted away, check to see it has been done.

The Annual Review

Whether you finally buy an existing home or one newly built, the home inspection is an essential component of the decision-making process. Once it's all over, however, don't file the report away and forget about it. Instead, think of it as an organic and living document. Take it out at least once or twice a year and "walk its walk." Reinspect everything and make sure you're keeping up with the maintenance, troubleshooting any new problems, and heeding the report's advice and suggestions. Every time you fix a problem, note it on the report, and include when it was done, who did the work, and what it cost. A list of all the improvements made to a house makes that house more marketable.

Most people leave the home inspection feeling dazed, overwhelmed, anxious about all these new burdens and responsibilities, in a panic about all the new expenses, and very, very tired. You may even feel a bit depressed and wonder if you've bitten off more than you can chew. This state of mind reminds me of an exchange I had with a student of mine at Manhattan School of Music after a very comprehensive three-hour lecture on taxes and the performing artist. His eyes looked glazed and kind of panicky and he leaned over and asked: "Janice, is it all right that I'm feeling stupid?"

"Todd," I replied, "if you felt smart right now, you'd *really* be stupid."

New and dense and difficult subjects need some getting used to. After some exposure, a few things make sense, and in a while more things make sense, and one day you honestly get a grip on the big picture and can fill in with a lot of crucial details. Even a person like me, who had no affinity for things mechanical, electrical, or physical, began to "hear the music." In time, you will too.

2. The Inner Mysteries, Part I: Plumbing and Electricity

"Hell," said Sartre, "is other people." Chances are he never stood in the furnace room of a new home and attempted to fathom a scary-looking boiler and that labyrinth of pipes. Now *that* is truly diabolical.

No part of homeownership made me more uneasy and intermittently paranoid than all the electromechanical equipment and all those pipes and wires branching out silently behind walls. (I'm not alone in these dark thoughts. Humorist Dave Barry feels that plumbing is the most intelligent life form on earth: it's just waiting until New Year's Eve when your house is filled to the rafters with guests to go into cahoots with the water heater and stage a total breakdown.)

Not only did my lack of knowledge cause me to suspect that every sound and gurgle was a sign of imminent disaster, but I looked like a dimwit to the tradespeople who came to work on the various systems. My worst moment came when an electrician attempted to explain something to me. The absolutely blank expression on my face prompted him to tease: "Hey, I thought you New Yorkers knew everything." In my very sensitive virgin state, I didn't laugh. I sort of winced and felt this awful blush rising in my face.

Well, certainly not one to sully the reputation of my fellow New Yorkers, I vowed never to be in that position again. I became animated by new goals: I wanted to understand enough to mitigate my fear and wild suppositions; I wanted to be able to troubleshoot problems and do simple maintenance; and I wanted to be able to *talk intelligently* with the tradespeople as they explained problems and solutions.

In fact, the more I talked with these tradespeople and the more I read, the simpler and more beautifully logical these inner mysteries all became, and this bogeyman that I'd fashioned in my mind disintegrated and disappeared. Imagine me, Janice Papolos, talking P-traps, circulator pumps, and straight-bus circuit breakers!

So, in the two chapters that follow, you too will attain an equally high level of understanding of these arcane matters. We're going to examine the major systems in a house and learn about a homeowner's part in their maintenance. By the time you're finished reading these chapters you should be able to open a clogged drain, reset a tripped circuit, deal with a heating system, restart a balky furnace, change the filter in the furnace, and bleed a radiator. Best of all, unfounded suspicions will be replaced with prescribed and timely action. You'll also not only understand what the professionals are saying and doing, but be able to evaluate the bids and estimates they offer you.

The simplest system, and the one in play twenty-four hours a day, 365 days a year, is the water-supply-drain-waste-vent system, so we'll discuss it first.

Faucets and Flushes: The Water-Supply-Drain-Waste-Vent System

People rarely ask me how many bedrooms I have in this house; they always ask about the number of bathrooms, though. And they've got their priorities straight. Modern sanitation lets us live with comfort and without the nightmare of cholera epidemics and other periodic plagues.

The path to modern plumbing was a bumpy one, however. The wheel had to be reinvented constantly. In this century, archaeologists uncovered the ruins of the palace at Knossos on Crete (one of the centers of the Bronze Age civilization) and discovered an incredibly sophisticated water-supply system as well as the ruins of a drainage system that included flushing toilets and traps and vents, similar to those used today. Unfortunately, around 1400 B.C., the Minoan civilization collapsed either because of a natural disaster such as an earthquake or a volcanic eruption or because of an attack by a foreign enemy, and these advanced principles of hydraulics were buried with the palace.

The next people to bring plumbing to a high level were the Romans. The city of Rome itself had close to 1,000 public and private baths, over 1,200 public fountains and cisterns, and an impressive number of public water-flushed toilets; 50 million gallons of water a day were brought in from the aqueducts in the countryside and fed into a network of underground pipes that were constructed of sheet lead or *plumbum,* the Latin ancestor of our term "plumbing."

Unhappily, these principles of sanitation fell with Rome in the fifth century. In the hundreds of years that followed, elaborate superstitions about bathing and sanitary precautions arose and any progress in plumbing came to a standstill. Europeans remained unwashed and lived in absolute squalor as plagues repeatedly swept through the populace. Queen Isabella of Spain (patron to Christopher Columbus) was terribly proud of the fact that she had taken only two baths in her lifetime.

These negative feelings about bathing also entered the New World with the European settlers. In fact, a law was passed in Boston in 1845 that forbade bathing unless prescribed by a doctor.

Plumbing finally got back on track in the 1800s, when physicians in England discovered the cause-and-effect relationship of waste and filth and infectious disease. The task was to create a plumbing system that supplied fresh water to a household yet rid the home of waste, bacteria, and dangerous gases without polluting the water supply. (Goethe was so right when he said: "Everything has been thought of before, but the problem is to think of it again.")

Today's plumbing comprises two completely separate systems: a **water supply system** that carries hot and cold water throughout a home, and the drain-waste-vent or **DWV system** that drains water and wastes from fixtures and appliances and safely escorts them below to a sewer or septic tank connection.

The water supply to your home comes either from a private well or the city and enters the house from an underground pipe. If you do have municipal water, this pipe—the **main**—connects to a meter that registers the amount of water flowing in so that you can be billed periodically for water consumption. Where the main first appears inside is a valve called the **main shutoff valve,** which allows you to stop all water coming into the house. This is the valve you want to identify with a big tag so anyone at home could stave off a flood by simply twisting it in a clockwise fashion.

The cold-water line runs throughout the house as well as to the water heater. (If you have a well, the cold water first is pumped from the well to a pressure tank, which maintains the pressure needed to move water throughout the system.) The water that flows through the heater becomes the home's hot-water line. From the water heater, pipelines conveying hot water run parallel to the cold-water lines up to fixtures such as sinks and bathtubs. Not all fixtures require both of the lines, however: the dishwasher uses only a hot-water line, and the toilets use only a cold-water line.

Municipal water enters the house under pressure from a street pipe that is 8 to 24 inches in diameter and moves into a 1-inch feed pipe inside the house. Still under pressure, the water moves up and around the home through pipes that are typically 1/2 to 3/4 inch in diameter. Riser pipes bring water between floors; connections are made with "tees," and right-angle turns are made with "elbows.

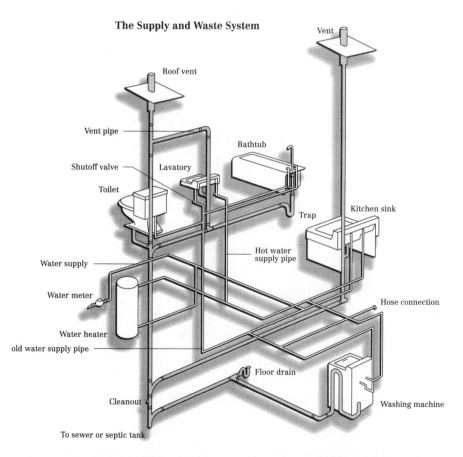

The Supply and Waste System

Throughout the first half of this century, galvanized piping was used in most homes. Galvanized pipes are made of iron and then coated with zinc. This limits the corrosion that water can cause when it comes into prolonged contact with iron. Yellow brass piping replaced galvanized; then came red brass piping, and finally, in the 1960s, copper came to be used almost extensively throughout homes. Copper pipe lasts about fifty years, is resistant to the mineral buildups that can cause clogs, and is relatively easy for a plumber to work with. While copper is used for hot-water pipes, some drainpipes are made of plastics such as polyvinyl chloride (PVC), acrylonitrile-butadiene-styrene (ABS), or chlorinated polyvinyl chloride (CPVC). I mention this because I remember an "Atomic Rooter" man asking me over the telephone what kind of drainpipes I had. Naturally, I didn't know, but when he found out they were galvanized, he reacted as if we had something out of the Stone Age.

Once water could be piped up to fixtures, a system had to be developed to carry used water and wastes down and out of the house. Enter the drain-waste-vent (DWV) system. This network of rather large pipes (ranging from 1 1/2 to 4 inches) collects used water from sinks, tubs, and showers, channels wastes down from toilets, and vents sewer gases up and outside the home. The water and wastes are carried downhill by gravity, joining pipes from other drains into a big vertical pipe called a **soil stack.** The soil stack is the main artery in this system. It not only directs all wastes and used water down to the sewer connection or to a pipe that connects to the septic tank, at the same time it terminates at the top end through the roof and vents the sewer gases and admits air in order to maintain atmospheric pressure in the drain lines (more about this below).

Today's drain-waste-vent system took quite a bit of developing and trial-and-error evolution. Downward-sloping pipes did a good job draining pipes, but two problems remained to be resolved: the very pipes that were allowing for the exit of wastes were allowing the entrance of foul and dangerous sewer gases into the house; and, at times, the pipes moved wastes too sluggishly.

Around 1840, someone invented the **trap,** the piece of plumbing that makes everything possible. You've no doubt been looking at this gooseneck curve of pipe under sinks your whole life, but if you're like me, you've never realized or appreciated the miracle of this utilitarian-looking object.

Go back and look under the sink in the bathroom. You will see a pipe that runs straight down from the drain, turns back up, and then either moves down again or curves back into the wall. Early versions of the trap looked like an S, and such a trap was called—unsurprisingly—an **S-trap.** Today's version is in the shape of a P lying on its side and is known as **P-trap.** Because some amount of water remains at the bottom of the curve, it acts as a plug and effectively seals off the waste line, preventing foul odors or poisonous and combustible gases from entering the home. As you'll learn in Chapter 4, these gases are produced by the action of anaerobic bacteria that live in sewer pipes and septic tanks.

Until the trap solved the problem of rising sewer gases, plumbing could not be brought inside the home. Traps also allow clog-cleaning access or contact-lens recovery, but those conveniences are secondary in importance to that water seal.

The S-trap had its problems, though. Sometimes the bend in the pipe didn't fill with water, because the water rushing through the drainpipe created a suction—a siphoning—of that water and pulled the water seal right down the system. Homeowners would have to remember to restore the seal by pouring some water down the drain after draining a sink or flushing the toilet, or smell the

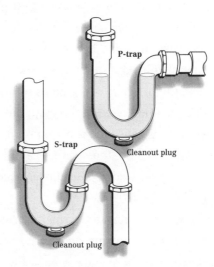

reeking consequences of their absentmindedness. The other problem I mentioned before is that sometimes the waste moved too slowly through the pipes—for the same reason that it's hard to pour tomato juice out of a can if you punch only one hole with the can opener. In the case of a can of tomato juice, a second hole acts as a vent that equalizes the pressure and allows an easier, more even flow of liquid.

Sometime around 1874, plumbers came up with the solution to both the siphoning problem and the sluggish waste removal by adding an additional pipe to the trap—a **vent**—that led out to the air above the roof and created a necessary pressure-relief system. Branch vents from every fixture are connected to the main **stack vent,** which protrudes through the roof. This 3-to-4-inch-diameter stack vent allows sewer gases to safely exit up and out into the atmosphere and maintains atmospheric pressure. Some houses have only one soil stack and all the fixtures are connected to it; others have two or more.

So a vent has three very important functions. It dissipates noxious gases harmlessly into the atmosphere; it equalizes air pressure throughout the drain system, preventing vacuums or back pressures that could interfere with the normal gravity flow of the system; and it maintains the water seal of the traps by preventing the siphoning of that water by the suction generated by flowing wastes.

Over time, the S-trap was replaced by the P-trap because its vent system was more reliable. The P-trap's more vertical rise prevented periodic clogs in the vents and any occasional siphoning of the water seal.

When Bad Things Happen to Good Pipes

Sooner or later, a homeowner experiences a clogged pipe somewhere in the drain-waste-vent system. It is rare that there's a backup in the soil stack or down below in the sewer service, but it happened to two of my friends. In Sasha's case in Los Angeles, the problem turned out to be the rapacious roots of a tree which had to be cut through to release their stranglehold. Unfortunately, it's a problem she's likely to reexperience. Joan and Larry in Pound Ridge, New York, had a different problem. It turned out that the pipe to the septic system was crushed and had to be dug up and replaced. They originally thought the whole septic system had failed, so they were very happy the solution was a finite sum of $500 for the pipe replacement.

The rest of us will experience the simple clogs of everyday life, mostly in the kitchen and bathrooms.

In order to prevent kitchen sink clogs, your constant vigilance will be required. All that grease. All those food particles. Grease coats the insides of the pipes and acts like a glue: food particles as well as any subsequent deposits of grease stick to it. Houses built before the 1960s may be particularly prone to clogs in the kitchen because their drain pipes were only 1 1/2 inches in diameter; 2-inch pipes have been used in the last thirty years.

Never pour off oil or butter into the kitchen drain. Put it in a coffee can in the refrigerator until it congeals and then dump it in the garbage. My mother always cautioned me to run cold water through a garbage disposal both before and after throwing in food. This I dutifully did, but I never knew why I was running that water. It turns out that the cold water helps grease flow through and not stick to the pipes and the force of the water pushes the ground-up food down the drain. Once a week, she ran very hot water through the drain to help remove any grease buildup.

Your first line of action for a clog in the bathroom is to reach for a plunger, but I polled about twenty people, and no one could tell me the correct way to use this fine clog-clearing tool. Most people pump it up and down a few times and are horribly frustrated when it doesn't work.

Sunset Books's *Basic Plumbing* describes the proper plunging technique for a clog in the sink or bathtub:

- Choose a plunger whose suction cup covers the drain opening completely.
- Fill the clogged fixture with enough water to cover several inches of the plunger cup.
- Block off all other outlets (the overflow vent, the second drain in a double sink, etc.) between the drain and the clog with a wet cloth or sponge or the water will shoot out all over you.
- Insert the plunger into the water at an angle so that little air remains under it.
- Use fifteen to twenty forceful strokes, holding the plunger upright.
- Repeat the plunging two or three times before giving up.

To this I add: Try it for fifteen minutes before mouthing expletives in defeat.

There's a great debate going on about the use of chemical drain openers. Some people think they're worth a try; others think they're useless, and, if the system has a septic tank, kill off all the necessary bacteria. There's no doubt, though, that these drain openers are among the most dangerous chemicals you could have in a house—fatal if swallowed and capable of causing great damage to eyes and skin. (If you insist on trying one, never use a plunger in conjunction with the chemical because it could splash the caustic chemical up into your eyes and face.)

Debra Lynn Dadd, an internationally recognized consumer advocate specializing in identifying products that are safe and environmentally responsible, advises against such products and suggests you try mechanical drain openers such as plungers or augers. Alternatively, you can try a natural solution: "Pour a handful of baking soda and a half cup of white vinegar down the drainpipe and cover tightly for one minute. The chemical reaction between the two will cause pressure in the drain and dislodge any obstructive matter. Rinse with hot water and repeat as needed."

If this doesn't do the trick, she advises another method: "Pour a quarter cup of 35 percent hydrogen peroxide down the drain. Wait a few minutes and then plunge. Repeat a second time if needed." The hydrogen peroxide causes a bubbling movement which may help loosen a light clog.

The Toilet

A toilet has a three-part mandate in life: it must carry away waste, clean the bowl, and prevent sewer gases from entering the house. Thanks to four enterprising Englishmen, Alexander Cummings, J. G. Jennings, Thomas Crapper, and Thomas Twyford, we enjoy the convenience and sanitary benefits of today's modern toilet.

Still, the toilet remained, for me, the greatest inner mystery. Decades passed without my understanding the minor miracle taking place inside our homes. I asked my plumber, Jim Rossetti, to come over and enlighten me and some of my readers.

So one Friday afternoon, Jim lifted the top of the tank of the toilet, and he and I spent quite a while staring inside at all the mechanical parts. Floating just on the surface of the water in the tank was a black rubber ball, and partially submerged in the water were tubes and valves and pistons. Jim flipped the flush handle and talked me through the chain of events that followed.

Depressing the handle activates a trip lever that lifts the **flush valve,** a kind of stopper, from its **valve seat** at the bottom of the tank. Water from the tank is now free to rush through this hole to the bowl below.

Once the tank is empty of water, the flush valve drops back into place. But that rubber ball, the **float,** has also fallen with the tank's decreasing water level and pulled open the oddly named **ball-cock valve,** which begins feeding fresh water into the tank through a refill tube. As the ascending water level in the tank reaches the correct level, the rising float closes the ball-cock valve and shuts off the water.

I realized while Jim was speaking that I was getting confused because the rubber ball looked as if it should be called the ball cock. No. The rubber ball is the float. Believe it or not, "cock" is another name for a valve operated by a ball. Once I realized that the ball-cock assembly pulls up the stopper and lets the water out of the tank and then opens the inlet refill tube to refill the tank, I was in better shape.

Meantime, back at the bowl, the cascade of water that was released from the tank above begins to push waste down the drain. A siphoning process takes place as water is forced through the back section of the drain, creating a suction that draws the remaining water and wastes down. Now you can see why the bowl completely empties with each flush, until the suction is broken when air moves into the drainpipe. The refill cycle that is triggered by the float not only fills the tank with fresh water, but also sends water to the bowl through a second refill tube that empties into an overflow tube. As the inverted trap of the bowl and the bowl fill with water, sewer gases are effectively sealed off from the house.

A day after this all seemed confusing, I was in awe of how simple and brilliant it was. Study the picture below, follow the text again, and sleep on it. See if you don't awaken with perfect clarity and proper awe.

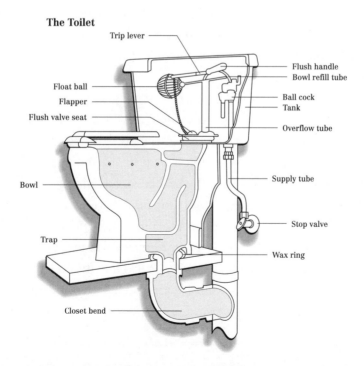

The Toilet

Trip lever

Flush handle
Bowl refill tube

Float ball

Ball cock
Tank

Flapper

Flush valve seat

Overflow tube

Supply tube

Bowl

Stop valve

Trap

Wax ring

Closet bend

The Afflicted Toilet

Prior to my enlightenment, the only time I spent thinking about toilets was if there was a clog, or if too much noise was occurring during the refill cycle. Jim and I spent time discussing both of these situations. First the clog you hate to know.

Jim had told me during an earlier visit that a plunger is not a good thing to use in a clogged toilet because it can break the wax ring that surrounds the horn of a toilet (this is the protrusion that helps seat the toilet into the floor flange). "Ninety-nine times out of a hundred you can get away with using a plunger," he said. "But your readers should know there is a risk of this breaking that wax ring and causing a leak that could damage floors and ceilings. A closet auger, or snake, is the appropriate tool for a clog in the toilet."

In preparation for our interview, I stopped at the hardware store and bought a closet auger (which I pronounced as in the word "owl"). I figured that Jim could teach me how to use it, I could pass this info onto you, and we'd all be the better for it. As I placed the auger in the car, I felt like a real homeowner with my new professional plumbing tool.

The day of our talk, and after examining and reexamining the flushing mechanism of the toilet, I told Jim that I wanted to learn how to use a closet auger and I produced my new one. Jim took one look and tried to suppress a smile. "That's a toy, not a tool," he said in his low gravelly voice. "That won't unclog anything!"

He went out to the truck and brought in his auger (only he pronounced it as in "awful") and proceeded to show me how to use it.

Unfortunately, using the auger requires skill and quite a bit of strength, and it extends to 6 feet in vertical length. Pretty impossible for me to use unless I want to stand on a ladder. (So. Anatomy really *is* destiny.)

Auger

"I'm going back to the plunger," I said with a sigh. Jim told me to try stretching out a coat hanger and finagling the toilet paper back up through the drain, and then letting the paper sit for an hour or so until it began to break up. Almost always the water in the bowl slowly drains through the clog, lowering the water level and making it safe to flush one more time. Then try to flush the toilet. Or assign this clog to a tall person living in your house who could use a good auger that is purchased in a plumbing supply house.

If the coat hanger doesn't work, and the tall person doesn't show, and your boss is coming for dinner, you might have to use a plunger and hope all goes well.

The last thing you want to do when there's a clog and the water level is still high is to flush the toilet a second time, because this will result in a revolting spillage all over your floor.

Jim told me that most toilet clogs are caused by children throwing toys in the bowl, or by their stuffing too much toilet paper or those pretty "hostess" paper hand towels down the drain. Paper towels are a real problem. They can ball up and get stuck down in the horn, which is only 2 1/2 inches in diameter; unlike toilet paper, paper towels do not break up. It's auger and plumber time. Get a Lid-Lock (see page 361) to protect the toilet, your child, and yourself.

The Case of the Running Toilet

Another mystery. What is all that noise coming from the toilet? Jim explained that the mechanical assembly of a flush tank will eventually wear out and you'll hear about it. It could be that the flush valve (the stopper) wears out or gets misshapen, or that the piston that sets the flush valve can no longer seat itself down. You hear the sound of continuously running water.

The life span of the mechanical assembly depends on how often it's used as well as on the hardness of the water coming into your house. Hard water can corrode parts, and lime deposits can clog things up. Fortunately, all flush-tank parts are available by the piece and are pretty standard.

I wanted to know what I could do to quiet all the racket, and I asked Jim about jiggling handles and bending lift wires—all the things I seem to remember my parents doing during my childhood (it's scary what your children remember about you, isn't it?). But he told me that lift wires are almost a thing of the past, the mechanics of toilets have changed, and if a part is shot, peace will be restored only after the ailing part is replaced.

Jim did give me a short-term solution. If the toilet is running badly, turn off the valve of the water supply (that's the tube that usually comes from the wall and it's how the water comes in to refill the tank and bowl). There will now be one flush left in the tank. After that's used in the next flush, turn the valve on, refill the tank, and turn it off again. Repeat as necessary until the plumber can come and save your sanity.

The 1.6-Gallon Ultra-Low-Flush Toilet

The toilets we all grew up with and those manufactured prior to January 1, 1994, used 5 gallons of water to create a good flush.

But concern about water shortages and the strain on municipal sewer systems created a movement that looked to the European 6-liter (1.6-gallon) toilet. After hot debate, Congress passed a legal mandate that has made it impossible to purchase anything but an ultra-low-flush 1.6 gallon toilet. (Have no fear. The toilet police won't come to your door and demand to know how many gallons you're flushing with; you just won't be able to replace a toilet with anything but one that uses 1.6 gallons of water per flush.)

Duane Johnson, author of *How a House Works,* does the arithmetic for us: "Assuming that each person flushes the toilet three times a day, homeowners can save from 5 to 10 gallons of water per day using ULF toilets. Even a small town can save between half a million and a million gallons of water daily!"

There are two kinds of water-saving toilets that you can purchase: the gravity ULF and the pressurized ULF. A gravity ULF toilet looks much like a standard toilet, but it has a somewhat modified tank. It may also have a slit along the bowl rim rather than holes, a reduced water reservoir, and steeper bowl sides that increase the speed and force of the flush.

The flush mechanism of a pressurized ULF toilet looks a bit like a plastic bomb suspended inside the tank. There's an additional closed compartment inside the plastic, and as the water supply fills the tank, the water pressure compresses the air inside that compartment. The compressed air acts to augment the velocity of the flush so that it is more forceful. These toilets are efficient, expensive, and rather noisy.

The Water Heater
Every house has a domestic water heater whose function is to receive cold water pumped into it, heat it, and send it on through the hot-water pipes. My house had two water heaters: one—an

Gas Water Heater

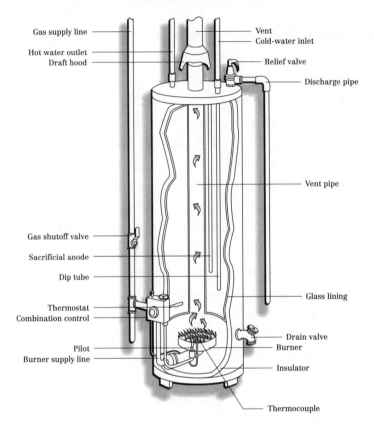

aquabooster—connected to the boiler, and an 80-gallon electric heater that was switched on when we closed on the house in early July. This was the "summer" water heater, used when the boiler was shut down after the heating season. In the fall, however, when we attempted to start up the aquabooster, the pump smoked and died. As did a replacement pump. Someone had piped the whole thing wrong. We settled for the full-time use of the electric water heater.

What a mistake. Our electric bills were running very close to $300 a month, and my blood pressure was heading up to accompany them. Eventually, my electrician did an energy audit and confirmed that the culprit was indeed that monster electric water heater. I replaced it with a 50-gallon propane-fired water heater and my electric bills dropped to $120! (My propane bill is about $50, but the propane feeds the stove and heater in the studio as well as the water heater. I still come out way ahead.)

I tell you this because you should know that the water heater is generally considered to be one of the greediest of all residential appliances. Only a central air-conditioning or heating system demands more energy and money. According to the U.S. Department of Energy, a water heater consumes some 20 percent of the energy used in the home. The electric water heater is a pig.

One time we ran out of hot water and the plumber who came to check out the problem peppered his diagnostic conversation with the phrases "lower heating elements," "dip tubes," and—most intriguingly—"sacrificial anodes." From that discussion, I came away understanding only that the lower heating element had died and needed replacing.

Once he restored hot water to a very disgruntled household, I began to get interested in the inner workings of that big lug of a tank. The phrase "sacrificial anode," with all its quasi-religious resonance, lingered in my mind long after the plumber left.

The majority of people in this country have gas water heaters. Their capacity ranges from 30 to 100 gallons, they are insulated internally, and they are glass-lined to resist corrosion. The products of combustion from gas-fired heaters are exhausted through a vent pipe into the chimney or flue pipe to the outdoors.

How is it that a reasonable amount of hot water is always available to your household? In a gas water heater, cold water is brought into the tank through a pipe called a dip tube. Now, this dip tube is very long, and it routes the water to the bottom of the tank, where it comes into close contact with the heating device, in this case the gas burner. The newly heated water is naturally more buoyant than the incoming cold, so it rises to the top of the tank—"on call" when anyone in the home twists on a hot-water faucet. Pressure is always supplied because the cold-water valve is always open.

An electric water heater is similar to a gas one except that instead of a burner, it has an upper and a lower heating element. These elements are controlled by individual thermostats that monitor the water temperature through the wall of the tank. Usually only one element operates at a time (your electric bill is bad enough). The upper element turns on first and heats the water in the top half of the tank, then it shuts off while the lower element raises the temperature of the water in the bottom half.

If you've barely executed your first aria in the shower and the water turns cold (and four people haven't showered before you, selfishly using up all the water), it's likely to be something relatively simple. In a gas heater, the **thermocouple,** a safety device that monitors heat and throttles the flow of gas if the burner shuts down, wears out. Or in an electric heater, as in our case, the lower heating element burns out. These components can be replaced by a plumber for about $50 to $100.

The common enemies of all water heaters, though, are sediment buildup, corrosion, and rust. The sediments come from the minerals present in water. They can accumulate on the bottom of the tank, trapping heat from the gas burner. The temperature will rise higher than it should and eventually stress the tank and its glass coating.

You can help fight the fight against sediment buildup by draining the tank, generally about once a year (some hot water heaters should be drained every other month, so read the instruction manual or call the manufacturing company). You also might want to have your plumber walk you through the process the first time.

Some newer models have a self-cleaning system to help reduce sediment. A curved dip tube causes the incoming cold water to create an eddy at the bottom of the tank. This prevents the sediment from settling and causes it to flow out of the tank instead. This is the kind I bought. In my Bradford-White water heater it is called a Hydro-jet system. It costs more but it's worth it.

The tank's inner glass coating helps defend against rust, but the other great rust guard is a rod suspended inside the tank, called—here it is at last—the **sacrificial anode.** This special rod is made usually of either magnesium or aluminum, and it exists simply as a decoy. Through the process of ionization, a sacrificial anode magnetically attracts the corrosion-causing minerals and elements in water that would otherwise attack the exposed metal of the tank. But, as its name implies, in the process of defending the heater, the anode itself corrodes. It can be replaced by your plumber for about $75, however, buying your heater a longer life.

Farewell, Old Faithful: Replacing Your Water Heater

A water heater usually lasts about thirteen years, but some do last quite a bit longer. How will you know when the water heater is about to bid you adieu? A pooling of water on the floor underneath the heater may signify that the tank has rusted and the end is near, but the leak could have other causes, so have a plumber rule out any fixable problems before relegating your heater to the ash heap.

I got very concerned about tank size when we replaced our electric heater. After all, most of my day is about appointments and deadlines, and there was no way I was going to schedule showers to ensure an adequate supply of hot water. But I'd also had it with humongous electric bills, and I needed to understand how we were using our hot water supply in order to calculate the tank size.

On an average, a five-minute shower consumes about 15 gallons of water, a tub bath about 20 gallons, a dishwasher about 14 gallons, and a load of laundry more than 40 gallons. A family of four should get along fine with a 50-gallon tank, as long as they don't do

The Water Heater

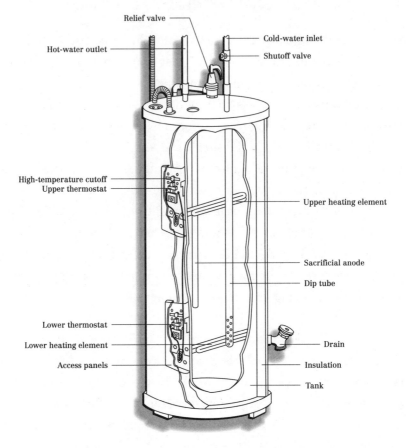

Relief valve

Hot-water outlet

Cold-water inlet

Shutoff valve

High-temperature cutoff
Upper thermostat

Upper heating element

Sacrificial anode

Dip tube

Lower thermostat

Lower heating element

Access panels

Drain

Insulation

Tank

the laundry with hot water, run the dishwasher, and attempt to complete three consecutive showers during the morning bathroom rush.

A very important factor in the decision on tank size is the recovery rate—the amount of time the heater takes to climb back up to the preset temperature after you've used up the standing supply of hot water. A gas heater recovers fastest and takes about an hour; an electric heater takes twice as long, so if you're going with electric, you'll need about an 80-gallon tank.

My neighbor Alan just told me he recently replaced his water heater and bought another electric model. When I asked him what his electric bill was, he answered: "About $100 a month." I couldn't understand that figure (it was $200 below my bill), and he ex-

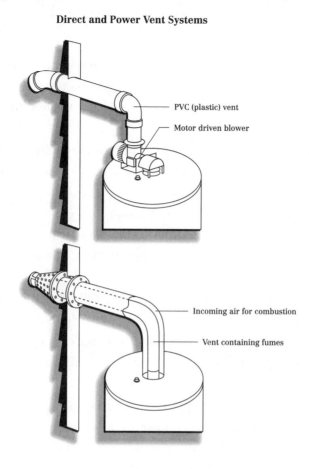

PVC (plastic) vent

Motor driven blower

Incoming air for combustion

Vent containing fumes

plained: "It's just Ruthie and me now, and we don't have as much laundry to do, or dishes to wash. A family with young children is constantly calling for hot water, so, naturally, the electric bills will be substantial."

One of the advantages of electric water heaters is that they don't produce combustion gases, so there's no need for a vent and they're easy to install. The other advantage is that there's no danger of backdrafting in a tight, energy-efficient house. (If there's too much air going out of the house and not enough able to come back in because it's tightly sealed and caulked, then the possibility exists that replacement air may be drawn down through the vent of a combustion appliance and pull the dangerous combustion gases down with it into the living space. See page 308 for a fuller discussion.)

Today it's possible to buy gas or propane water heaters that are either "power-vented" or "direct-vented" so they both eliminate the need for chimneys and practically eliminate the dangers of backdrafting.

The **power vent** uses a blower to pull the combustion gases from the heater and exhausts them outside the house through a 3-inch PVC pipe that runs out through the wall. This is what I purchased. The fan keeps the combustion gases directed up and out—they can never be sucked back into the house by an upset in the air pressure balances (see Chapter 10, "Ventilation Is the Name of the Game").

The **direct vent** uses a double pipe. It pulls the combustion air into the unit through the outer chamber and exhausts the combustion gases out of the house through the chamber in the middle. So it too can exhaust through an exterior house wall and doesn't backdraft.

Because the vent pipes of this type of gas or propane heater cannot be extremely long, you have to be able to place the water heater near an outside wall. You should also understand that a power-vent or direct-vent unit will cost at least twice what you'd pay for a standard gas model, but, in my opinion, the safety features are well worth it.

Integrated Systems for Boiler Owners

No longer in use in my boiler, but still present as a vestige of how hot water was once supplied to this house, is a "tankless coil." This is typically a copper coil running through the middle of the boiler capable of producing domestic hot water as a co-product of central heating. Tankless coils are still fairly common in the New England area.

A previous owner of my house installed the now-infamous

freestanding electric water heater next to an aquabooster. An aquabooster is an insulated tank that stands alongside a boiler and is piped to the boiler's tankless coil. It stores hot water and thus gives you a fighting chance at a hot shower if someone runs the dishwasher at the same time you decide to lather up. Apparently, the electric heater was used in the summer when the boiler was shut off, and the aquabooster was supposed to be used during the heating season. I realize now that an aquabooster would have been a good solution for us, if only the pipes hadn't been put together backward, so that the water pressure kept blowing the pump.

I was having a propane tank installed for a gas stove, so I went ahead and purchased a freestanding propane-fired water heater as I mentioned at the beginning of this section. But two months after the installation, I met my plumber, Jim Rossetti, and he told me that I should have purchased either a new aquabooster (piped correctly) or something called a Boiler Mate. A Boiler Mate, manufactured by Amtrol in Rhode Island, also works off the boiler. When the water inside the inner storage tank of the Boiler Mate falls below a certain temperature, the boiler kicks on and circulates water through a coiled heat exchanger in the Boiler Mate. The recovery rate is about thirteen minutes, so you have an abundant supply of hot water, and the boiler has to run only a few minutes at a time, two or three times a day, so this integrated system is highly efficient. The Boiler Mate also has a long life span and its manufacturer offers a lifetime warranty against leakage.

At any rate, discuss all the options in the water heater department with your plumber or your fuel-supply company when it comes time to make a decision on a replacement. There are safe and efficient choices, and an expert can give you valuable advice.

Why Do Plumbers Charge So Much?

Once you buy a house, you need to form a special relationship with a plumber—immediately! Talk to the former owners and ask them who worked on the house and did quality work, or survey your new neighbors. Don't wait until there's an emergency to go looking for one. Eventually you may learn to do some simple repairs yourself, but in the beginning, learn from the experts.

People seem to roll their eyes when they talk about plumbers and exhale some expression about how expensive they are. There are some reasons for the high fees.

Plumbing is a complex business today, and becoming a plumber requires a very protracted period of study. In fact, the full training period takes much, much longer than the time you spend completing a law degree. I called Keith Stadler, the department head at the Wright Technical School in Stamford, Connecticut, and he talked me through the extensive training of a plumber-in-the-making in the state of Connecticut. "The actual training begins with five years of theory in a classroom," he explained. "Some of the courses taught are physics, mechanical drawing, pipe fitting and welding, and fixtures installation and design, as well as heating system design and maintenance. Then there's a five-year apprenticeship under a licensed master plumber. After completing the coursework and the apprenticeship—a minimum of 12,000 hours of combined theory and field work—a novice plumber can get a journeyman's license by taking and achieving passing scores on a rigorous exam. Two years after receiving a journeyman's license, a plumber can apply for a master's license by passing yet another set of exams."

Think of all of this the next time you get a bill.

The Electrical System of a House

Thanks to the power of electricity, you now hold this book in your hand. No, not because I wrote it on a computer, or because electric light cast its glow and enabled me to see what I was writing, but because I was almost electrocuted.

As I mentioned in the Preface, I came up with the idea to write this book in front of the fireplace one winter Sunday afternoon. About a week later, there was an unusual ice storm in the Northeast and my car began to fishtail into one that was oncoming. I managed to avoid a head-on collision, but I must have put my foot on the brake, because my car flew off the road and smashed into a utility pole, snapping it in two and bringing down a canopy of live wires above the roof. Naturally I had to hit the pole that held the transformer box (that canister that looks like a tall gray garbage can), and 13,000 volts of live electricity dangled above my head.

Now, even though I was a city girl, I had read somewhere that you never get out of a car anywhere near downed power lines—the rubber tires offer insulation. But when a Good Samaritan drove by and determined that the wires weren't touching the car but that my car was on fire, I had seconds to make a decision. Too many TV and movie car explosions informed my choice. I stepped out.

That I wasn't a crusty mummy on the roadside and a memory to my family and friends is something no one can understand. The policeman who came and helped me home just sat in the patrol car, looked at my car and the wires, and every so often put his head down on the wheel and seemed to shudder.

I hadn't understood that electricity is looking to return to the ground, and my first step out onto the ice could have completed a mighty fine circuit. Nor did I know that the wires did not have to touch me or the car: electricity is capable of arcing several feet to get to that circuit (especially in wet conditions).*

I was pretty shaky for a long time afterward, but in the days that followed, I decided that since my life plan might exceed my life *span,* I was going to do everything I'd ever said I'd do—and do it quickly. Thus, I pushed ahead with this project. (It was sort of life-affirming, and my way of turning the horrible into something positive. Plus, I had to pay for that damned utility pole and my increased insurance rates.)

Anyway, I now have this powerful respect for the positive as well as the negative aspects of electricity and I am of the firm opinion that one should know all about it and be able to reset a tripped circuit breaker and understand why ground-fault circuit interrupters (GFIs) are so important in preventing electrocution (see page 91). But I also think that anything involving the electrical wiring of a house should be left up to the professionals. There are many other projects you could turn to should the handyman/handywoman urge come upon you. Go fix a pipe, recaulk your bathtub, or drain your hot water heater. But don't read a book and attempt to turn yourself into an electrical apprentice. It's just too risky.

But enough with the scary stuff. We're going to take a closer look at those gray canisters perched atop utility poles. (They're called step-down transformers, and their function in life was never to finish me off, but to provide electrical power to all of our

---

*If you're ever—God forbid—in this situation, where you must leave the car because of a fire, get up on your haunches at the doorway and jump out of the car with both feet tucked up in the air underneath you. Jump as far away from the car as you can manage, and land on both feet so there is no circuit between you, the metal on the car, and the ground. If there's no fire and you have to stay in the car for six hours, stay in that car! Don't get out until the utility company helps you out.

dwellings.) But before we do, let's review a few definitions and characteristics of electricity for anyone who, like me, daydreamed through this unit in high school.

Electricity for Dummies

An electric current is actually a great jostling of negatively charged electrons along a conductive pathway. In fact, a throng of electrons flows through metal in much the way water flows through a pipe, so it may simplify matters to extend the plumbing metaphor in order to define some terms.

As water flowing through a pipe is measured in gallons per minute, the volume of electric current flowing through a circuit is measured in amperes or **amps.** (Put another way, amps are the measurement of the number of electrons per second flowing past a given point.) While water pressure running through pipes is measured in pounds per square inch, the amount of "pressure" or push in electric current is measured in **volts.**

But this is where the plumbing analogy breaks down. If a pipe contracts a hole or a break, water will continue to spurt out indefinitely, but if there is any break or interruption in an electrical circuit, the electricity will simply cease to flow. An electrical current can travel only in a continuous loop from its source, through various receptacles and devices, and back again to its original starting point.

The other electrical term we'll be talking about in this chapter is **watts.** This is the sum total of energy in a circuit at any given moment in time. If you multiply the number of amps an electrical appliance consumes by the voltage in the power line, you arrive at the wattage. Amps × volts = watts.

(Is it all coming back to you?)

Bringing Electricity Home

Electricity is generated at a power plant and transmitted to homes and businesses over high-voltage lines. In order to send electricity over long distances, a transformer steps up the strength of the current. But this strength would totally overwhelm a house unless it was stepped down incrementally and reduced in strength before entering the dwelling. This conversion is done by a distribution network along the way, and—at those familiar gray canisters right outside your home—approximately 13,000 volts of electricity is stepped down to two usable, "hot" supplies of approximately 120 volts each.

Homes today need to be linked up to both supplies. This way, one supply of 120-volt power can be used in combination with a neutral wire to power lamps and hair dryers, vacuums and electric shavers; and a combination of the two 120-volt supplies with a neutral conductor can provide power to larger equipment that requires 240-volt power, such as an electric range, an electric water heater, a well pump, or a central air-conditioning unit. (For very complicated reasons, this kind of service is not referred to as "240 service," but as "220 service." This is mostly because the voltage coming into a home can deviate from the normal 120 volts, depending on the house's proximity to the step-down transformer.)

You can still come across older homes with 120 service—they are connected only with one of the 120-volt supplies from the transformer and a neutral conductor—but this is insufficient for today's vast number of appliances and electrical equipment. It costs about $800 to $1,000 and requires about a day's work from two electricians to upgrade the electrical system to 100-amp, three-wire service.

If you go outside your house and look for the wires that

arrive from the local transformer, you will most likely see the three lines affixed to your house near the roof. Two of the three wires are the live 120-volt lines that carry power into the home, and the other one is the neutral conductor line that acts as a return path for electricity, completing its circuit. I'd always noticed that there's a sort of sloppy-looking sagging of these wires just before they attach to the house, but I never knew why. It turns out that they are drip loops to prevent water from entering the service head.

Once the electric lines go through the service head, they run down a metal conduit and through an electric meter which records the household's electrical consumption, and then enter the house through a gray metal box on the wall of a basement or garage called the **service panel.** The service panel is the heart of the home's electrical service. It is command central.

The Anatomy of a Service Panel

Inside the service panel are three metal bars called **bus bars.** A bus is anything that takes electricity from one place to another. Two of these buses carry the electricity from the 120-volt service wires entering from outside the home and are thus called the **hot bus bars.**

The service panel then divides the incoming electricity into branch circuits that dispatch electricity throughout the home. All the 120-volt branch circuits that provide power to the outlets in your home begin at one or the other of the two hot bus bars. Larger appliances, such as your water heater, electric stove, or well pump, require 240 voltage, and are powered from both bus bars.

All these branch circuits complete their circuits inside the service panel, at the third metal bar, called the **neutral bus bar.** This neutral bus bar is connected to the neutral service wire outside the home as well as to something called a **grounding conductor.** This grounding conductor is a wire that is hooked to the water supply pipe that brings water into the home, or to some sort of metal rod driven into the earth near the house's foundation. The grounding wire offers any excess or misdirected household current an uninterrupted metal pathway to the earth and thus helps avoid shocks and fires in the event of a short circuit.

More About the Branch Circuits

The cable that is used in residential wiring for circuit branches also carries three or more solid wires. The hot, *live* wire carrying 120 volts from the service panel bears insulation that is covered either black or red. The "neutral" wire is usually covered in white or gray insulation. Comparable to the neutral service wire, it provides "used" current a pathway back to the service panel. The third

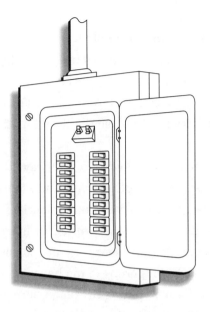

wire—the equipment ground—is either uninsulated or sheathed in green insulation. Should any problem crop up in the circuit, the equipment ground wire channels rogue current back to the service panel and then to the water pipe and to ground.

Don't expect to see the hot or neutral bus bars when you open the door to your service panel. While the hot wires from the service entrance are directly attached to the hot bus bars, the hot wires of the branch circuits are not. Instead, they are attached to either a screw-in plug fuse or a circuit breaker, and it is these "overcurrent protection devices" that you will be staring at. These fuses or circuit breakers will disconnect the supply of electricity to any circuit that begins to heat up because it is drawing more current than the fuse or circuit breaker is programmed for. When such an overload occurs, the fuse "blows" or the circuit breaker "trips." Current ceases to travel until you correct the problem and replace the fuse or reset the circuit breaker.

Shutdown at Command Central

This shutdown occurs in two situations. The first is if there's a short circuit because of a faulty piece of equipment or a frayed cord, and the second is a circuit overload. Let's discuss a short circuit first, because we so often use the term but its meaning is a bit fuzzy to people.

Current automatically flows if a pathway is forged between a hot wire and anything grounded—even if it is unplanned and accidental. When this situation arises, and an accidental path provides a shorter route to ground—in other words, the longer, safer, *intended* route has been bypassed—a "short circuit" has occurred. And this unplanned pathway is dangerous to the house and its inhabitants.

A frayed cord or wire or a faulty plug is a recipe for a short circuit. If the insulation of a wire has deteriorated and the wires inside touch each other or the grounded metal frame of an appliance, they can create a strong surge of current that would be extremely dangerous to you if you came between the hot conductor and the grounded contact appliance or device. You would become a part of this circuit and complete the pathway to ground, receiving a strong shock, possibly even winning an instant trip to the heavenly spheres. Also, your house would be in danger of sparks flying and a fire starting.

If you notice frayed or charred cords, disconnect the lamp or appliance immediately and do not use it again until it's been properly repaired.

The second, more common cause of a shutdown on a circuit is a circuit overload. A circuit is designed to handle only a certain amount of amperage. The sky is not the limit. If you attempt to get more current out of a circuit than it is capable of handling, the wires could overheat and start a fire. Fuses and circuit breakers are the fail-safe in the system, because they interrupt the circuit once your demand exceeds the amount of amperage the wires are designed to transport.

It's likely that your home is wired predominantly with 12- and 14-gauge wire (in this case, 12-gauge is physically larger than the 14-gauge), and these wires nicely handle lights and electric clocks and other small appliances. The National Electrical Code (NEC) permits 14-gauge wire to transport up to 15 amps and 12-gauge wire to transport up to 20 amps. To ensure that overloads don't occur, each "circuit" is defended by either a 15-amp or 20-amp circuit breaker or fuse in the service panel. The power-hungry appliances I mentioned above, such as the electric clothes dryer, the well pump, and the electric stove, use larger conductor wires and so must have higher-rated overcurrent protection devices, usually 30-40-, 50-, and even 60-amp fuses or circuit breakers.

The first time I attempted to fathom my service panel, I saw those circuit breakers marked 15 or 20 or 30 and 50, and I remember telling John Krozer, our electrician, that we didn't have modern 220 service. He explained that 220 is the voltage or the push of electricity arriving from the transformer, and the 15, 20, 30, 40, and 50 markings are referring to the amperage—the measure of electrical current.

Whereas earlier we multiplied amps times volts to arrive at wattage, there's also a formula to determine amperage: divide the number of watts an appliance consumes by 120 volts. Thus, a 1,200-watt toaster draws 10 amps of electricity ($1,200 \div 120 = 10$). But if I plug a 9-amp iron into a 15-amp outlet at the same time as I'm browning some toast, I'd be drawing 19 amps on a 15-amp outlet, and the fuse would blow or the circuit would trip immediately. This is why the NEC now requires kitchens to have at least two 20-amp circuits to handle the appliances used there. (Of course I *could* give up ironing. . . .)

So naturally, the next question is: How do fuses and circuit breakers know that I'm toasting and ironing at the same time and have exceeded the amount of power I can draw from that circuit and am at risk of a meltdown inside the wiring?

A circuit breaker contains a bimetallic strip that becomes a link in the circuit when it is installed in the panel box. If too much current passes through a branch circuit, it creates heat, and this heat bends this metal strip, causing a release to trip and open the circuit. The flow of electricity ceases. When a circuit breaker trips, the toggle moves either to the "off" or an intermediate position. All you need to do to reset a tripped circuit breaker is to move the switch all the way to the off position and then press it back to the "on" position.

A plug fuse contains an alloy strip that has a low melting point, and it also becomes a link in the circuit when installed in the socket or fuse holder in the service panel. If the amperage moving through the circuit exceeds the fuse's rating, the alloy strip melts and opens the circuit. But a plug fuse gives you an even more detailed report on the condition of the circuit it protects. If the metal strip inside the fuse is separated, you'll know that an overload has occurred. If the window of the plug fuse is blackened or discolored, there's a short in the system.

I asked John Krozer if fuses should be replaced with circuit breakers, and he told me that fuses are not inferior to circuit breakers. In fact, they sense overloads a bit faster than circuit breakers. Their drawback is that you've always got to keep a supply of various-amp fuses around the house, whereas there's no such store of supplies required with circuit breakers.

However, you can't just reset a circuit breaker or plug in a new fuse. First you need to find out what's causing the overload and correct it.

No More Overloads

The simplest way to avoid spending your day resetting tripped circuits is to simply plug the appliance that's causing the problem into another circuit. I found this out whenever I attempted to vacuum the back bedrooms at night, when all the lights and TVs were on. For some reason, when I plugged the canister into the receptacle in the master bedroom, we'd all find ourselves in the dark and loud outcries were sounded in the peanut gallery, where my sons were watching such important shows as *Full House* and *Roseanne.*

Blown Fuses

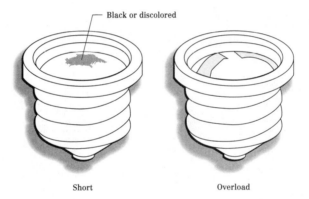

Black or discolored

Short   Overload

It's tempting to think that this blackout was a sign from God that I was to lay down my canister forever, but it's probably just due to the fact that the vacuum draws 10–12 amps and that there are too many other pieces of electrical equipment demanding current from that already loaded circuit. Add up all the amperage and my kids are missing their Must-See TV. Now I vacuum in the day or just use a hallway receptacle.

Of course, my other option is to have John run another circuit from the service panel and install a new receptacle that expands my ability to draw power. We did this when we put a 17,500-BTU air conditioner in the family room. Since it draws 16 amps of electricity, he suggested we put in a 20-amp receptacle dedicated only to the air conditioner. It cost about $200 to add this circuit. Another circuit in the bedroom and I can vacuum into the wee hours of the morning.

You can get an idea how many amps the common electrical appliances are drawing when you use them and why certain circuits may be overloading from the chart below:

Current Needed for Household Appliances

Appliance	Current (in amps)
window air conditioner	8–16
table saw	13–15
refrigerator	6–15
toaster oven	12
microwave	6–12
hair dryer	10
clothes washer	10
toaster	7–10
coffee maker	6–10
garbage disposer	5–10
clothes iron	9
dehumidifier	7
freezer	5
vacuum	10–12

(Adapted from "How a House Works," *Family Handyman*, March 1995)

Many of us are guilty of using multiple-plug extension cords—the "extension cord octopus"—which artificially increase the number of outlets on a circuit beyond the eight to ten the circuit was designed to handle. THIS IS A FIRE HAZARD!

If you create a map of the circuits and you know which outlets are controlled by each circuit breaker or fuse, you can then figure the continuous load on each circuit and figure out why and when there's an overload.

Identifying Circuits

If no one has identified the circuits on your service panel, you can map out the whole electrical system in less than an hour. First buy an inexpensive voltage tester in a hardware or electrical supply store. Then, working with a partner to make it easier, turn on all the lights in the house. Turn off one circuit at a time by flipping the circuit breaker to the "off" position or unscrewing a fuse. Noting which lights go off gives you a big clue as to the area of the house serviced by that particular circuit. But the voltage tester can be plugged into vacant receptacles so you can identify the circuits they are on, also. Always record your discoveries on a map of the house's floor plan, and keep repeating the process until you've mapped out all the circuits. (Remember that the circuits or fuses marked for 30, 40, 50, or 60 amps are powering something big like the electric stove or hot water heater or central air conditioning, and you'll know which is which when the appliance fails to respond.) Then mark the circuit breakers or fuses on the service panel with a fine felt-tip pen.

Our service panel was thoughtfully marked when we arrived with phrases such as "guest bedroom," "master bath," "garbage disposal," "dryer," "living room," "electric range," etc. Play the Sher-

lock Holmes game yourself and mark each one of the circuits on
your service panel.

Once you've identified each circuit, make a list of every appliance and fixture that is always plugged in there or wired into the
circuit, and also a list the wattage each appliance consumes. Add
up the total of the wattage, then divide the sum by 120. The continuous load should never demand more than 80 percent of the circuit's capacity printed on its circuit breaker or fuse. For example,
it's reasonable to demand up to 12 amps on a 15-amp circuit, or 16
amps on a 20-amp circuit. The 20 percent margin beyond this continuous load permits you to occasionally plug in another piece of
equipment without overloading the circuit.

Upgrading Your Electrical Service

According to Monte Burch, the author of *Basic House Wiring,*
"the consumption of electricity in the home has more than tripled
in the past twenty years, yet very few homes are wired to cope with
this extra burden."

Today, most local codes require a 100-amp service entrance
as the minimum, but a typical 3,000-square-foot home, complete
with an electric stove, a dishwasher, a microwave, central air conditioning, recessed lighting, computers, printers, a fax machine, a
workshop, etc., needs 200-amp service and a forty-circuit panel
box. (Some of the very large new homes built today have 400-amp
service with two forty-circuit panel boxes.)

According to John Krozer, this upgrading takes two electricians a full day to upgrade to 200-amp service. The size of the
wiring from the weather cap outside into the panel box is enlarged
so that there is more capacity, and the existing circuits are put into
a bigger panel box. This increase in capacity costs about $1,200,
and you should understand that any work beyond the service

panel—such as the installation of a dedicated circuit for the dishwasher or the computer or the air conditioner, and any installation of electrical outlets—is all charged for separately.

Keeping the Home Owner-Safe: Ground-Fault Circuit Interrupters and Three-Wire Grounded Receptacles ("Monkey Faces")

While circuit breakers and fuses protect wires and appliances, they don't protect *you*. If one of your electrical appliances or tools breaks down in some way and begins to leak current, the grounding wire will channel most of that deviating current away. But "most" is not good enough. If you happen to be standing around with that appliance or tool in an area that's wet or where you could touch a metal faucet, you would make an excellent channel for a bit of that errant electricity also, and a smidgin of it—as little as 200 milliamperes—could kill you. That's why the National Electrical Code requires that all new bathroom circuits and circuits installed next to a kitchen sink, as well as all new 15- and 20-amp outdoor receptacles, be protected by a device invented about twenty years ago—a ground-fault circuit interrupter, known affectionately as a

Ground-Fault Circuit Interrupter

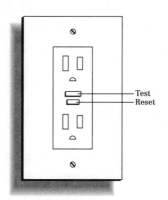

GFI. It's the interesting-looking outlet you may recall seeing in bathrooms near sinks, and it's marked with little buttons that say TEST and RESET. GFIs are lifesaving.

I have this very dangerous habit of wanting to do two things at once, and not always thinking things through. Once, while blow-drying my hair, and in the interest of saving time, I got the urge to sprinkle cleanser and scour the sink. So I ended up touching the metal faucet and running water while holding an operating electrical appliance in my hand. If there had been some fault in my hair dryer and electricity had began to leak, the metal and water would have been wonderful conductors to help the electricity return, *through me,* to the ground where it longs to go. Death would have come for the Happy Homemaker.

The GFI keeps me on this planet because it senses misdirected current and reacts within 1/40 second to trip the circuit before a devastating dose of electricity comes my way.

How does it do this? There's a doughnut-shaped transformer inside the GFI which senses the currents passing through the hot and the neutral wire. Although they travel in opposite directions, they should always be equal. If, however, there is a current leak because of a faulty appliance or frayed cord, the current flowing through the hot wire will be stronger than that flowing through the neutral wire. An imbalance occurs. The GFI detects an imbalance as small as 0.005 amp and trips the circuit, shutting it down. It senses the ground fault and "interrupts" it, thus earning its name. Pretty remarkable.

You may be left wondering why the GFI is set to sense an imbalance at 0.005. Well, a shock of 0.006 is enough to upset the electrical impulses in your heart and disrupt its beating rhythm, causing death. That's why.

Make sure you have GFIs in your kitchen, bathroom, basement, workroom, pool area—anyplace where water or moisture could pose a danger to you. Your electrician can install one in about ten minutes for approximately $50. As I have a strip of plug outlets near my sink, John installed a GFI in the service panel. This "circuit breaker" variety protects every outlet on that circuit.

You should test a GFI regularly—perhaps once a month. Push the test button. This will create a small electrical fault and a GFI in good working order will react by shutting off the circuit. You'll hear a click. Push the reset button when you want to use your hair dryer or juicer or any other electrical appliance.

You should also know that new hair dryers have a square-looking plug on the end of the cord—it's a built-in GFI, and it's a good idea to replace an older model with a new one that offers this safety feature.

I had noticed that some of the outlets looked different around my house. Some were typical two-prong outlets, but others in the kitchen and down in my office and laundry room had three openings that look like little sad or startled faces (Think of this a Rorschach test.)

I asked electrician John Krozer what these differences all meant, and he began with what he calls "monkey-face plugs." They look like this:

John explained that the longer vertical slot is the neutral connection, the shorter slot is the hot side of the plug, and the little half-round mouth is the mechanical ground. This half-round mouth is bonded to the neutral bus bar in your circuit panel box.

How does this protect you? If you are using a heavy-duty appliance or power tool, and the hot wire breaks free from the connection and lies against the metal part of the motor or appliance—and there is no mechanical ground—then the frame of the appliance or motor becomes energized. It becomes "hot." If you then touch that appliance or tool (a vacuum, a dryer, a dishwasher, an electric stove,

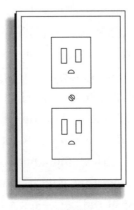

a toaster oven, a power tool, etc.), the circuit could be completed by running through you and then down to the earth. Definitely not good.

The monkey-face plug protects you because the third prong—the half-round one—is connected by a separate green wire in the cord to the metal housing of the appliance or tool. When you plug the appliance in, that third prong fits a slot connected to the neutral bus bar in the circuit panel box as I mentioned above. This then routes any leaking or errant current safely back to the neutral bus bar, where it will trip the circuit or blow the fuse, and cease to be a danger to anyone or anything.

John told me that most new houses are built with monkey-face plugs as the standard, but older homes may not have them. He advises that you have them installed in the rooms we've discussed above as well as wherever you plug in the vacuum cleaner or use some kind of appliance. It is fairly inexpensive to change a two-pronged receptacle into a safer, grounded three-pronged receptacle.

Shutting Off All Power

It's unlikely you'll ever have to shut off the electricity to your entire house, but you should know how to do it in the event of an emergency or a dangerous situation. If you see your lights cycling way up and down in brightness, it's a sign that you have an open or floating neutral. This means that there is a break in the neutral line and the voltage is fluctuating. You'll want to shut off all electricity to the house and call your utility company right away. Otherwise you'll have current surges and all your major appliances could blow out.

If a storm or tree branch brings wires down outside your house, you're also going to want to shut off all the power and call the power company with—forgive the pun—lightning fingers. Keep your children and pets inside the house and *do not* go out to inspect the situation.

To shut off all the power, return to the service panel in your basement or garage. On the top of the panel is a switch, called the "Service Disconnect," or "Main." Push the switch to "off" and all power will cease flowing.

If you have an older service panel with fuses, there won't be a switch to push. Rather, you'll find a main pull-out block with two cartridge-type fuses mounted on its backside. Just pull out the block and wait for the power company.

Deciphering Your Electric Bill

New Age philosophers tell us we should love our bills. After all, they're a great affirmation of our creditworthiness or ability to pay. Well, I just couldn't feel all warm and fuzzy about my electric bills because they were running sky-high, thanks to my former electric water heater.

But now that I'm paying about $150 less a month, I open each one with great satisfaction and smug delight, although I do realize that this is not quite what the metaphysicians had in mind.

There's no doubt that I need a great deal of spiritual work, but

Electric Meter

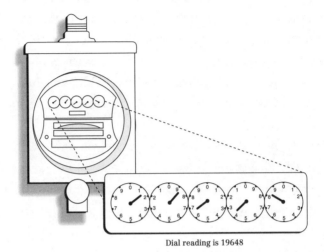

Dial reading is 19648

before I trek off to some retreat center, let me tell you how your electric bill is computed each month.

Outside your house, where the service lines enter, is a meter that measures the consumption of electricity you and your household use in kilowatt-hours. One kilowatt represents the consumption of 1,000 watts for one hour. While some meters on homes resemble an odometer like that on a car, the majority of homes have a pointer-type meter which looks like five one-handed clocks abutting each other. It all involves disks and gears and motors, but your bill is drawn up after a periodic reading of these numbers on the clock faces.

Since I just clawed my way through the bushes on the side of our house to get a peek at our meter (in high heels, no less), I'll demonstrate how these figures are displayed on ours:

Starting at the left, you read the first pointer clockwise, the second counterclockwise, the third clockwise, and so on. If the pointer is between numbers, the lowest one is notated.

So, my reading on June 7, 1995, is 19648. A month later, the clocks are checked again, and the current reading has advanced to 20321. The difference between the readings equals the total kilowatt-hours consumed in that one-month period—in this case, we consumed 673 kilowatt-hours. We are charged at the rate of 10.599 cents per kilowatt-hour, there is a $9 service charge, and we also pay a share of the oil used to generate the electricity (the fuel adjustment). Thus our bill for that month was $80.83. (When I had my 80-gallon hot water heater, we consumed more than 2,500 kilowatts on a good month, and the bill could be close to $300.)

JUL 07 1995		Account Status
Account Number Statement Date		
Service Used At		

CL&P ELECTRIC RATE 001

METER #	BILLING PERIOD FROM	TO	DAYS	METER READING PREVIOUS	CURRENT	KILOWATT HOURS USED
	JUN 7	JUL 6	29	19648	20321	673

TOTAL 'OLD' RATE	24 DAYS		$64.614397
TOTAL 'NEW' RATE	5 DAYS		$13.850218
FUEL ADJUSTMENT	673 KWH X	$0.002430	$1.635390
GU ADJUSTMENT	673 KWH X	$0.001080	$0.726840
TOTAL CHARGE RATE 001			$80.826845

AMOUNT NOW DUE CL&P

$80.83

JUL 7 1996	Account Status
Account Number Statement Date	
Service Used At	

CL&P ELECTRIC RATE 001

METER #	BILLING PERIOD FROM	TO	DAYS	METER READING PREVIOUS	CURRENT	KILOWATT HOURS USED
	JUN 7 1995	JUL 6 1995	29	19648	20321	673

TOTAL CHARGE RATE 001 $80.83

The Day the Power Died: Is There a Generator in Your Future?

More and more people are looking into and installing small generators to keep their homes and in-home businesses running during power failures. A standby power system consists of a generator set and transfer switch which is usually mounted before the main distribution panel of the home. It continually monitors the flow of electricity. If for some reason there's no voltage moving through, the transfer switch disconnects itself from the utility source and transfers to the generator—restoring power to all predesignated electrical equipment.

Generators are commonly fueled directly through the home's natural gas lines or with on-site liquid propane gas, although some do run on diesel fuel. Eight kilowatts would run an entire house, but 6-kilowatt systems are the most popular. With a 6-kilowatt system, a homeowner decides to power only certain electrical systems or appliances, say the heating system, the water heater, the well pump, the refrigerator and freezer, the security system, the computer, the fax machine, some lights, the stove, and a television. Enough to keep the house and homeowner safe, the business up and running, and the kids from driving you crazy.

An electrical contractor can help you do a load survey and choose which systems and appliances to power, as well as order the generator and arrange for the installation. A concrete pad must be poured in order to mount the generator, and this generally takes a day.

While you'll undoubtedly be the envy of the neighborhood, none of this comes cheap. An installed generator with an automatic transfer switch (you don't have to be home to switch on the generator) costs between $7,000 and $9,000 for a typical three- or four-bedroom home. If you are frequently away, or this is a country home, think of a generator as an insurance policy against frozen and broken pipes and the damage they can cause if the power fails and the furnace shuts off or as insurance against serious—and no doubt costly—disruption of your business. Kohler, Onan, and Generac are the names to look for.

3. The Inner Mysteries, Part II: Heating and Cooling

In all our weekends of house hunting, we must have looked at forty houses, but I couldn't have told you a thing about the kinds of heating systems they used. In fact, I didn't even know what the heating system in *this* house was when we put in our remarkably hasty bid. Later, when I found it was oil-fired hot-water baseboard heating, I repeated this parrotlike to any one who asked, but I was clueless as to what the phrase actually meant.

I—a person who could literally *live* in an electric blanket—didn't bother to figure out how comfortable I'd be in the internal climate of our home, based on its system of heating.

Fortunately, we are incredibly comfortable—in the *winter.* Baseboard hot-water heat is nondrafty, nondrying, even heat. But I'm trying to hang on to that thought in the midst of an atypical and sweltering heat wave that has gone on for over four weeks now. If we had a forced-warm-air system like the majority of the homes in this country, we would have ducting already in place and central air-conditioning could be installed at a somewhat reasonable price. Not only would we be refreshingly cool on sultry days, but the central air-conditioning would dehumidify the house and I would not be skiing up and down all the floorboards swelling with humidity. Nor would I be running a dehumidifier in my office constantly in order to wage a never-ending battle against mildew.

As you'll see in this section, each type of heating system has advantages and disadvantages. Out of this country's approximately 64.4 million single-family homes, almost two out of three, or about 41 million, have forced-air systems, so we'll discuss these first.

Forced-Air Heating

Heating systems are generally classified by the medium they use to distribute heat from the furnace or boiler to the living space of the home. And though a forced-air system can be fueled by natural gas, oil, or electricity, it is air that is heated and moved through ducts to the registers of each room.

It works as follows. A furnace, sitting most likely in your basement or utility room, has a **return air duct** that feeds air into a bottom metal compartment that houses a **filter** and a **blower,** or motor-driven fan. Once the air has been filtered of particles such as dust, pollen, and some bacteria, the blower pushes it into a second compartment one level up, where it is warmed by a heat source.

In the heart of the furnace, the burner fires into a **combustion chamber,** producing hot flame gases. These gases then rise into a metal drum called a **heat exchanger.** As the hot gas flows through the *inside* of the heat exchanger, circulating air passes over the *outside* surfaces and is heated through the hot metal. The warmed, circulating air then leaves the furnace and rises to the **plenum.** The plenum is a sheet-metal box that has several supply ducts radiating from it. Warm air is delivered through this network of ducts to

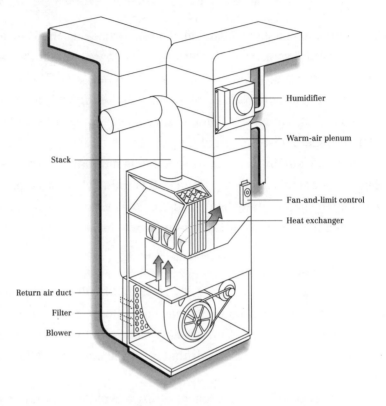

Humidifier

Warm-air plenum

Stack

Fan-and-limit control

Heat exchanger

Return air duct

Filter

Blower

each room of a house. (The combustion gases are routed through inside passages to a flue pipe and out the chimney. These gases do not mix with the circulating air, because the route that they take is totally sealed from the circulating air space.)

Return air registers, one on each floor or several, then return cool air to the bottom quadrant of the furnace and the process begins again.

Gregg Gilbertson, the service manager of Hoffman Fuel Company in Bridgeport, Connecticut, and Dan Quinlan, Hoffman's service supervisor, gave me an intensive two-day tutorial on furnaces and boilers and the fine points of heating plants. One of the first things I asked them was how the return air "knew" to go down this rather passive-looking return duct and start the process again.

Dan told me that the blower creates a pressure differential within the duct system, so a vacuum is created on the return side and air must come in to equalize it. The law of physics, as you'll see in Chapter 10, "Ventilation Is the Name of the Game," is that if one cubic foot of air goes out, one cubic foot of air must come in to replace it.

Both Greg and Dan mentioned how much they liked forced-air systems, not only because they could be so easily adapted for air conditioning, but because you could truly "condition" the air. A humidifier can be mounted up on the plenum, which will help make up for the dryness of winter air. There are motorized units that spray a fine mist of water directly into the stream of heated air, those that spin a water wheel through the air, and units that draw the air through a moistened pad.*

Also, an electronic air filter can be attached to the furnace (on the return air side), and this can remove far more pollutants in the air than the filters usually mounted just before the blower. By the process of ionization—giving tiny particles a strong positive charge so that they will be attracted to a series of negatively charged plates and will stick to the plates until they are washed away—the filter provides you with air that is almost 95 percent pollutant-free. Understandably, this is a great boon for allergy sufferers and anyone interested in breathing healthier air. Also, this kind of filter helps your equipment work more efficiently. The price tag is around $500 to $700, however. (If you have an ionizing air filter, you don't need any other kind of filter in the forced-air system. An ionizing filter should be cleaned every four to six weeks.)

---

*If you do have a central humidifier, make sure you clean it weekly during the heating season, or it can become a breeding ground for mold spores and germs. If your schedule does not allow for this maintenance, remove the unit and purchase room humidifiers that can be seen and cleaned easily.

Inside a Gas Furnace

During my first conversation with Greg and Dan, we focused on the compartment in the furnace where the air is warmed. If we call this level two of the three-level stack and open it up to view, you would see the burner, the heart of the system. Many homes in the Northeast heat with oil, but the majority of homes in this country produce heat with natural gas.

If your furnace has a gas burner at its heart, and you push the thermostat up and call for heat, the contacts of the thermostat close and a current—a 24-volt circuit—sends a signal to the furnace control circuit, and it in turn provides power to the ignition circuit and opens up the gas valve. This gas is routed to the burners, and just at the opening of the burners, it is mixed with air. (Air supports the

Gas Burner

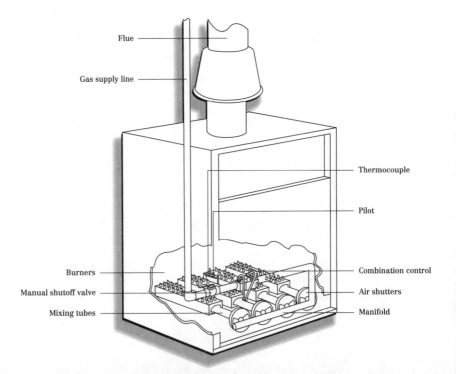

proper combustion of the gas.) This mixture than moves to the burners of the furnace, where it is ignited by a pilot. The heat that is generated is transferred to the circulating air via the heat exchanger.

There are several safety devices. One is the **pilot sensor.** Should the pilot go out and become incapable of igniting the burners, this unit automatically shut off the gas.

A second safety control, the **limit switch,** is set in the airstream of the furnace. This prevents any overheating of the heat exchanger. For instance, if the blower motor should fail and no air is blown over the heat exchanger, the temperature of the heat exchanger would climb so high as to be a fire hazard. The limit switch prevents that from ever happening.

A **roll-out switch** is another safety feature. If the combustion flames should ever roll back out of the burner (say in a negative air situation), the roll-out switch would cut off the gas valve and throttle off combustion.

The company that supplies your gas will read a meter every twenty-eight days or so and bill you for your gas consumption. Most gas companies also offer yearly contracts that cover service on parts. Because gas furnaces have few movable parts and gas burns cleanly, they need cleaning only every four to five years, and this service is usually paid for separately—it does not come with the yearly contracts.

Still, I would have someone from the gas company check the furnace every year to make sure there are no cracks in the heat exchanger (which could disseminate carbon monoxide into the living space) and that everything else is in tip-top shape. See page 306 in Chapter 9, "The Healthy House," for what should be checked on a gas furnace to ensure safety.

A gas burner is less costly to install than an oil burner, and you don't have to depend on an oil-delivery truck's ability to get up your hill in a blizzard to fill an empty tank. Though we heat with oil, one reason a gas pipe might have been on my wish list is that then I would have had a gas stove and wouldn't have had to go to all the expense of installing a propane tank and a new gas stove.

Inside an Oil Furnace

If you compare an oil-fired forced-air heating plant to the gas-fired furnace described above, you will see that the oil-fired plant is a more complicated device. It has quite a few more movable parts and specific components that increase its efficiency and properly ignite its fuel. Though an oil-fired furnace sports a filter-and-blower unit similar to that of the gas furnace described above, the oil burner also has a second motor that drives a pump and blower wheel for combustion air. The pump pulls oil from a storage tank and pressurizes it for proper combustion. Greg Gilbertson explained to me: "You can't just ignite oil—it's a liquid with a high flash point. If you dropped a lighted match into a bowl of oil, it would simply sputter and die out. First, the oil must be atomized—suffused with air—so that fine droplets are formed. When these droplets evaporate, it is the vapor that can be ignited with an electric spark produced by a pair of electrodes."

The result of this oil-mist ignition is a superheated flame that fires continuously into the combustion chamber beneath the heat exchanger. This flame is 2,200 degrees F., but the heating plant is so efficient that by the time the gases leave the unit, they have been reduced to a temperature of 300 degrees. All that heat has been wrested from the combustion process and used to heat your home.

All oil-burning equipment has one of two types of safety device in case of a flame failure. One is a cad cell eye that keeps watch and shuts the burner down if it doesn't sense combustion. The other

Oil Furnace

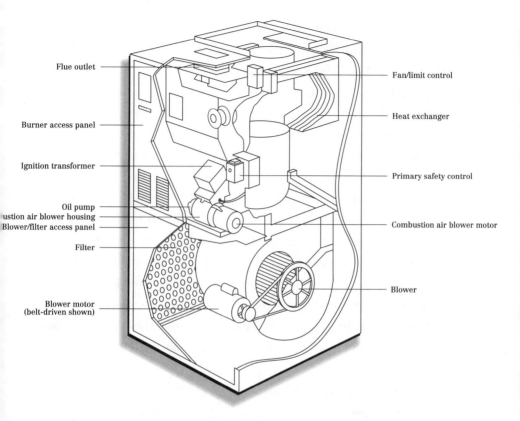

Flue outlet

Burner access panel

Ignition transformer

Oil pump

ustion air blower housing

Blower/filter access panel

Filter

Blower motor
(belt-driven shown)

Fan/limit control

Heat exchanger

Primary safety control

Combustion air blower motor

Blower

is a helix-shaped device that is set in the flue pipe. It also detects a flame failure by sensing a drop in temperature in the flue pipe.

For safety and efficiency, an oil furnace should be inspected and serviced every year. The annual servicing of an oil-fired furnace includes checking for air leaks; cleaning and examining the filter system, the combustion-air blower, and the burner motor; checking the firing system (the burner nozzle and ignition electrodes); and adjusting the draft regulator on the stack (the pipe leading from the furnace to the chimney). All the safety devices should be checked, and instrument tests should gauge the smoke density and carbon dioxide level of the flame, as well as the temperature of combustion exhaust inside the stack.

Have your sweep out to the house to clean the chimney before you schedule your oil burner tune-up so that soot isn't knocked down into the just-cleaned smoke pipe.

All of the procedures above are performed by a licensed heating technician, but if you have a forced-warm-air system, you have a monthly maintenance chore also—you must pay strict attention to the filter and clean or replace it. A severely clogged filter can cause an inadequate air flow over the heat exchanger, and this will cause the limit switch to repeatedly cut off the furnace.

Just pull out the old filter once a month and hold it up to the light. If you can see light through it, it's still usable. Cleanable dry-foam filters can be vacuumed or washed. Dan Quinlan told me that it's possible to buy a more sophisticated honeycomb filter that does a better job. Your heating company can install it and replace it once a year at the annual tune-up. If you have the more expensive ionizing filter, it will need hosing off every four to six weeks.

Inside an Electric-Resistance Furnace

Over 12 million homes in this country heat by electricity alone. That is, they either have an electric-resistance furnace which heats air and pushes it through a plenum to the ducts and registers of each room, or there are electrical baseboards that heat the house. Electric heat is by far the most expensive way to provide warmth to a home. According to Richard Trethewey of *This Old House,* "Compared to the price of fuel oil or natural gas, electricity is the Cadillac of fuels. At eight cents a kilowatt hour it's equivalent in heat value to oil priced at $140 a barrel!"

If you have electric heat, I hope you live in a tightly built, well-insulated house in an area of the country that barely breaks a frost, or that this is your summer house that you close up in October or rarely visit in the cold weather months.

Electric Furnace

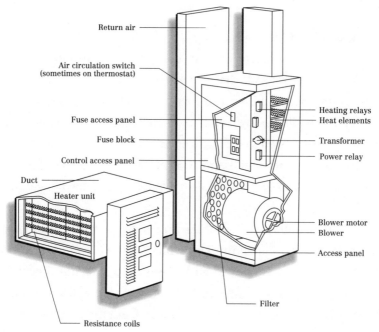

Return air

Air circulation switch
(sometimes on thermostat)

Heating relays
Heat elements

Fuse access panel

Fuse block — Transformer

Control access panel — Power relay

Duct

Heater unit

Blower motor
Blower

Access panel

Filter

Resistance coils

An electric-resistance furnace works like an oversized toaster with a fan blowing through it. The furnace is much like the gas furnace I've discussed above, but there is a series of heating elements—between three and six—in the compartment above the blower. These heating elements are high-resistance electric wires or rods that glow much as the smaller ones in your toaster do. The blower pushes air up through these elements, the elements heat the air, and the warm air rises up through the plenum and is distributed through the ducts throughout the house.

Because no combustion takes place within an electric furnace, a flue or heat exchanger is unnecessary. This kind of furnace is also practically maintenance-free, because, with the exception of the blower unit, there are no moving parts. Only the filter, blower, and humidifier require maintenance.

Baseboard Electric Heaters

Baseboard electric heating consists of long, narrow units, mounted at floor level, that have heating elements inside. Heat transfer fins surrounding the heating elements release the heat into the room, displacing cold air by convection. Baseboard electric heating is often used in add-on rooms because it is relatively easy and inexpensive to install and it produces clean, even heat. It is, however, costly to operate, and the room had better be well insulated to retain the heat.

Each baseboard heater is wired directly to the house's electrical supply—usually 240 volts, but there are 120-volt models also—and is controlled by either an internal thermostat or one mounted on the wall. A wall thermostat should be mounted on the inside wall, as far away from the heating units as possible.

During the summer months, dust, lint, and animal hair will accumulate on the heating elements of the units and will create a foul odor for a short period of time when you first feel the chill of autumn and turn on the system. To avoid this, vacuum or brush the heating elements before touching the thermostats.

Baseboard heater

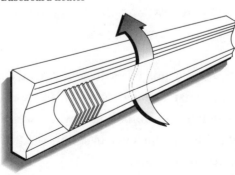

Heat Pumps

Many, many homes in the South and Southwest have a kind of heating/air-conditioning plant known as a heat pump. In the win-ter, a heat pump extracts heat from the outside air and transfers it into a home; in the summer, it reverses jobs and air-conditions a house by moving the heat from the inside to the outside. There is no combustion or burning of fossil fuels inside the home. Instead, a heat pump uses electricity to recycle heat from the sun into your home.

How does it do this? First you have to keep in mind that a liquid absorbs heat from its surroundings when it evaporates into a gas and that a gas releases heat when it condenses to a liquid. In the winter, a refrigerant in the outdoor coils of the heat pump absorbs heat from the air, and as it does, the refrigerant is converted to a gas. That gas is then channeled into a compressor where the heat level is intensified (it may become as hot as 200 degrees). This hot vapor is then pumped to the indoor coils, and it is here that a blower circulates indoor air over the now-heated coils. Warm air is soon available for distribution throughout the home. Concluding the process, the vapor runs from the indoor coils into an expansion valve. There it condenses back to liquid form and returns to the outdoor coils to begin the cycle again.

Heat Pump in Heating Mode

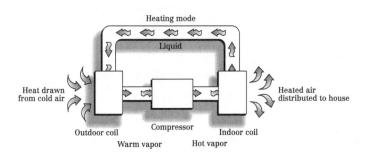

In the summer, the cycle and the direction of the flow are reversed, thanks to the reversing valve. The refrigerant flows intially to the indoor coils, where it absorbs warm air inside a hot and sticky house. It then transfers and jettisons that heat outdoors in a manner similar to central air-conditioning.

Systems with outdoor and indoor components are called split-system heat pumps, but there also exist single-unit heat pumps that house all the components in a single outdoor cabinet. The compressor, the fan, the two coils, the reversing valve, and the blower unit fit into this cabinet. There is no furnace, and only the system's main supply and return ducts penetrate exterior walls.

This all sounds great, but I kept thinking: "Where's the heat? You're turning on a heat pump because it's cold outside. If the temperature outside is 35 degrees, how does the pump get heat from cold air?"

According to thermodynamics, I found out, air contains trace amounts of heat all the way down to –459 degrees F. Even at 0 degrees F, air still has more than 80 percent of the heat available at 100 degrees, and the heat pump can tap this heat.

However, heat pumps work best if the temperature doesn't get below 35 degrees F. Their efficiency declines sharply as the thermometer plummets and the outdoor condenser coils frost over. When the temperature drops below 30 degrees (this point is referred to as the balance point), the heat pump cannot always handle the entire heating load, and a supplementary backup heating system—usually an electric resistance coil—is pressed into action to create heat while the condenser coils are defrosting. Unfortunately, your electric bill travels in the opposite direction of the plummeting outdoor temperatures.

Heat pumps are just grand for people who live in hot, humid climates with mild winters, such as in Florida, Louisiana, Mississippi, and Georgia. In fact, I was just down in South Carolina and an engineer was working on an air-conditioning system, so naturally I was eager to strike up a conversation about them. He told me that most of the homes in that state were heated and air-conditioned by heat pumps. I told him that my cousins Linda and Scott built a house in Lutherville, Maryland, that has a heat pump. Scott told me that the only time his hands are warm in winter is when the toaster oven pops open and he runs to warm them up inside (and that's only if he beats out all the rest of the family and gets there first).

The engineer said heat pumps are really for areas much farther south of the Mason-Dixon line than Maryland—regions where the average winter temperature is above 40 degrees, and where the heat pump is used primarily as a cooling device in the long, sultry summer seasons. I was relieved to hear that Scott and Linda could convert their heat pump into an oil-fired hot-air system if they chose, and I rushed to pick up the phone and tell them. But Scott told me that they've gotten used to the chill and dressing in layers

Heat Pump in Cooling Mode

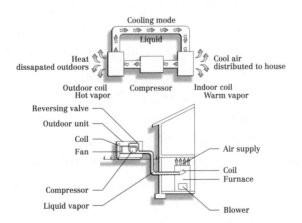

Anatomy of a Split-System Heat Pump

in the cold weather. Still, he wishes that they'd been savvy, like their neighbors, who told the builder that there was no way they'd heat with a heat pump; they'd pay the extra for an oil-fired warm-air system right from the start.

There's another kind of heat pump that can overcome the problem of declining air temperatures. There are now pumps that circulate water through pipes in the ground to pick up heat, then extract the heat from the water. Because the earth and groundwater maintain a more stable year-round temperature than air, they're more efficient and may not require the expensive backup heat source mentioned above. They also use a certain amount of the excess heat gathered by the pipes to produce domestic hot water.

However, a ground-and-groundwater-based heat pump requires several deep vertical loops of pipe in a well or several horizontal loops of pipe buried in the ground, and this can be a difficult, and therefore expensive, installation. In fact, 1,200 to 2,400 feet of plastic pipe usually has to be buried at the bottom of a 6-foot-deep horizontal trench. The average system of this kind can cost anywhere from $7,000 to $10,000.

Recently, a newer kind of geothermal heat pump has come on the market. These have ground-loop coils that sort of resemble a giant Slinky. They also have more efficient components, and they are buried with "trenchless" boring techniques. All of this serves to lower the high ticket price, but even this kind of heating plant costs almost $3,000 more than a conventional heating/air-conditioning system. (However, you should know that some utility companies are offering as much as $2,000 in rebates to homeowners who install these heat pumps, so call your local utility company before making a decision about a heating plant.)

Red Alert: The Cleaning of Air Ducts

Now that I've discussed all the heating plants that use a ducting system to distribute warm (and probably cooled) air, I need to alert you to the fact that, in the interest of breathing better air, the ducts should be cleaned by professionals about every seven to ten years. Microbials—mildew, mold, dust mites, and bacteria—can grow in the ducts and be blown about the house, exacerbating asthma, other respiratory problems, and allergies.

I had a conversation with Michael Vinnick of Duct and Vent Cleaning of America in Springfield, Massachusetts, and he explained that an HVAC (heating, ventilation, and air conditioning) engineer makes access holes throughout the ducts and vacuums them with an industrial vacuum that has HEPA (high-efficiency particulate air) filters. The ducts are then misted with a sanitizer that kills molds and spores, and the access openings are resealed. This all takes about half a day for a typical three or four-bedroom house and costs somewhere between $300 and $700.

Circulating-Hot-Water Systems

As I told you, our home is one of the approximately 6.7 million homes in the country that has baseboard hot-water heating. While the house has no ducts and can't be adapted easily for central air-conditioning, Richard Trethewey, one of the experts from the *This Old House* television series, is convinced that "hot-water heating is more comfortable than forced-air. Nothing blows and stirs up dust, there is no pressurization and depressurization in a house which could draw cold, dry air in, it's quiet, and it heats evenly." So, take heart, all my in-the-minority hot-water-heat brethren out there!

Hydronic systems are characterized by a central boiler or

Hot Water Boiler

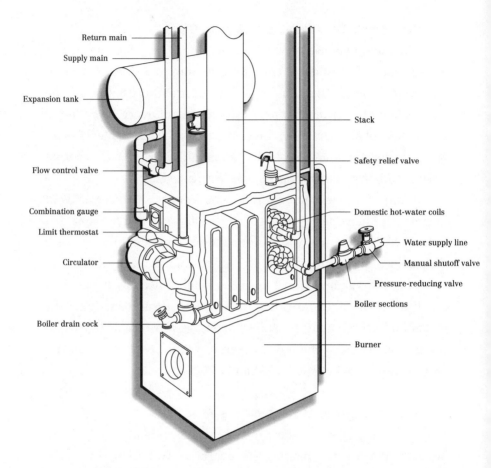

Return main

Supply main

Expansion tank

Stack

Safety relief valve

Flow control valve

Combination gauge

Domestic hot-water coils

Limit thermostat

Water supply line

Circulator

Manual shutoff valve

Pressure-reducing valve

Boiler sections

Boiler drain cock

Burner

water heater, which uses gas, oil, electricity, propane, wood, or coal to heat water. The resulting hot water or steam is then distributed through pipes to a radiator, which releases heat into the room. The heating cycle is completed when the water or steam has given up its heat in the radiator and is channeled back to the boiler.

Modern systems use an electric-powered circulator—either on the return or supply piping—to circulate hot water out of the boiler and through the radiators, and return cooled water to the boiler to be reheated. Thus the name *forced*-hot-water system. (Note we use the term "boiler" when discussing a forced-hot-water or steam heating plant, and "furnace" when we're discussing a forced-warm-air system. Some technician or engineer is going to be very impressed with you if you get the terms right.)

Steel or cast-iron boilers are frequently used for home heating. The most common design is the "fire-tube" boiler in which the hot combustion gases flow inside long tubes surrounded by water. These fire tubes can be arranged up-and-down or horizontally within the boiler water. The burner fires into the combustion chamber and the hot gases are directed inside the tubes. The boiler water is on the outside of the tubes and the heat passes through the walls of the tubes from the flame gases to the water. The hot water is then pumped throughout the house, wherever there is a call for heat.

The cooled flame gases are collected at the top of the boiler as they leave the fire tubes. The flue pipe then carries these exhaust gases to the chimney and out of the house.

Installed above the unit is a juglike **expansion tank.** Water expands as it is heated, and the extra volume moves into the expansion tank, rather like an overflow reservoir. This tank also helps control the pressure in the system. As the heating system water cools, the water contracts, pushes out of the expansion tank, and returns to the heating system.

An **aquastat** tells the boiler how hot to heat the water. Typically, an aquastat might be set at 180 degrees F. for the high limit and 160 degrees for the low. If you have a tankless coil that heats the house's domestic water, and you have a new baby or young child in the house, a tempering valve (sometimes called a mixing valve) can mix cold water with the very hot water to reduce or eliminate the possibility of scalding. This is placed outside of the tankless coil.

There are two very important safety controls in a boiler. Should the pressure ever get too high, a spring-loaded valve called a **safety relief valve** opens and allows excess pressure to escape. This valve

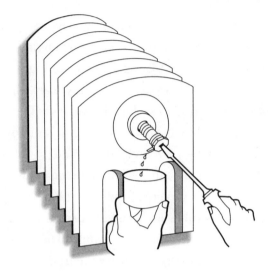

also opens if the temperature of the water ever climbs to a boiling temperature. It prevents it from turning to steam. The preset water pressure, water temperature, and water level in the boiler are all indicated on a **combination gauge** that is on the front or top of the unit.

How I Overcame My Fear of Bleeding Radiators

The people who built our house wanted to be able to control the heat in every room, so they installed nine zones. There are nine thermostats in this house!

The only problem was that when I called for heat in my son Alex's room, there was no hot bubbly response. The baseboard remained stone cold.

I mentioned this to a contractor doing some job here at the time, and he told me to "bleed the radiators." It sounded as if I should be shopping for leeches. Whatever this process was, it certainly seemed beyond my abilities as a virgin homeowner, and I balked at his suggestion.

He laughed and explained what was going on. Water contains

a certain amount of air, and when you heat it and send it through a hydronic system, some of that air can form an air pocket that blocks the pathway of the warm water needed to heat the room. Bleeding the radiator releases this air so that the heat is unimpeded.

This was so easy to do, I was embarrassed by my initial reluctance. Inside each radiator is a small air valve that can be opened with a screwdriver or special key available at hardware stores. I placed a cup under the valve and opened it with a twist of the screwdriver. Air hissed out, and when water began to squirt out, I twisted the valve closed again and felt the radiator grow warm.

You may need to bleed the radiators each fall, especially those units at the end of the pipe runs. You should also vacuum the radiators from time to time with the wand attachment of your vacuum cleaner.

Steam Heating Systems

We lived with steam heat for sixteen years in our prewar apartment in the city. The system produced so much heat that we had the windows open constantly in the winter, and I always found the banging and hissing noises oddly comforting when the boiler was fired up each fall and turned on each morning. (And boy, did those bathroom radiators dry panty hose quickly and warm towels delightfully.)

Many houses in the Northeast that were built during or before the 1940s still sport steam heating systems, and they are marvels of engineering and plumbing. When balanced correctly, a steam heating system produces heat efficiently and so quickly that the steam can get to the second floor before a running homeowner can (it's estimated that the steam travels at 30 miles per hour).

The boiler of a steam heating system typically sits in the basement and uses gas or oil to convert water to steam. The steam then surges under its own pressure up through black iron pipes and inlet valves to all the radiators in the home. Once the steam comes into contact with the cooler metal radiators, it releases its heat energy and condenses back to water. And because water is heavier than steam, this condensate trickles back down the same pipes to the return main (the upcoming steam shoots right past this water trickling down the sides of the pipes). The returning water feeds the boiler and is once again reheated to steam. As long as you call for heat, the cycle continues.

A system that is plumbed this way is called a "one-pipe" distribution network, but occasionally you find a "two-pipe" arrangement in which the steam shoots up one set of pipes to the radiators, and the water exists the radiators and trickles down another set of pipes in order to get to the return main.

What accounts for all the noise of these systems? As the steam surges up the pipes from the boiler, it runs into air, and it pushes this air ahead of it and out the vents of the radiators. Thus the hissing. Hammering can be caused by a dozen different things, but it usually occurs because the radiator valves are only partly open. It's likely that someone throttled back a valve to limit the heat enter-

One-Pipe and Two-Pipe Systems

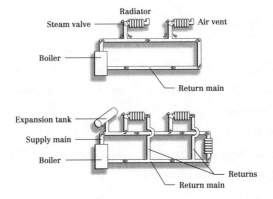

ing the room. Simply opening the valve may put an end to this banging.

Frequently, hammering occurs when a radiator is not pitched correctly. It should be pitched toward the inlet valve. It's not uncommon, however, for the constant expansion and contraction of a radiator to dig a small hole in the floor and cause the radiator to pitch the wrong way. This can be remedied by levering the legs opposite the inlet valve with a piece of wood.

If neither of these interventions work, call your plumber and let him or her do an advanced diagnosis and cure.

What's Going On In and Around the Boiler?

In order for the boiler to work safely and effectively, it is equipped with several components. The ones we need to talk about are known as the **pressure relief valve,** the **water gauge glass,** and the **low-water cutoff.**

A gauge installed on top of the boiler measures steam pressure. The pressure is controlled by the pressuretrol. It should not require more than 2 pounds of pressure to heat your house. If the pressure gets too high (over 15 pounds) the **pressure relief valve** will open automatically to protect the boiler.

An optimal amount of water must be in the boiler if it's to work properly and safely, and on the side or the front of the boiler is a round glass tube that reflects the water level in the boiler. Normally, it varies between one-third and two-thirds full. This gauge glass has a gauge cock (valve) at its top and another at its bottom. If the water in the boiler falls to a dangerous point—where the heat from the burner would "cook the tank" and damage the boiler—a float within the **low-water cutoff** chamber drops with the descending water level and shuts down the boiler, via an electrical float switch.

That is, if the reservoir of water surrounding the float is not so clogged with sediment as to impede the operation of the float. This is why a homeowner with a steam boiler must take ten seconds a week and open the **blowoff valve** at the bottom of the low-water cutoff chamber and flush out about 1 1/2 quarts of this sediment-filled reservoir of water.

Where does all this sediment come from? Whenever you boil water, minerals are left behind (take a look inside your teakettle one day—if you dare); and it's these minerals that you're flushing out in this weekly trip to the basement.

Be careful when you're handling the hot, dirty, sediment-filled water. Wear gloves, use a bucket, and don't pour the water away all over your prized perennials or into your new porcelain sink or toilet. A utility sink in the basement is a better idea.

This flushing of the sediments is not an optional activity. If the low-water cutoff is not maintained, it will fill with sediment, and if you go into a low-water condition, the low-water cutoff will not shut off the burner. So the burner stays on and boils all the water out of the boiler. And now you have a burner that's firing on a hunk of steel or cast iron, getting hotter and hotter and hotter. It heats the pipes red-hot and the pipes come into contact with wood in the house, and, gee, I don't even want to describe what happens then. If this were to happen while you were home, you'd smell a terrible odor from the boiler and shut it down immediately. The problem is if you go away and leave the heat on but don't have anyone maintaining the low-water cutoff or smelling the consequences of maintenance failure.

If you don't have an automatic feed on your boiler that automatically replenishes the water supply, check the water level when the boiler has cycled off. The water level in the gauge glass should be between the 1/2 to 2/3 mark. If this is not the case, open the fill valve and close it when the water level is just right. (Do you see why

Water Gauge and Cutoff

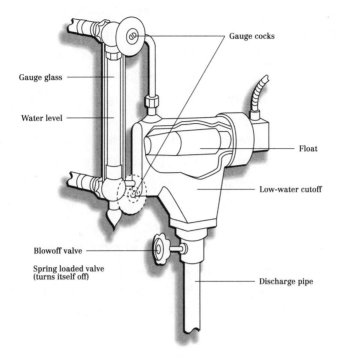

you'd better show up at the home inspection with serious intentions and an inspector who really wants to teach you all these things?)

It just so happens that my editor, Gerald Howard, has steam heat in his 1920 stucco home. I asked him how he feels about flushing the blowoff valve every week and what he does if he and his wife, Susanne, go away in the winter. He said, "It's a simple enough chore to manage once a week, easier to accomplish than the garbage and the recyclables. Besides, it keeps me in touch with the heating plant. As for those *very rare* winter vacations, we are blessed with fine neighbors who keep an eye on the house for us."

I also had a conversation with Steve Gladstone, the home inspector profiled in Chapter 1, about steam heat, and he told me that about 20 percent of the houses he inspects heat with this kind of system. He likes steam heat a lot and thinks it is a good, dependable, fast, and efficient means of heating. He tells his clients not to be afraid of the maintenance—it takes so little time—and he teaches them how to flush the blow-off valve and check the gauges. He also warns new homeowners that the radiators can become very hot, and he advises that they protect crawling babies or toddlers against burns by installing radiator covers.

Once a year you should schedule a professional tune-up for your boiler—in the spring before you turn the heat off. The oil companies do this, or a plumber or heating contractor can do it. The boiler should be flushed during this annual checkup, although some oil companies charge extra for the service.

There's a very informative and entertaining book describing the rich history and practical aspects of steam heating systems. It's called *The Lost Art of Steam Heating* and it's written by Dan Holohan. It's available from Dan Holohan Associates, Inc., 63 North Oakdale Ave., Bethpage, NY 11714 (800-853-8882).

Heat for Feet: Radiant Heating

One of the little mysteries of our house noted on the home inspection report was that there was a thermostat in the family room, but no baseboard radiators. Naturally, I thought we had no heating system in this rather large space, but soon found out that the room was warmed with radiant heating. This is a serpentine loop of hot-water lines or tubes that are embedded in the cement slab flooring or looped through wooden joists and that heat from the ground up. (The Romans used this kind of heating in their baths in the first century; today, it is the system of choice in 60 to 70 percent of all new homes built in Germany.) Thanks to a technology developed for telecommunications in the 1960s, the tubes used today are made of a cross-linked polyethylene reputed to last 200 years without leaks.

What a delightful experience. The entire floor is a radiator. You walk barefoot into the room, and your feet feel nothing but warmth. The children sit down to watch television and their fannies are warm as toast. My friends Mark and Wiga put radiant heating under the tiles in their kitchen, and they told me that coming into this room, barefoot, for coffee in the morning is a great way to start the day.

The drawback is that many radiant heat systems take some time to get going. If the thermostat in my family room is off and I want to crank up the heat, it will be hours before the room is fully heated. This may be because my system is old; Mark tells me his kitchen is warm inside of twenty minutes. However, most people do mention the time lag with a radiant system.

Who Ya Gonna Call?: How to Choose an Oil Company

If your house is heated with natural gas, you have no choice in fuel companies. The supplier of gas in the region pipes it into the home and bills you for the amount of gas you use.

Those of us with oil-fired heating systems, however, can buy our fuel from any of a number of companies, all leafleting and promising and offering. How do you settle on a fuel company?

There are several things I advise you to examine besides the price of the oil. The quality of the oil is one of them. While the law mandates that heating oil cannot contain more than .05 percent sulfur, look for a company that processes oil until the sulfur content is .02. This burns cleaner and doesn't gunk up the environment or your heating plant.

As you'll read in Chapter 9, "The Healthy House," aging underground oil tanks are a major problem for the homeowner because the possible envirnmental hazard of a leaking tank. Until you can afford the approximately $3,000 to unearth that tank and place a new one above ground in your basement or crawl space, I advise you to purchase environmental insurance that would cover any (and possibly catastrophic) EPA clean-up costs. So look for a company that offers this benefit. It should cost about $80 a year, but a sizable leak could cost $100,000. (I only sleep at night because of my tank insurance.)

Next I would look at the service contract offered by the company. You want to see that a technical staff is available twenty-four hours a day with no additional charges for calls made after 5:00 P.M. and on weekends or holidays. Some smaller companies charge $50 an hour after the working day and on weekends.

Hoffman Fuel paid us a visit shortly after we moved into our home, because it was the supplier of the oil to the previous owners. We liked its representative, Mr. Ipacs, very much, but when he began to describe their service contract, Demitri and I began silently to signal each other. We were unable to determine if this was something we needed or yet another "warranty" for the hapless homeowner.

What a shame we didn't have someone to advise and assure us. We should never have doubted the supreme wisdom of a service contract. It's a *mighty* important thing to have.

I can't tell you how many times the heat has gone off at night or early in the morning, and one call to Hoffman brings a serviceman to the door within an hour—for no charge.

Every spring, a member of the office staff calls me and schedules the annual tune-up of the boiler, and the company renews the environmental insurance on my intact (we hope) oil tank. When I'm ready to have it dug up, Hoffman has an environmental staff equipped to do that.

Hoffman also has a computer system that calculates degree days and my usage and automatically spits out a ticket and routes an oil delivery to my home.

We were offered a three-for-one (new customer incentive) contract: we paid for one year and got a three-year service contract. So check out the company and see what it's offering. Ask your real estate agent or your home inspector for a reputable oil company in your area and then have a meeting and listen carefully to the explanation of the company's services.

Once you have a service contract, you can call the fuel company anytime the heat doesn't go on, but before you make that call, there are several things you should check out first:

1. Are other lights or electrical fixtures on and running? A power failure knocks everything out, and a service person can't help; only restored power can get the furnace up and running.
2. Check that the thermostats are set 5 degrees or more above room temperature.
3. Check the master switches of your oil burner. One is on the burner, another may be in the furnace room, and a third may be at the top of the stairs. A guest or family member may have turned it off mistaking it for a light switch.
4. Check your circuit-panel box to make sure you don't have a tripped circuit or a burned-out fuse. Flip the circuit breaker to the "on" position if it has tripped, or replace the fuse.
5. Press the restart button on the motor—just *once!* Do not keep pressing it or oil will flood the combustion chamber.

If nothing works, call the service company and report what you checked out and what you did. Bundle up until the service person gets there and gets things going again.

Several times my boiler shut down immediately after an oil delivery. It turns out that sediment was being stirred up, clogging the filter, and shutting the machine down. A serviceman had to clean the filter to get it going again. This tends to happen only with older tanks.

Flagging a Fuel Line

1994 was a terrible year to move. After decades of mild, almost snowless winters, we hit town and it didn't *stop* snowing. My neighbors kept pointing out that there hadn't been a winter like this in over thirty years. (I was reminded of *The Witches of Eastwick*—did this have something to do with our moving into town?)

So one morning we got up, Jordy was sick, Demitri was out of the state, and the house was stone cold. I called the fuel company and we found we were out of fuel. But no one had told me to flag the fuel line, and it was buried by ice and snow mounds, courtesy of the ever-present plowing company.

We had coordinates for the fuel cap, and I was outside with an ice pick stabbing away for forty-five minutes—just missing it by a quarter of an inch each time. (I remember a lot of expletives and muttering about moving back to the city, I wasn't cut out for this, etc., etc.) At last—blue with cold—I struck pay dirt and the man was able to give us some emergency oil.

But I learned my lesson. In November of the next year, I ran around to all the hardware stores looking for a proper stake, and the minute it snowed, I was out there shoveling and clearing the area around the stake and fuel cap.

Stake it and rake it is my new philosophy.

Shopping: What to Look For, What to Buy

Furnaces and boilers manufactured today are substantially more efficient than the models churning out heat in basements for the last fifteen to thirty years. This simply means that the newer units extract the same amount of heat from less fuel. In fact, any furnace or boiler that you can purchase is rated with an Annual Fuel Utilization Efficiency (AFUE) percentage, and federal law mandates that the AFUE be at least 78 percent.

To what do we owe all this new efficiency? In the case of hot-air systems, the introduction of three new components: a **secondary heat exchanger,** a **multiple-speed blower,** and a **sealed combustion chamber.**

The **secondary heat exchanger** deals with the combustion gases that used to exhaust up the flue, and wrings some more heat from them before they escape. The **multiple-speed blower** lowers your operating costs by calibrating its speed to the ever-changing heating requirements of your home. It doesn't have to operate continuously at full throttle as the older blowers do. And the **sealed combustion chamber** means that the furnace is not drawing combustion air from the furnace room or house. It draws air right from the outside and channels it directly to the burner, and subsequently it exhausts combustion gases directly back to the outdoors. Not only does this boost efficiency, but it prevents the possibility of backdrafting, which could send carbon monoxide and other potentially lethal gases back into the living space. (A thorough discussion of backdrafting and sealed combustion takes place in Chapter 9, "The Healthy House." Sealed combustion heating units are a must in any tight and energy-efficient home.)

All these innovations quite naturally increase the price of a new furnace. While a midrange efficiency gas furnace with an AFUE of 80 to 86 percent costs somewhere in the range of $1,500 to $2,000, a high-efficiency unit with an AFUE of over 90 percent can cost upward of $3,000. While a gas furnace can have an AFUE rating of 96.6 percent (in this case they are called supercondensing furnaces), oil furnaces never have a rating higher than the mid to upper 80s. Still, as we discussed earlier in this chapter, an oil furnace is more complex and will cost several hundred dollars more than a comparable gas model.

Newer boilers are more efficient because of improvements made in burners and heat exchangers and because of sealed combustion chambers (which also make the boiler safer).

While writing all this, I became curious to know what the AFUE rating on my Burnham boiler was, so, even though boiler rooms give me the creeps, I just tiptoed in at the crack of dawn and made out the number. It read 84 percent. At first I was terribly disappointed to think that we are so un-state-of-the-art. But I subsequently found out that boilers have lower AFUEs than furnaces, because they have to heat water to a high point to provide adequate heat. So 86 percent is about as high as an oil or gas boiler goes. We're sitting pretty, I guess.

Should you replace your old furnace with a superefficient model when the time comes? Richard Trethewey writes: "It doesn't always pay to buy the most efficient equipment on the market. Paying $1,000 extra for a high-efficiency gas furnace may make good sense in a Minneapolis, where the length and severity of the winters could provide a quick paycheck. But the same investment in a Dallas home—where the heating season is relatively short—could turn out to be a flop. The length of the season, fuel prices, the size and condition of your home, and the number of years you plan on staying in that home should all play a part in deciding how much efficiency you want."

The following chart will give you an idea of the annual savings on a new furnace or boiler:

Annual Savings for Every $100 of Fuel Costs

Original Efficiency — **New or Upgraded Efficiencies**

	55%	60%	65%	70%	75%	80%	85%	90%	95%
50%	$9.09	$16.76	$23.07	$28.57	$33.33	$37.50	$41.24	$44.24	$47.36
55%		8.33	15.38	21.42	26.26	31.20	35.29	38.88	42.10
60%			7.69	14.28	20.00	25.00	29.41	33.33	37.80
65%				7.14	13.33	19.75	23.52	27.77	31.57
70%					6.66	12.50	17.64	22.22	26.32
75%						6.50	11.76	16.66	21.10
80%							5.88	11.11	15.80
85%								5.55	10.50
90%									5.30

(Source: The Energy Efficiency and Renewable Energy Clearinghouse)

If you're purchasing a new furnace, boiler, or heat pump, Richard Trethewey advises you to look for a strong warranty: "For oil and gas furnaces, look for a minimum twenty-year warranty on the heat exchanger. Some manufacturers offer a 'lifetime' warranty, meaning the life of the furnace. For heat pumps, I'd want at least a five-year warranty on the compressor (some manufacturers guarantee it for ten)."

Look for the names Thermopride, Lennox, Carrier, Trane, and Amana when you're shopping for a gas-fired furnace or electric heat pump. If you're in the market for an oil-fired furnace, look for Thermopride, Armstrong, Oneida Royal, DMO Industries, Hallmark, and York.

In the boiler department, Mr. Trethewey is a great admirer of the Viessman line (the Rolls-Royce of boilers) and feels that Weil-

McLain, Burnham, Hydrotherm, and Slant Fin are names to trust.

Air-Conditioning a Home

Most homes are air-conditioned in one of two ways: either individual units are installed in the windows or walls, each cooling just a single room or small area (the "oasis method"), or a forced-air furnace or heat pump is adapted so that cooled air is delivered through the ductwork to the entire house. Since we've already discussed a forced-air central heating plant, let me describe how the central air-conditioning system works first.

When you turn the thermostat and call for some relief from summer's heat and humidity, the air-handling unit switches on and pulls room air through the return ducts of the house. After the air is filtered, it rises to the plenum, where a chilled evaporator coil has been installed. Once the warm house air hits the evaporator coil, it cools and condenses and the moisture is drained away in a drain pan. Thus, the air is dehumidified. Now cooled and dehumidified, the air is distributed through the ductwork of the house.

But what chills the evaporator coil, and where does the heat from the house go to? If you look at the diagram, you will see that every air conditioner has four basic components: a **chemical refrigerant,** a **condenser,** a **compressor,** and an **evaporator coil.** As I just mentioned, the evaporator coil is positioned in the plenum— the sheet-metal box—above the furnace, and the condenser and compressor are outside, where their noise and heat are less bothersome. The outdoor components are connected to the evaporator coil by two runs of copper tubing and a thermostat.

In order to plot the cooling process, we need to keep two basic laws of thermodynamics in mind. The first is that a liquid absorbs heat from its surroundings when it evaporates into a gas, and that

Split Air-Conditioning Unit

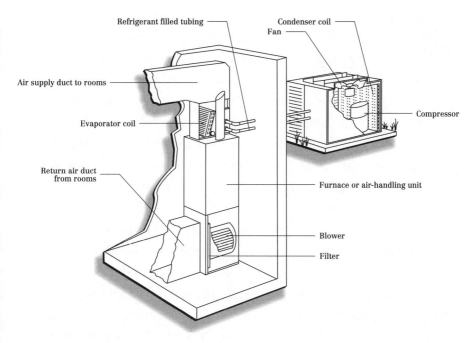

Refrigerant filled tubing

Condenser coil

Fan

Air supply duct to rooms

Evaporator coil

Compressor

Return air duct from rooms

Furnace or air-handling unit

Blower

Filter

a gas releases heat when it condenses to a liquid. The other is that heat always flows from a warm place to a cooler place. We also need to realize the unique properties of a chemical refrigerant. It is volatile. This means that it is able to boil from a liquid to a gas at low temperatures.

When you can't take the heat any longer and you switch on the thermostat, the unit starts up by sending a refrigerant in a vaporous form to the outdoor compressor. Here it is compressed into a high-pressure, high-temperature gas. Next this heated vapor travels to the outdoor condenser coil. As it flows through the coil, air is constantly blown over it by a fan. Consequently, the vapor condenses inside the tubing to a liquid form. The hot gas has cooled a bit.

The liquid refrigerant is then routed through the smaller-diameter tubing into the house, where it passes through a metering device—a small orifice—to the indoor evaporator coils. Now the pressure drops dramatically, and with this change in pressure comes a corresponding drop in temperature. The cold refrigerant converts to a mixed liquid/vapor state as it moves through the circuits of the indoor evaporator coil. Here this mixed-state refrigerant transfers its coldness to the metal of the coils. As the warm, humid air of the house is blown over the now-cold coils, two things happen: Moisture is extracted from the air as the air condenses, and the heat, moving from a warm place to a cold one, is absorbed by the cold refrigerant.

But this transference of the heat to the mixed-state refrigerant converts the refrigerant once again to a completely vaporous state. In the final leg of the cycle, the vapor exists the house through the larger-diameter copper tubing and heads back out toward the outdoor compressor. As it moves through the outdoor coil, it discharges the heat it's picked up from the sweltering house and the cycle continues.

So, contrary to popular opinion, an air-conditioner does not blow cool air into the house; rather, it blows warm air out.

Some manufacturers of quality central air systems are Carrier, Trane, York, and Lennox. It costs about $2,000 to $4,000 to adapt a warm-air furnace to central air conditioning and requires about a day's work.

Room Air Conditioners

The $2,000 to $4,000 it will cost you to adapt a warm-air furnace to central air-conditioning is not a bad investment for years of cooling, dehumidifying, and comfort. But if it's not in the budget just now, or if you're in my position and have no ductwork (in this case I've gotten quotes that range upward from $15,000 to equip this house with central air), you and I have to rely on the oasis method and install window or wall units in the rooms we most decide need cooling—a bedroom, a family room, a kitchen, or whatever.

A room air conditioner has a condenser, a compressor, and evaporator coils, as well as a fan; it's just that they're all present in one unit—nothing is out and away from the house—so they are not whisper-quiet by any means.

Inside the cabinet of a window unit there are two separate sections. The outdoor coils are positioned in the part of the unit that hangs out your window, and the evaporator coils are up front, behind the grill.

The cooling process is the same as the one I've just described for central air conditioning, it's just that the route the refrigerant takes is much abridged.

The moisture that condenses from the humid air in the house is handled a bit differently in a room air conditioner, however. It collects in the bottom pan of the unit, where there are two or three little alcoves that tilt the condensed water to the outdoor section of the air conditioner. In today's newer models, this water is picked up by the outdoor fan and flung against the hot outdoor coils. Not only does this flicked water evaporate and help cool the hot outdoor coils, but it makes the unit run more efficiently. So don't worry if

Room Air Conditioner

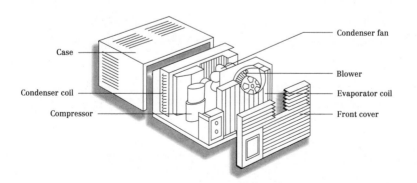

you don't see big damp stains outside underneath your new air conditioner.

You'll need to clean the filter at least once a month in the summer. Some filters can be vacuumed, others can be wrung out with
water, and some must be replaced. Read the instruction pamphlet
that comes with the machine.

Sizing a Unit

We moved a 5,000-BTU air conditioner from our city apartment and stuck it in the window of our family room, expecting to
enjoy some respite from the summer's heat. No chance.

The room is very large, moving out into an all-windowed so-
larium. A lot of heat radiates in through those windows, the ceilings are quite high, and there are two doors and a little hallway
moving out from the room. A tough cooling problem. We ended up
buying a unit with 17,500 BTUs, and after it's run for an hour or
two, the room is just about "comfortable."

The chart below will act as a guide to help you calculate the
number of BTUs needed to cool a space. You arrive at square
footage by multiplying the length of the room times its width. If your
ceilings are over eight feet high, buy the next-larger size:

Cooling Area	Capacity
265 sq. ft.	6,000 BTUh
300–350 sq. ft.	7,500 BTUh
350–450 sq. ft.	9,000 BTUh
450–520 sq. ft.	10,000 BTUh
520–600 sq. ft.	11,000 BTUh
600–750 sq. ft.	12,500 BTUh
750–900 sq. ft.	15,000 BTUh

900–1,050 sq. ft.	16,500 BTUh
1,050–1,250 sq. ft.	19,000 BTUh

It's never a good idea to oversize a unit, figuring you'll get more cooling power. A unit too large for its space will cool in short, energy-wasting bursts and then shut down for extended intervals. The humidity will climb and the room will begin to feel clammy.

When you shop for an individual air conditioner, look at the energy efficiency ratio (EER). The higher the EER, the more cooling per dollar you can expect. Thus, if the 15,000-BTU unit I looked at had an EER rating of 11, and I also priced another 15,000-BTU unit with a rating of 10, I would be better off buying the air conditioner with the EER rating of 11. Its efficiency would result in a 10 percent savings.

If you are going to remove a unit from the window or wall for the winter and store it, make sure you lay it down just as it sat in the window (don't up-end it). If you store the unit in the wrong position, you put a strain on the copper tubing connection to the compressor and you may bend the mounting bolts. You also risk the refrigeration oil in the compressor migrating into the tubing and coils, effectively destroying the compressor.

I got tired of moving the window unit in and out and up and down the stairs, losing the view and ventilation of a free window, and watching bugs determinedly crawl their way past the side panels, so we decided to put a unit through the wall. I painted the frame white to match the wall, and it doesn't look half bad.

But then I began to worry about drafts in the dead of winter. I found out, however, that most home centers and hardware stores sell an outside cover that is made of plastic or canvas and attaches to the unit with Velcro (some can be tied on). All you have to do is take the inside dimensions of the unit and show up at the hardware store.

It cost us about $250 to have the unit installed in the wall, and $200 for the electrician to run a new circuit dedicated only to this unit.

I understand that different models with similar BTU capacities may require either 120 or 240 volts, and that it's a better idea to choose the 240-volt equipment, as higher-voltage air conditioners use a bit less electricity.

Split Systems for Oasis Cooling

A new option in room air-conditioning is something the Japanese have been using for several years now: a split system. These systems have an indoor air handler that is about 20 inches wide by 14 inches high and that protrudes out from the wall only 5 inches. This air handler is attached to a rigid conduit (2 to 3 inches in diameter) that runs down the outside of the house to an outdoor unit that contains one or more compressors. Inside the insulated conduit is a power cable, liquid, and suction tubes for the refrigerant, and a condensate drain.

One day this type of system will go in my family room and the dining and kitchen area and produce quiet, cooled air, but it is an expensive option—the installed price of a split system runs from about $1,500 to $2,500 for each 12,000 BTUs of cooling produced. Quiet, but not cheap. But cheaper than adding ductwork to the entire house. . . .

Dynazone, Environmaster, and Klimaire manufacture powerful split-system air conditioners that can run up to four separate air handlers. Burnham, Freidrich, Toshiba, Hitachi, Sanyo, and Mitsubishi manufacture models that handle from one to three rooms.

Well, if you've absorbed even half of all this information, you'll make a pretty impressive conversationalist—even with *my* electrician.

I've found that my initial dread and fear of the mechanical systems of a house have been transmuted by understanding into real awe and respect, and I hope that this is the case for you, too.

I've also found that I feel a great debt of gratitude to the thousands of people whose names are lost to history, but whose thinking and inventing and tinkering have allowed us to live at home, with dignity, in comfort and safety.

But we're not done yet! For many people, there's the tail end of the drain-waste-vent system that concludes its pathway in the backyard: the septic tank and leaching system. This is a fascinating entity deserving its own chapter, and it is to this that we turn next.

4. To Rid-X or Not to Rid-X: You and Your Septic System

As I sat at the computer attempting to broach the subject of septic systems, I was wondering how I was going to talk about waste and sludge and scum in an adult and gracious manner. I found I felt more like a third-grader charged up with bathroom humor. How to talk—how on *earth* to talk—about all these heretofore unmentionables?

Interestingly, all of the books and pamphlets speak glowingly of septic systems and use phrases like "the magic box," "ingenious," and "a phenomenal design of nature" to describe the tank and leaching fields. It's true, you know. Once you understand the workings of a septic system, you'll no doubt add some admiring phrases of your own.

How It All Works

More than 25 million American homeowners have an on-site sewage treatment system. This translates to mean that they are not hooked up to municipal sewer systems. Instead, each household de-composes waste and returns good-quality water to the watershed, via an individual on-site system.

There are typically four major components of a septic system:

1.   A house sewer line that carries the waste to a septic tank.
2.   A septic tank that prepares the waste material for dispersal into the leaching system.
3.   A liquid distribution box to uniformly distribute the semi-processed liquid, called the "effluent" through a leaching sys-tem.
4.   The leaching system, which is a trench or bed excavated be-yond the septic tank. It normally consists of a series of perfo-rated pipes resting on crushed stone. This unit allows the effluent to percolate into the soil where it is purified as it fil-ters through the soil.

Septic Tank and Leaching Field

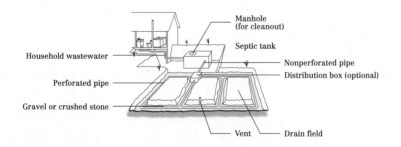

People in a home bathe, shower, wash clothes, use the kitchen and bathroom sinks and the toilets. All of this wastewater is dis-charged through the house drain line and into a septic tank buried somewhere in the yard.

A standard rectangular 1,000-gallon tank is 11 feet long by 4 1/2 feet wide by 5 1/2 feet high and is usually made of concrete or fiberglass. It reminds me of a giant coffin.

The wastewater coming from your home moves rather rapidly into the septic tank and enters a virtual stilling pond. Inside the tank, anaerobic bacteria (the kind that flourish in the absence of oxygen), yeasts, fungi, and other microbes feed on and attempt to digest the organic solids—feces, urine, detergents and soaps, and food bits. While doing so, these organisms produce a variety of gases and heat. Much of the waste is liquefied, but any undigested or undigestible solids sink to the bottom of the tank.

These gases bubble to the surface and pull up tiny particles of solid matter, which mix with oils, waxes, and grease, as well as other floatables to form a layer of scum over the surface of the liquid.

Now, this scum is remarkable because it helps prevent air from seeping below the scum level. So, the underside of this floating layer of scum becomes an ideal incubator for the anaerobic colonies. (In case you're wondering where all these anaerobic bacteria come from, they come from *you!* The composition of feces is primarily bacteria.)

The gases escape back through the sewer line and are routed up the stack vent in the house and dispersed harmlessly above your roof.

Let me resketch this picture. Inside this still and dark place there are three layers. Closest to the surface are the grease and other lighter-than-water materials, on the bottom are the solids (the sludge) that cannot be digested, and in the middle of this appetizing sandwich is a quantity of partially treated wastewater. When the wastewater rises to a certain level, it spills out of a baffle or Tee-baffle and enters the leaching system as effluent. As the effluent

Inside a Septic Tank

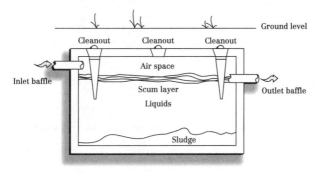

trickles through the pipes and seeps into the earth, its impurities are neutralized.

Once More unto the Leaching Field

Even after the septic tank has sequestered the sludge and other solids, the clarified effluent still contains high levels of bacteria, viruses, nitrogen compounds, and phosphorus, among other things, which must be removed or inactivated before the water is returned to the water table.

As I mentioned before, the effluent flows from the septic tank into the leaching field—the network of porous pipes (usually perforated plastic or loosely joined clay) that are bedded in trenches of crushed rock or coarse gravel. These trenches are covered over with soil and turf.

Once the effluent enters the leaching fields, it becomes a part of, and is purified by, nature's amazing balancing act. Soil may look inert to you, but it's absolutely teeming with life. And this life is competing for nourishment and aiding in the process of water purification at the same time.

For instance, half a ton of worms are generally undulating around and aerating an acre of land, and it is estimated that some 5 million bacteria are present in a single teaspoon of common back-yard soil. The aeration of the soil by the worms provides oxygen to the aerobic bacteria—the kind that live in the presence of oxygen—so that they can flourish and feed upon the organic waste still present in the effluent. The aerobic bacteria chemically oxidize their food, and their wastes become, in turn, food for plants. Penicillin and other antibiotics are produced by the soil bacteria and fungi, and these antibiotics help destroy the pathogens, or disease-causing microbes.

Soil is a home to worms and aerobic bacteria, and it acts as a physical filter for larger particles. But soil has an even more complex and fascinating action. It is composed predominantly of tiny pieces of stone and decayed organic matter such as leaves. When the stone pieces are extremely fine, the soil is said to be clay.

Each of the clay minerals carries a tiny electric charge. Many pathogens, however, have a coat of protein that carries an opposite electrical charge to that of the clay minerals. Opposites attract. The pathogens cannot resist the pull of the clay minerals, and once matched, they are held tightly in place. Away from their hosts, viruses die.

Water filtered through soil becomes purified. (And you thought winemaking was interesting!)

While some 85 percent of all on-site wastewater disposal systems are septic tanks functioning as I've described in the preceding pages, there is a "cousin" system used in some parts of the country that relies on aerobic bacteria—which need oxygen to grow—in a tank that is multichambered.

In some home aerobic unit designs, the waste is treated in the first chamber as it is in the septic tank I've described above, but then the effluent is forwarded into a second chamber through a pipe outfitted with a filter or baffle. In this second chamber, an aerator blows tiny bubbles into the effluent, promoting the growth of aerobic bacteria. These aerobic bacteria then feed on the organic matter and decompose it.

The partially treated effluent next moves into a settling chamber, where the bacteria and by-products drop to the bottom. Because this chamber bottom has a sloping floor, the bacteria flow back into the first chamber, where they will continue the decomposition process. Eventually, the final stage of effluent purification takes place in the leaching field, or soil absorption system, just as it does with the septic tank.

The advantage of home aerobic systems is that they can purify wastewater even more thoroughly than a septic tank—sometimes removing as much as 90 percent of organic material and suspended solids. However, they require much more frequent servicing and maintenance than septic tanks, and power failures significantly affect their proper functioning. In addition, they are more expensive to install than septic tanks and are powered with electricity that a homeowner has to pay for. But they can be a good choice for homes in areas where septic systems are impractical due to soil conditions.

All God's Creatures, Great and Small: Our Part in Septic Maintenance

Now that you're duly impressed with these magnificent systems, we need to lay out the human role in this drama. Much of what you do or don't do throughout the day determines the life span and proper functioning of the system.

A few days after we moved into our house, a plumber was hooking up the dishwasher and he cryptically muttered something under his breath about the garbage disposal. I *think* he said they were illegal with a septic system and I shouldn't have one (so why was it here?). I only use it once a week to clear little bits of food clogging up the sink, but I always feel guilty flipping the switch. While researching this chapter, I drove over to talk with Charles Bassman, the owner of Kaiser-Battistone, a large septic company up here. I pressed the play/record button on the tape recorder and asked him why I couldn't use a garbage disposal.

"It can be terrible for your system," he told me. "We redid a system last year that failed after only five years because of the disposal. Everything and anything went down it. It was used as a garbage pail. The entire tank was plugged from top to bottom, along with 40 percent of the leaching field. It was jammed solid and backed up completely."

He approved of my light and infrequent use, and we moved on to the subject of grease. Charles told me that grease is the archenemy of septic tanks and drain fields. First of all, the kind of bacteria you need to flourish in the septic tank do not thrive in solidified grease. Not only does grease slow down the bacterial action in the tank, but it constricts the sewer line passage. What it does to your arteries it does to your septic system.

Grease also goes on to jeopardize your leaching fields. Soils get sealed off when grease and suspended solids work their way past the outlet baffle and move out into the leaching area. Your leaching fields become inoperative. Charles summed up by saying: "Anything you can do to avoid large quantities of grease from getting into the drainpipe is important."

Immediately my thoughts raced to that pot of chicken soup I had made two weeks before, and I remembered spooning out all those fat globules into the sink. I confessed this to Charles, and he assured me, "You can't avoid some grease in your kitchen drain. Just don't fry a pan of bacon and dispose of the fat through the septic system. Pour it into a can, let it solidify in the refrigerator or freezer, and dispose of it as garbage, not sewage."

There are many rumors and apocryphal stories about what you can and can't put in a septic system, and I decided to ask Charles about them all. What about coffee grounds, fruit peelings, kitty litter, cigarette butts, dental floss, tampons, and condoms?

"Don't put them in the septic system!" he cautioned. "Most of these items can't be broken down easily and will flow out into the leaching field and clog up the pipes or plug up the soil around them, causing an eventual failure."

I brought up the subject of laundry. Several books and pamphlets I had read tell you to space out your laundry—don't do a lot of loads in a day. "Do you mean I can't do a dark and white wash consecutively?" I asked him. (My voice was developing a distinct whine.)

"Each load of laundry discharges as much as 44 gallons of water," he informed me. "If too much water cascades into the septic tank all at once, the solids can be washed out of the tank before they are allowed to settle and they can then clog the leaching field."

While we were on the subject of surges of water into the leaching field, he mentioned running toilets. Apparently a faulty plumbing fixture such as a running toilet can force hundreds of gallons of wasted water through the tank and into the leaching field. The earth will become totally saturated and the system will stop working. About two months ago, the toilet off our master bedroom ran for about twenty-four hours. I had no idea of the grave danger this was posing to the leaching fields. I now know that I should have turned the shutoff valve behind the toilet until the plumber arrived the next day (see page 66 in Chapter 2).

While I fiddled with the tape recorder, Charles handed me a list of household items that I unthinkingly use every day. Labels carrying any of the following warnings may kill off the important, crud-digesting bacteria in the septic tank, reducing its effectiveness at processing waste:

- Harmful or fatal if swallowed.
- Avoid contact with skin.
- Do not get in open cuts or sores.
- If comes in contact with eyes, call a physician immediately.

Particularly noxious to septic tank flora are paints, paint thinner, oil, gasoline, pesticides, and antifreeze. While these you can avoid depositing down the drain, bleach, ammonia, cleansers, polishes, and drain cleaners also have labels carrying these warnings. And cleansers, polishes, and some amounts of bleach and ammonia are not negotiable. You *have* to use them if your mother is ever going to come to your house for a visit. And this brings us to the controversial subject of biological additives.

To Rid-X or Not to Rid-X

Charles and almost every other septic company employee I spoke with feel that after using a large amount of some household cleaner, one should repopulate the bacteria colonies with an enzyme treatment.

There are two schools of thought about adding enzymes and additives to beef up the bacterial count in septic tanks and to chomp away at grease. Septic contractors who clean systems seem to recommend them; engineers who develop systems don't think they do anything beneficial. Actually, septic tank additives have been around since the 1950s. Even earlier, some folks used to feed their tanks egg shells because they believed the shells would augment the biological activity inside the tank.

I first heard of additives when my friend Sonya showed me a box of Rid-X that she pours down the toilet once a month. I was so impressed it was one of my first purchases when we bought the house. (I found it near the cleaner and laundry section in the grocery store.)

Now mindful of the additive controversy, I recently examined the packaging of Rid-X and learned that it is "formulated to liquefy solid organic wastes to keep septic systems free-flowing." The package copy goes on to note that "certain of today's household chemicals kill some of the bacteria necessary for the breakdown or liquefaction of organic solids, and if solid organic waste matter remains solid instead of liquefying, the result could be clogged pipes, offensive odors, or sewage backup. Rid-X adds hundreds of millions of the beneficial bacteria and enzymes needed to keep your system operating at full efficiency. Rid-X breaks down solidified mixtures of fat, protein, starch, and paper—which can block drains or seal the side walls of cesspools—into liquids that can be washed away in the flow of water."

The final exultant claim at the bottom of the box reads: "One Pound of Rid-X Can Liquefy up to 25 Pounds of Organic Waste Overnight."

Sounds good to me. You flush a box down the toilet once a month and have peace of mind for only $4.59.

Naturally, there's a catch. There doesn't seem to be incontrovertible evidence that these products work or are necessary at all. For instance, listen to these varying points of view quoted in an article by Kevin Wilcox for the newsletter, *Small Flows,* of the National Small Flows Clearinghouse:

Harold Ball, president of Orenco Systems in Oregon: "A lot of manufacturers have sent us their products. We've added them to septic tanks according to their instructions. We've tested discharge from septic tanks, and we've never seen discharge significantly improved, or worsened for that matter. There are billions of bugs in these tanks. I don't see what adding a few thousand more does. As far as we're concerned, they're useless."

Theresa Sears, manager of Valley Research in Valley Bend, Indiana: "We put a pipeline into an average household septic system and we test the discharge each week for a year. We test for ammonia level and biochemical oxygen demand. Our product (an enzyme additive) hits on everything. It lowers the amount of ammonia and the biochemical oxygen demand in the discharge from the septic tank."

Harold Schmidt, consulting engineer and pioneer of septic tank and effluent pump (STEP) systems: "People ask me if they should throw in yeast. I'd say throw in yeast if you want. But I'd rather throw in a dime. At least that way you get your money back."

John T. Winneberger, Ph.D., engineer in New Mexico with over thirty-four years of experience in septic tank technology: "The only way yeast could benefit a septic tank is if you eat it first."

While this is hardly as serious a matter as whether one should take estrogen after menopause, I am still puzzling out my course of action (or inaction). However, I am beginning to feel that I have inherited a third child, what with all this care and nurturing of the system. (Charles Bassman did reassure me by reminding me: "You can't let a septic system dictate your life.")

It's Anyone's Guess: Tank Location

At the conclusion of our discussion, I made an appointment to have our tank pumped, because it had been fourteen months since we'd bought the house. Charles said that we should have the tank inspected yearly to determine if it needs pumping and to check that all the baffles are working and that there are no cracks in the tank.

The date was set for the following Wednesday. A few days before, Demitri and our neighbor Karen and I sat out on the patio eating salsa and chips and placing bets as to where this mystery tank might be. I could have gone to the department of health in the town and asked for a sketch of the property, but Karen said the septic people poke around with a stick until they hit a metal access hole cover that lies under the grass. "They just *know,*" she assured us. I was beginning to think that this line of work demanded or produced otherworldly powers.

Demitri was convinced the tank was down the hill near the crabapple tree, because there was some interesting clover growing there, a spot different from the rest of the lawn. I couldn't see how it could be down the hill. Besides, what I thought was the stack vent was on the side of the house, so the tank must be over there. I was pretty sure the leaching area was on the hill, because the snow melted there first and that was probably where all the aerobic bacteria were creating heat.

The picture of the three of us poking around and making major pronouncements about tank placement is all the more funny when I tell you that the day we were up here for the home inspection, the septic people were out on the lawn—in front of our very eyes—pumping or inspecting or something. It came back to us through Jill Bregy, our Realtor, that the system was in working order, though the tank size was not up to present code, but we paused only for a second in our conversation with our contractor to note that bit of news. It never occurred to us to go out and get the card of the septic company, inquire about pumping intervals, or even ascertain the location of the tank. I guess we thought the company would contact us in a year or so. This major lapse on our part is extremely worrisome. (Is it us, or are all virgin homeowners temporarily insane?)

Well, the company never did contact us, and, as I told you, I made an appointment with Charlie's company. By this time I was really curious to know the "lay of the land," and I couldn't wait until the septic guy showed up on Wednesday.

The Lay of the Land

Come Wednesday, John pulls up with this huge truck and a long, green, pythonlike hose. After introducing myself, I watch quietly while he lands his heavy metal pick into various spots on the lawn, hoping he'll strike the metal top of the access opening. Nothing.

He wanders around a bit, questions me about the bathroom layout, and pokes some more. I encourage him with Demitri's clover theory of septic tank placement, but he waves that one away with a sort of snort. A half hour passes. The tension is building.

I root around and find the deed from our closing, and—what do you know?—there is a map with coordinates of what might be a tank, but naturally, we can't make out the numbers, and the sketch of the now nonexistent back driveway and dog run convince me that this map was drawn in 1943.

Shadows are lengthening on the lawn now, and we still haven't located the tank. John suddenly decides to take the matter in hand. We march off to the bathroom and he throws a radio transmitter into the toilet. He directs me to stand there and flush the toilet three times. I am now totally fixated on finding this tank (inquiring minds want to know), and I'm nervously hoping that this little "sewer rat" makes its way safely through the drainpipe and out into the septic tank that surely lies somewhere on our property.

At the Beep

I move quickly through the house and out to the lawn, where John is roaming with a receiver, waiting to pick up the waves of the transmitter. At first, nothing, and then—faintly—we hear beeps. It feels like the games of hot/cold we used to play as kids. Suddenly, loudly and insistently, right beneath my chrysanthemum bush just off the patio, comes the clarion call. I am shocked. Is this anyplace to put a septic tank?

Apparently it is. In no time John moves the patio step, digs into the earth, and removes the top of the upriser to the tank. Our gaze is met by the release of a dense cloud of septic flies. John seems to chuckle at my recoil and tells me that they're blind and live under the access openings of septic systems (makes you wonder what they did in a past life).

So, with success now ours, John begins the inspection by measuring scum and sludge levels and determines the tank needs pumping. He hooks up the hose and proceeds to vacuum everything out of the tank—sludge and scum as well as effluent. John uses a big shovel to dislodge the sludge and keeps shaking his head. At last he pronounces that it's been a while since this tank has been cleaned. "Fourteen months," I tell him, but he has a skeptical look on his face.

Before paying the $213 bill, John tells me two things. Our tank is only 750 gallons and should be 1,500, and we'll probably need to have it cleaned every year. First let's talk about tank sizing.

Bigger Is Better

A septic tank must be large enough to contain a three-to-five-day quantity of sewage. Because bacteria work more slowly as temperature lowers, the tank needs to be larger in colder climates.

There are other advantages to a larger tank. The effluent remains longer in the tank, resulting in a greater degree of bacterial digestion and the breakdown of solids. So the effluent entering the leaching fields is cleaner and poses less threat to the service life of the field.

Each person uses about 95 gallons of water a day (this includes cooking, washing, and toilet flushing). If five people are living in a house, their water usage would amount to $5 \times 95 = 475$ gallons. Three days would bring the total to $3 \times 475 = 1,425$. Five days would bring the total to $5 \times 95 = 2,375$.

Again, unless you live in warm-weather states, it's best to go with a larger tank.

The U.S. Health Service recommends the following tank capacities, allowing for normal wastes plus the use of a washing machine:

Number of bedrooms	Minimum capacity (gallons)
1 or 2	750
3	900
4	1,000
5	1,250

We're in trouble with our 750-gallon tank. Right now everything is copacetic, but the minute we decide to do some construction and apply for a permit, the board of health is going to force us to bring the tank size up to code.

I asked Charles Bassman what an excavation and reconstruction would cost. In our part of the country a 1,500-gallon concrete tank is about $3,000 installed; a fiberglass tank that might work in our soil might cost a bit more; and new leaching fields run about $8,000–12,000, depending upon the degree of restoration, back-filling, and reseeding of the grass. Thus, we're looking at an expense of close to $15,000 before we even begin to dream of home improvement.

Of course, our system could conk out at any time. It is now forty-one years-old, and the life span of most septic systems is twenty to thirty years, though some have been known to last fifty years (Go, baby!).

But, in the meantime, in order to ensure my septic system's continued good health, we will definitely have it inspected once a year and pumped when needed.

There seems to be a lot of confusion regarding pumping cycles. The size of the tank is the big factor here. If the tank is properly sized for the household, it should be pumped every three-to-five years. Of course, if you have a weekend house and it's sized properly for the house and fifteen people are not in residence every weekend, a longer interval between pumpings may be justified. The National Small Flows Clearinghouse in Morgantown, West Virginia is an excellent resource for a homeowner and you can call them at 1-800-624-8301 with any question pertaining to on-site sewage treatment systems.

Death of a Septic System

Nothing lasts forever. My neighbors Rusty and Karen's system is failing, and I keep saying to them, "But how do you know something is wrong?" They apparently have some very mushy parts on their lawn where the leaching fields are.

These are the warning signs of a failing system:
- Sewage surfacing over the drainfield (especially after storms)
- Sewage backups in the house
- Lush green growth over the drainfield
- Slow-draining toilets or drains
- Sewage odors

If any of these awful signs is occurring, have at least two septic contractors and the local health department or other local permitting agent come over and give you an opinion. Failure of septic systems tends to be slow and gradual, and you may be able to limp along for a while until you get the financing together. The contractor can best advise you about this. No doubt you'll be told to put water conservation techniques into play by taking the laundry to a laundromat and flushing the toilet less frequently. Whatever you do, don't plan an at-home wedding and invite a hundred guests until you replace the system.

Your Very Own Map and Personal Maintenance Record

Before you go back to your life, please take a minute to sketch a map of your house and septic tank and leaching field (with all the positioning coordinates) into this book. Some kind of stone marker would make things extremely easy. (Every time I see those stones with the word "Imagine" engraved in them, I have visions of the word "Septic" floating on one. Or maybe the word "Access" would offer spiritual as well as practical value.)

Our Septic Map

Also keep a record of the company you used, the dates of inspections or pumpings, and any recommendations your septic contractor makes.

So, when all is said and done, was I wrong when I said a septic system is something to be admired? If you have a home with a septic system, I hope this information keeps it healthy and lengthens its life span. If you don't have a septic system and still waded through this chapter, think what an impressive and truly considerate guest you'll make when you visit your friends in the country. Word will get around and invitations will come pouring in, and you won't have to spend all that money on a weekend house and deal with all of this yourself!

septic company: ....

telephone number: ....

dates of pumping: ....

recommendations: ....

....

5. Creosote Is a Dirty Word

"Did you know you could have a fire in your chimney?" my mother breathed urgently into the receiver one day. Since I thought that's exactly where you were *supposed* to have a fire, and I was looking forward to the sound of kindling warming the now-cool nights of autumn, I couldn't fathom what she was talking about.

Well, she wasn't talking about the romantic kind of a fire, to be sure. She was talking about the Smokey the Bear type—caused by a buildup in the chimney of a substance called **creosote,** a word I'd never come across before.

Creosote, a black, tarry substance, is a by-product of wood-burning. The combustion gases of a fire condense initially as a liquid, but soon cool into creosote and begin to accumulate inside the chimney. Creosote can block the flue and corrode the mortar joints, but more important, the substance is highly combustible itself. In your worst nightmare, it can ignite a huge fire in your chimney, burning your house to the ground.

But the good news is that you never have to fear this awful possibility if you have your chimney checked and cleaned out each year. If you thought a chimney sweep was a relic from Victorian days or a singing-dancing friend of Mary Poppins, you're only half right. A chimney sweep is an important member of today's annual house team.

Sweeps and the dangers of creosote were new to us, and we also didn't know a lot about the actual construction of a fireplace and the dynamics of airflow. And I certainly couldn't pass any tests about the proper building of a wood-burning fire. This chapter will focus on all of the above.

Fireplace Facts

A chimney has two important jobs: it supplies fresh air to the fire, and it carries off smoke and harmful combustion gases. Because there is always a temperature difference between the heated air in the chimney and the cold air outside, an upward flow is created, and the smoke and gases are sucked up and out of your house. This suction is referred to as a "draft." (Here's that law of thermodynamics we talked about in Chapter 3 again: Heat will always flow from a warm place to a cooler one.)

The **flue** is the long channel in the chimney that conveys the smoke and combustion gases of a fire to the air outside. Flues are usually lined in order to operate efficiently and safely. Local building codes will specify certain materials for the lining of the flue. It is usually made of rectangular terra-cotta or round, glazed (vitrified) tile. Some flues, however, have a stainless-steel, insulated lining system.

Now take a good look at the diagram on page 160 so that the following descriptions of a fireplace's structural components will make some sense.

The Fireplace

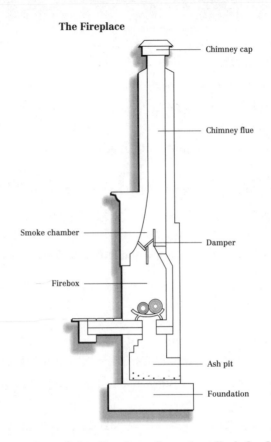

The extension of the fireplace floor is called the **hearth.** The hearth protects the area directly around the fireplace from flying sparks and ashes. It is built of noncombustible materials like brick, stone, or marble. Hearths are built at or above floor level.

The space formed by the back and sides of the fireplace where the fire is laid, is referred to as the **firebox.** The walls surrounding the firebox are constructed of solid masonry or reinforced concrete, and building codes usually require them to be a minimum of 8 inches thick in order to withstand the enormous heat of the fires. The lining of these walls is usually a 2-to-four-inch-thick layer of firebrick set with a heat-resistant form of mortar called fireclay, or a steel lining not less than 1/4 inch thick. In addition to protecting the structure, firebrick is a refractory brick that retains and then throws heat back into the room.

Above the firebox is the hinged lid that fits into the throat of the fireplace. It is called the **damper.** The damper's main purpose is to allow the smoke to reach the flue area and exit the house. But it also serves to prevent the warm air in the house from escaping when the fireplace is not in use, and to keep debris and rain from falling into the firebox. Always keep the damper closed when you're not using the fireplace.

Most people are somewhat familiar with terms like "hearth" and "damper" and "flue," but there are some other slightly more esoteric components to a fireplace that you should know about. For instance, the **smoke shelf.**

The smoke shelf is actually a shelf that lies directly behind the damper. It provides the foundation for the **smoke chamber**—the space between the smoke shelf and the flue. The smoke chamber is the transitional point between the fireplace and the flue where the smoke and gases collect and wait their turn to exit up the flue. They don't all fly up the flue at once. Rather, they are funneled up a pathway that begins at the smoke chamber.

I'll mention one more term because it's so poetically descriptive: The overhanging lip of masonry that forms the upper edge of the fireplace opening is called the **chimney breast.**

And you thought a fireplace was just a hole in the wall with a chimney extending from it!

Once the flue gets hot, a good draft occurs, and it continuously sucks air and smoke and gases from the fire and exhausts them out through the chimney.

In the best of all possible worlds, that is. Sometimes things don't work as they should. And this is where we come to the draft lecture.

Smoke Gets in Your Eyes

If your chimney isn't drawing well—if smoke is pouring into your room rather than being drawn up and out—you'll really need to do an analysis of your draft situation. First, so you don't feel like a fool later, check to see that you've not forgotten to open the damper. If it's not as simple as a forgotten damper, put the fire out with a small fire extinguisher, and when everything is cold, do a little sleuth work on your own.

Protect your eyes with glasses and cover your hair. Then with the damper opened, shine a flashlight up and around the smoke chamber, looking for any blockages such as leaves and sticks. If there's no chimney cap (more about this later), a chimney can be a wonderful nesting place for birds, raccoons, or squirrels. Wonderful for them, eventually perilous for you. If you discover shards of tile or bricks, they're a sign of a deteriorating chimney, and you need expert attention immediately. Do not even attempt to light a fire until after the expert has given you the green light.

Backdrafts

If the chimney seems in good shape physically and there is no animal-housekeeping blockage, the next item to investigate is the possibility of airflow *down* the chimney. It's not uncommon to have a reversed airflow—a **backdraft**—especially in today's newer homes. This downward flow of air may be caused simply because the chimney is on an outside wall and is cold. Preheating or priming the chimney as described on page 170 may quickly counteract the downward current of air and get things flowing in the right direction. But backdrafts can be caused by a host of other situations or conditions, inside as well as outside the house.

For instance, if you have a furnace, a clothes dryer, and a bathroom or kitchen fan exhausting air out the house, at the same time, then air to compensate for this loss must be drawn back in. (The law of physics is that if a cubic foot of air goes out, a cubic foot of air must come in to replace it.) Older homes are drafty and offer multiple avenues for air to seep back inside the house—cracks in foundations, gaps in windows and doors galore. But newer, tighter homes have air barriers and energy-efficient doors and windows, and every hole and vent is sealed and caulked, so the house has a difficult time searching for that replacement air and equalizing the negative pressure created by all those appliances and fans. One of its last great options is to draw air down the nice smooth, straight drop of the chimney, resolving its problem at your peril. The natural draft from a fire is overwhelmed by the strength of this downward drop of air, and the result is a fire that casts smoke and combustion gases into the living space.

You can confirm that the problem is backdrafting by cracking open a window when you light a fire. If this form of air replacement relieves the negative air problem, then you'll have an answer to the question "Why are my eyes burning and tearing?" Once the fire gets going, you can close the window. Your sweep or a plumber or a furnace technician can install fresh-air ducts in the furnace room that will help solve the problem of negative air, and you should be mindful not to run ventilating fans if possible.

However, if the preheating or the cracked window does nothing to stop the smoke from spilling into the room, you have to consider several possibilities. The chimney may not be drawing because it isn't tall enough, or the house may be positioned up on a hill or down in a valley and wind may be causing an adverse inversion of air. Trees hovering over your roof also may be restricting air. Or the smoke chamber could be too shallow.

According to my sweep, Steve Oldham of Chimney Swifts in

Wilton, Connecticut, these downdrafts can be either sporadic or constant. "If the problem is sporadic," he said, "it can be counteracted with something called a draft inducer. This is a cone-shaped baffle which is installed at the top of the chimney. This device costs about $200. However, if the problem is constant, it may require a fan inducer, and you'll be looking at a price tag closer to $1,000."

If you feel your dreams of romantic evenings in front of the fire sputtering out, don't despair. Whatever the unique problems and dynamics of your fireplace and chimney, Steve told me, they can usually be corrected.

Just Say No to Rainwater and Animals

As I mentioned above, there's another safety device we really need to talk about: A **chimney cap.** I'm having one made for my chimney, and not a moment too soon. Although I haven't had any animal guests—yet—every time we have a heavy rain, water drips down the chimney into the fireplace.

The first time it happened, I was on the phone with a neighbor, and we concluded that it wasn't doing any harm, so I didn't think much about it. Wrong. Wrong. Wrong! I later found out from Steve that water dripping into the bricks makes them porous, and then your mortar joints—the cement between the bricks—crack. If the bricks loosen, you will have a huge masonry repair bill and the dangerous situations we discussed above. Talk to your sweep about a chimney cap. These caps are sold according to size, and the cost is anywhere from $60 to about $1,000 for one that is custom-made.

Not only do chimney caps block the entry of rainwater, but they are normally constructed with a metal spark arrester which breaks up any sparks before they would drift to your roof or nearby trees.

But there's an even more urgent reason why chimney caps are not in the nice-to-have but rather the need-to-have category. My chimney has a double flue. One side exhausts the combustion from the fireplace; the other exhausts the combustion gases of the oil-fired boiler in the basement. If an animal nests or dies in one of the flues, the combustion gases in that flue would be blocked from their exit and carbon monoxide could come down the flue and into the living space when the heating season begins and the boiler fires up. We wouldn't necessarily know about it, because carbon monoxide is odorless and colorless and we might mistake the symptoms for the flu.

I recently attended a press conference on carbon monoxide that was organized by the First Alert Company, the manufacturers of smoke detectors and carbon monoxide detectors. The program began with an impressive presentation and education by doctors who are experts in carbon monoxide poisoning. But several families had been flown into New York City that day to speak with the press also, and they told unforgettable stories of tragedies experienced and barely averted.

In several of the cases, animals had expired in the flue or left behind nesting materials and this very dangerous scenario actually unfolded. I take up these subjects at greater length in Chapter 9, "The Healthy House," and Chapter Ten, "Ventilation Is the Name of the Game." I cannot stress too strongly, though, the importance of carbon monoxide detectors and chimney caps.

So, you have one extremely compelling reason to call the chimney sweep. Now I'm going to tell you about another.

Why Creosote Is a Dirty Word

Fire after fire, creosote is deposited inside the chimney, and—like plaque—begins to harden. It can block the flue and dissolve mortar joints, and it is also incredibly flammable. If it ignites inside your chimney, you'll think you have died and gone to hell. A chimney fire flares with a hideous roar. According to Jim Holbrook, a chimney sweep interviewed for an article in the magazine *Martha Stewart's Living,* "It can get up to 2,000 degrees inside the chimney. These balls of flames like meteors come shooting out into the room and out the top of the chimney onto the roof. It sounds like a freight train."

This kind of chimney fire can burn so furiously that the chimney may be unable to contain it. It can heat the wood beyond the flue and chimney to flashpoint and burn your house to the ground. Believe me, this is one of life's experiences you never want to have. And you'll never get close if you have the chimney inspected and checked for excessive creosote buildup each year. Just call a sweep at the end of the heating season, and let him or her (yes, there are many female sweeps) check where danger lurks.

Spring is the best time, because deposits of creosote can be removed before they harden and begin to corrode the masonry, and if you need repairs, you've got the time and good weather in which to make them.

How to Find a Chimney Sweep

To locate a sweep near you, look in the Yellow Pages and find one who has been tested and certified by the Chimney Safety Institute of America (CSIA). Sweeps are schooled not only in cleaning, but in repairs, building codes, installations, and formulas of drafts. So not only will a sweep clean, but he or she will make a safety inspection and point out any signs of deterioration and recommend repairs. A cleaning/inspection costs between $75 and $100.

Today, sweeps use flexible fiberglass rods, specially engineered wire brushes, and a huge vacuum to remove every ounce of soot.

My sweep, Steve Oldham, questioned me about the draft, cleaned and checked the chimneys, coached me on building fires that don't increase creosote deposits, and ordered and installed a custom-made double-flue chimney cap with a spark arrester. He also recommended that I leave the bed of ash in the fireplace, as it may still harbor live embers for quite a few days. Only when the ash had been cold about a week was I to scoop up the ashes in a dust-pan and transfer them into a pail to dispose of or to use as fertil-izer on plants and bushes.

When I asked him about glass enclosures for the fireplace, he said they helped keep the warm air in your living room rather than allow it to be sucked up through the flue along with the smoke.

But I was absolutely charmed by something else he said. Ap-parently it's a centuries-old tradition in Europe that if you see the brushes of a sweep or you shake hands with a chimney sweep, you're in for a spell of good luck. I hope so, because I intend to see Steve and those brushes every April or May. But I'm already lucky if my family and home are safer for his visit. Anything else in the way of good fortune would be delightful, but is absolutely not required.

How to Build a Fire That Would Make a Boy Scout Weep

There are quite a few reasons why it's important to know how to build a good fire. Not only does your prowess impress your date, your mate, and your relatives and friends, but a properly built fire burns hotter and leaves less creosote behind (a mellow flame doesn't shoot the sooty by-products up and out before they condense on the chimney walls). A smart fire is a safer fire, because you have more control. Besides, it's demoralizing to go to all this work and then spend most of the evening staring at cold logs.

I spoke with Thomas Swan, owner of the Black Swan Hearth and Gifts in Newtown, Connecticut, about how to build a proper fire. We started with a discussion of the wood you need to have on hand to assemble your pyre.

"The best logs come from deciduous trees," he said. "The ones that lose their leaves in the fall." These logs are dense and strong and are referred to as hardwood. Coniferous trees—pines and spruces—are softwoods. Softwoods are much lighter, and don't contain as much wood fiber as hardwoods, and so log for log, they deliver significantly fewer BTUs of heat.

He went on to say, "Softwoods are highly flammable, but their flammability factor is due to their high resin content. And it's the resin that spells trouble. It never burns completely, and it collects on the chimney walls, forming creosote. So use the softwoods for kindling only and learn how to ignite the hardwoods. Oak, maple, ash, beech, and birch are hardwoods. So are the fruit and nut trees—cherry, pear, and pecan—and if you can find them in your area they'll burn with a beautiful aroma."

Not only do you have to buy the right kind of wood, you have to have wood that has been aged properly. If the wood is too freshly cut, it will contain too much water and your fire will hiss and smoke and burn unevenly. Thomas Swan suggests that you buy a cord (a stack of wood 8 feet long, 4 feet high, and 4 feet wide) that has been aged for at least six months. "Deal with reputable people so you can trust that the wood has been aged for that period of time," he advised. "Properly aged wood should have 'checking' on its ends. These are hairline cracks that result from drying and shrinking. The ends of the cut wood should also be dark-colored—gray—*not* white. This means it's weathered."

He also cautioned against buying wood that has been aged for too long a time, for instance for over two years. "If wood gets too rotted, it can cause a creosote buildup in the chimney," he said.

Once you get your cord delivered, it should be cross-stacked—off the ground—with the logs at 90-degree angles to each other, so that air flows freely through the pile and keeps it dry. Cover only the top with a tarpaulin. The ground is constantly evaporating moisture, and a fully covered pile will simply trap the moisture and keep the wood damp (you'll create a kind of greenhouse effect). Not only will your wood rot, but the insects in your area will be eternally grateful to you for providing them with a perfect home.

So you've seen to the seasoned hardwood logs. Now you need two other kinds of wood: kindling and fatwood. Kindling is nothing more than thumb-diameter pieces of chopped-up logs. You can split down some of those logs you've got stacked, or if you don't have a Paul Bunyan yen (or an ax handy) you can purchase a bag of kindling at the hardware store.

I originally thought that fatwood was wood laced with some sort of lard, but Thomas enlightened me about fatwood's interesting history. It actually comes from the naturally resinous pine stumps of the American South. Decades ago, loggers came into an area and slashed the southern yellow pines. They let the trees weep sap for six months before they cut the trees down (the sap was then distilled into pine tars and turpentine). Once the trees were cut, however, 4-to-6-foot stumps were left standing, and the root bases of these originally 70-foot trees continued to send sap up to the stumps. Over time, the stumps became saturated with the petroleum-based pine tar. Cut into sticks, the fatwood from these stumps is extremely flammable.

I asked Thomas Swan if I should look for any particular brand of fatwood, and he said only to make sure it comes from the Southern states of this country, never from Central or South America. Products from the United States are coming from the stumps of trees cut long ago, while in Central and South America, loggers are moving into the rain forest to cut living trees.

Now that you've got your hardwood, your kindling, and your fatwood at fireside, open the damper full-throttle. Some chimneys—

because of location on an outside wall, construction, or the baro-metric pressure at the time you wish to enjoy a fire—have to be pre-heated to counteract a downdraft. (You'll know if you have to preheat if you feel a current of cold air coming down.) Simply crum-ple a sheet of newspaper, light it, and hold it up near the damper. "When it burns down close to your hand, let go of it," Thomas said dryly. Once the downdraft is neutralized, you're ready to go.

Lay up the fire with two pieces of approximately 4-inch-diameter split logs. Lay them parallel to each other on the andirons, the metal supports. You're going to start small and build larger later. Next crisscross these logs with several pieces of fatwood.*

On top of the fatwood, and also crisscrossing the logs, goes your kindling. Light the fatwood first—it's the most flammable, and as the fire burns upward, it will ignite the kindling. Once things get going, add four to five small-to-medium-size pieces of wood. Save the larger logs for later when the fire is well established with a good, strong draft. Leave the damper wide open throughout the burning period.

Whew! After all that, you should have a fire you can be proud of and a real feeling of accomplishment. Sometimes, though, the thought of all this assembling and timing makes me a bit tired, and I'm tempted to pop a Duraflame log on the andirons and return to my book and tea. I asked Thomas if this is a bad idea, and he said no, not at all. In fact, they're even a bit more environmentally cor-rect. But he did tell me that compressed-paper logs give off a more mellow flame, which, as you remember, doesn't shoot the sooty by-products up and out of your chimney as well. Thus, creosote will accumulate a bit faster. But as long as you clean out your chimney every spring, the lazy person's approach to fire-building—though probably more expensive—is not the worst thing you could do in life.

---

*You can use newspaper instead of fatwood as a firestarter, but fatwood burns longer, thus in-creasing your odds of getting the fire going. It also burns cleaner.

Some Final Safety Tips

You're going to want to visit a fireplace accessory store and take a look at your options in fireplace accouterments. First of all, you'll want to purchase some tools. They most often come in sets that include a brush, a shovel, a poker, and tongs. The poker and tongs let you manipulate the logs as you're adding to the fire, and the brush, of course, helps you sweep the ashes up. You might also want to invest in a pair of fireplace gloves to protect your hands from rough woods and hot logs.

A fireplace accessory store will also have fire extinguishers that are small and unobtrusive and more decorative in style. It's always a good idea to have such a device at hand. And to make sure you know exactly how to use one, see page 394 of Chapter 12, "The Great Escape."

If you've gone the Duraflame route with your fire and you have to leave the house for any reason during its two-to-three-hour run, do not try to extinguish the log. Just close the glass doors to your fireplace, or make sure your screen is positioned very carefully around the fireplace. Don't, however, make a habit of this. Reserve your hearth times for those cozy nights at home when your public activity ceases and you can relax in front of a fire that warms both body and soul.

6. The Sorcerer's Apprentice; or Water, Water Everywhere

....

There's a memorable scene in the middle of the movie *Fantasia* when the Sorcerer's Apprentice decides to attempt some magic of his own and commands a broom to fill and carry water buckets to the cauldron. Unhappily for the little apprentice, he takes a nap and awakens as an unimaginable flood threatens the castle floor and walls. The relentless broom cannot be stopped—not by the apprentice's desperate spells—not even by brute force.

Fortunately, the sorcerer returns and restores order to the situation, but the wide eyes and frantic activity of the sorcerer's apprentice reveal his absolute terror and loss of control.

Homeowners can experience that same degree of panic when that drip-drip-drip pattern reaches their ears. There's nothing like a roof that leaks or basement walls that spring water to undermine your feeling about the soundness of your structure. As David Owen writes in *The Walls Around Us,* "Being the victim of a leak is like being the victim of a robbery—you feel violated. There's something nightmarish about dripping walls."

How true. But even without a glowering wizard to save the situation, there's a lot you can do to contain the problem, fix it, or prevent it from happening in the first place.

"Is There a Problem with Your Flashing?"

It wasn't two months after our move-in day (and, naturally, after the entire house had been freshly painted) when I began to notice a leak in the living-room ceiling during a particularly heavy rainfall. I was so anxious and disturbed about it I must have mentioned it to everybody and anybody I saw in the next couple of days. Several people asked me the strangest question: They wanted to know if there was a problem with my flashing.

Well, had I known what flashing was I might have responded with a thoughtful, considered, "in-the-know" type of answer, but I think my reply was more on the order of an irritable "What the hell is flashing?" I was starting to feel very tired.

Roofing problems seem to be a source of deep angst for many homeowners. By the time you finish this chapter, however, not only are you going to be able to discuss flashing with the best of them, but you'll appreciate that your roof is really a marvel of engineering, a truly fine canopy for your home.

Anatomy of a Roof

A roof is built up layer by layer on top of the rafters. First, in order to give the roof a rigidity, the roofer nails on a plywood **sheathing.** This is also called **decking.** Then, to protect the decking from moisture, some roofers lay **roofing felt.** On top of the felt, a succession of shingles is laid, each one atop the one below, like a duck's feathers.

The Roof Revealed

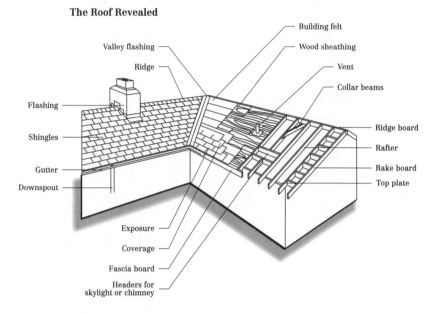

By far the most popular shingles are made of asphalt. In fact, some 85 percent of the homes in this country have some form of asphalt shingles. They cost less than slate and wood shingles and terra-cotta tiles, and they are more fire-resistant than wood shingles.

Asphalt shingles are either organic or inorganic. Organic shingles have a composite mat core composed of wastepaper and wood by-products. The mat is then saturated with asphalt in order to resist moisture and coated with mineral surface granules to reflect sunlight and provide color. In 1959, however, Owens-Corning introduced a shingle with a fiberglass core. This inorganic fiberglass core is sandwiched between two asphalt layers before it is topped off with mineral surface granules, and these shingles cannot absorb moisture.

In fact, Owens-Corning has a press kit about its "Heart of Pink" fiberglass core which has samples of organic felt and fiberglass mat. The homeowner is challenged to put each in a glass of water. Naturally I had to check this out, so I trooped upstairs and conducted the experiment. Sure enough, the organic felt absorbed water and the "Heart of Pink" did not. Of course, the asphalt saturation does render the organic shingles pretty waterproof, they are less brittle, and the highly respected builder Jim Locke (author of *The Well-Built House)* has written that he actually prefers organic shingles, but fiberglass shingles have become the roofing standard, and their Class A fire rating is a great advantage.

Asphalt roofs may not look as cozy or architectural as wood shingles and shakes, but they last for about twenty-five years and require little maintenance beyond removing fallen leaves and pine needles.

The chart on page 176 compares the various roofing materials and details the life spans, maintenance, and pluses and minuses of each choice.

I was interested to learn that asphalt shingles withstand all kinds of foul weather quite admirably, but their greatest enemy is the sun. Those ultraviolet rays are killers. If you begin to see too many mounds of the mineral surface granules collecting in the gutters, or too many shingle edges curling in all directions, you'll know your roof shingles have lived their life span and—sometime in the next few years—you'll have to pay for the next generation to be installed.

Flat roofs, or those with shallow slopes, present a different roofing problem: you can't use asphalt shingles on them. Water from melting snow will back up right under them.

Until recently, asphalt roll roofing was used on shallow-sloped or flat roofs. Asphalt roll roofing is similar to asphalt shingles, but it comes in long, 36-inch-wide rolls. The problem is that it rarely last more than five years.

Today, there are two new classes of **single-ply membranes** which are a great improvement for these kinds of roof structures.

The Run-Down on Roofing

Material	Pluses	Minuses	Expected Life
Asphalt shingles: (Felt or fiberglass base impregnated with asphalt and coated with granulated minerals.)	Inexpensive to purchase and install, fire resistant, many color choices, little to no maintenance, easy to repair.	They don't have the architectural and rich look of wood, tile, or slate.	15 - 20 years
Architectural or laminated shingles: (Multiple overlapping layers are laminated to give the illusion of more shadows and texture as in a wood or slate roof.)	As their name implies, they are more "architectural" looking, and they last longer than asphalt shingles.	Expensive.	30 - 40 years
Wood shingles and shakes: (A wood shingle is sawed and a wood shake is split from logs and therefore more rustic looking. Western red cedar covers most roofs, but Alaskan yellow cedar, Eastern white cedar, and Southern pine are other options.	Extremely beautiful, not difficult to repair or replace.	They are not fire-resistant unless treated (some areas of the country ban wood roofs of any kind), very expensive to purchase and install, requires special decking and maintenance.	20 - 40 years
Tile roofing: (Made of clay, concrete or fiber cement.)	Aesthetic appeal, very fireproof, long lasting.	Expensive to purchase, ship and install, heavy and so may need roof reinforcement; a cracked or chipped tile can be difficult to repair.	20+ years

The Run-Down on Roofing continued

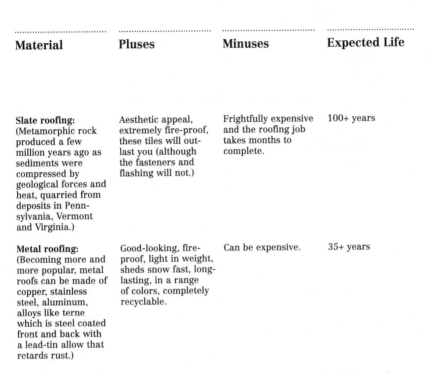

Material	Pluses	Minuses	Expected Life
Slate roofing: (Metamorphic rock produced a few million years ago as sediments were compressed by geological forces and heat, quarried from deposits in Pennsylvania, Vermont and Virginia.)	Aesthetic appeal, extremely fire-proof, these tiles will outlast you (although the fasteners and flashing will not.)	Frightfully expensive and the roofing job takes months to complete.	100+ years
Metal roofing: (Becoming more and more popular, metal roofs can be made of copper, stainless steel, aluminum, alloys like terne which is steel coated front and back with a lead-tin allow that retards rust.)	Good-looking, fire-proof, light in weight, sheds snow fast, long-lasting, in a range of colors, completely recyclable.	Can be expensive.	35+ years

Note: Except for metal, these materials are appropriate on sloped roofs only. Flat roof coverings are discussed on page 175 and below.

The first kind is modified bitumen. This membrane is modified asphalt, laminated to either a kind of polypropylene or fiberglass and torch-applied to the roof by a professional. The second, EPDM (ethylene propylene diene monomer), is a purely synthetic rubber membrane that is applied with adhesives. Both have important advantages. They expand and contract without cracking, they are ultraviolet and ozone-resistant, and they will outlast any rolled roofing by many years. In fact, the EPDM membranes are expected to protect a roof for more than thirty-five years. Also, both classes of single-ply membranes limit the damage caused by ice damming. They are initially more expensive than roll roofing, but are, in the opinions of experts, the only way to go.

Flashing Explained (Finally)

If a roof were just a roof, all nicely layered with shingles, then earth would be a simpler place. But a roof suffers many intrusions. Chimneys, attic vents, plumbing vents, skylights, and dormers all jut up through the roof and compromise its integrity. These uprisings, as well as the valleys (the places where two slopes of a roof come together), all create seams. And seams, unfortunately, provide access for water. To keep water out of these vulnerable areas, all the seams must be covered with strips or sheets of metal called—ah-ha!—flashing.

The correct installation of flashing is the most important part of roofing. When a roof leaks, it is often because of a failure in the flashing. And very often the culprit is the flashing around the chimney.

Why so? Well, the chimney is so heavy that it must have its own foundation, and this foundation can settle and move, causing the flashing to thin out and tear.

Moreover, flashing and restoring the flashing of a chimney requires patience and professionalism as the flashing must be tucked into mortar joints in order to prevent water from pouring down behind the flashing. It's quite probable that, in the history of the roof, a first-rate job of repairing the chimney flashing wasn't paid for. Or a do-it-yourselfer opted for a cheap fix and plugged any gaps with a plastic roof cement. After a few years, the cement hardens and cracks and leaks become your legacy.

Figuring out the source of the leak can be like finding the source of the Nile. Water that penetrates the roof can meander for many feet, snaking along sheathing and down rafters and joists before dribbling into the insulation and making an appearance on your ceiling or wall.

If you climb up to the attic, you may be able to track down the point of entry. Water stains in insulation, framing, or sheathing will narrow your focus, but keep in mind that any leak will originate higher than the area where it first becomes visible to you.

Another option is to wait for a sunny day and see if you notice any tiny pinholes of light streaming through the attic. There's the culprit! If you do find one, push a wire up through it and call the roofer for the repair job.

If you're lucky, the problem becomes readily apparent, but there's an uncomfortable reality in this roof-leaking business: You may *never* locate a leak, and be obliged to live with a chronic condition. My prayer for you is, if it has to be, may it be only an infinitesimal leak, and may it manifest only during torrential rains that come every seven years.

Unsightly Stains

It turns out that the leak in our ceiling was caused by a nail some dodo had driven through the roof. The roofer fixed it, but now I was left with this unsightly rusty-looking water stain on the just-painted ceiling. We lived with it for about six months because we thought we had to have the entire room redone. Until Tony "You Name It—We Do It" Kelly came into our lives and fixed just that patch, quite satisfactorily.

Here are the steps Tony took to repair only this water-stained part of the ceiling:

1. First he retaped the ceiling where there's a seam in the sheetrock. (Water, looking for the path of least resistance, tends to work its way through the seams.)
2. He smeared a mudlike taping compound on the retaped seam.
3. He sanded it down.
4. He applied a primer with stain kill (prevents the stain from bleeding through).
5. He painted that part of the ceiling with the original white.

Always keep an extra, unopened can of your ceiling paint in your basement, and mark it "Living Room Ceiling" (or "Dining Room Ceiling" or whichever room it was used for). Our leftovers were in the unheated garage during one particular winter from hell, and they froze and unfroze and became an unusable glop.

Damn Those Ice Dams

Now that I've brought up the subject of winters from hell, we can chat about the dark and loathsome subject of ice dams.

I first ran into this phrase when I called my friend Elin in upstate New York to see how she was faring in February. She sounded uncharacteristically grim and intense, and when I asked her what was wrong, she described the terrible leaks she and Bob were experiencing in their beautiful new home. All due to ice dams. Later, when we talked about my ideas for this book, she kept repeating in a voice straight out of Conrad's *Heart of Darkness: "Tell them about the ice dams . . . just tell them about the ice dams."*

All right, all right. Ice dams get started on snowy roofs when too much heat escapes from the living space below and begins to melt the snow cover. Initially, the water trickles down and doesn't refreeze, because the heat is rising steadily through the roof and the blanket of snow provides a kind of insulation from above. But eventually, as this trickling water hits the colder edges of the roof—the eaves that extend beyond the home's exterior walls, or the area just above the eaves, or the gutters—it refreezes and forms an icy border. As cold days pass, and as this thaw-and-freezing processional continues, the icy wall becomes more massive, and any new meltwater (which would ordinarily drip off the edge of the roof) is dammed inside. Since shingles can shed only *running* water—they cannot cradle a pond—the water backs up and begins to leak down between the shingles into the living space below. Ice dams cause massive damage to the roofing materials, to framing, and to siding, as well as to exterior and interior paint and wallboard.

How can one prevent this horrible chain of events from occurring? I spoke to Pat Huelman, the coordinator of the Cold Climate Housing Center at the University of Minnesota, who has written extensively on this subject, and he told me: "To successfully prevent ice dams, the roof deck and shingles should be the same temperature from the eave to the ridge. Any heat loss from the attic must be minimized, and a three-pronged approach is needed to accomplish this. First, there must be adequate insulation throughout the attic. Then, all air leaks and holes that might carry warm air into the attic must be sealed. And finally, there must be proper ventilation beneath the roof deck."

Pat then got more specific. He said that it is especially difficult—but essential—to insulate the area where the roof sits on the outside wall. "This perimeter area is the place most prone to heat loss. Because there is not much height there, however, it is critical that a careful insulation job be done."

Houses that are newly built in colder climates are built tightly and with polyethylene air barriers. But older homes don't have the advantage of these air barriers and often have holes and plumbing vents that must be sealed if warm air is to be prevented from leaking into the attic and warming the snow cover above it. I wondered how these holes are sealed, and Pat said, "We seal large holes with a rigid board insulation and use a polyurethane foam around the edges. Medium holes can be foamed with this expanded polyurethane foam, and small holes can simply be caulked."

The other major (and I mean very major) component to this anti-ice-dam triumvirate is the installation of **continuous soffit- and-ridge vents.** The soffits are the underside of the roof overhang, and when continuous vents are placed here, combined with a long vent all along the high peak of the roof (the ridge), the air enters the roof at the soffit and moves up along the roof sheathing and exhausts out the ridge (no matter which direction the wind is blowing). And this constant and equally distributed airflow keeps the roof at a correctly cool temperature and—hallelujah!—ice dams don't form. (This kind of ventilation is discussed fully in Chapter 10, "Ventilation Is the Name of the Game.")

This kind of ventilation system doesn't cost an ungodly amount of money, if it's installed during construction. Pat Huelman told me it costs $300. But the retrofitting of an existing house could run four to five times that figure.

If ice dams do come into your life, you're going to hear about resistance-type heating cables, which you buy and attach in a zigzag pattern to the first course of shingles, just above the eaves. Supposedly they heat and prevent ice dams from getting a toehold on your roof. But Pat Huelman told me that they can make ice dams worse—they merely shift the pattern around. Now you have ice dams both above and below the cables. And if ice dams are higher on the roof, they can cause more water damage inside the areas you really care about in your house. This is the case with eaves flashing, also. It does help some snow slide off the roof, and it is fairly watertight, but ice dams can still form above the metal.

I also asked Pat if we should be raking the snow off the roof with an aluminum snow rake, because I'd read about this maneuver. But he expressed real concern about anyone trying to do this unless he or she could stand on the ground and *delicately* do the raking. "Roofs in winter are slippery and dangerous places," he warned. "Don't try to get up on one." I think his point was that as bad as an ice dam is, a broken back is worse.

He also advised that you never try to "beat up the ice dam" by hacking it apart, as you'll surely destroy the shingles and roofing while you're doing your Norman Bates impersonation.

If you are reroofing, you can try a relatively new product to limit any damage caused by ice dams. Talk to your roofer about self-adhering waterproof membranes. These are tough, rubbery sheets that can be installed between the roof deck and shingles or tiles in areas prone to leaks, for example the eaves, valleys, and flashings. They automatically seal around nail holes, also. These membranes don't prevent ice dams from forming, but they resolutely "stand their ground" and don't allow the backed-up water an entrance to the house. They are an insurance policy "in the event of . . ." But proper insulation, the sealing of any air leaks, and the cooling of the roof with a continuous soffit-and-ridge ventilation system are the real solutions to your ice dam blues.

Gutter Talk

Rainstorm after rainstorm, thousands of gallons of water a year pound away at your roof. The shingles may shed the water the way a duck's feathers do, but if the water isn't diverted from the house's siding, it can ravage the paint, foster mildew and rot, destroy mortar, and proffer an open invitation to insects. Enter the world of gutters.

Gutters are installed on the eaves of a house to collect rain or

The Gutter

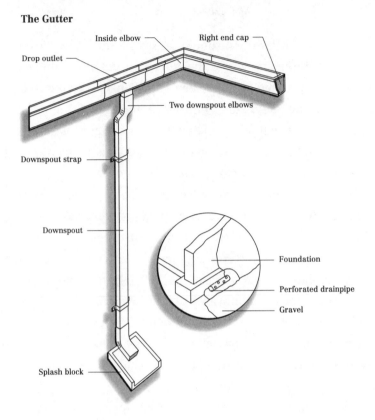

melting snow from the roof and channel it into downspouts that direct the water away from the house's siding and foundation. They can be made of galvanized metal (common but requires periodic painting), wood (used infrequently today), or aluminum or vinyl (the best because they require little maintenance besides cleaning).

All gutters must slant just a bit toward their outlets. The route of the flow is as follows: An **elbow**—just like the crook of your arm—directs the water through a **leader,** connects with another elbow, travels down the straight shoot of the **downspout,** and curves around yet a third elbow that ushers the water away from the wall by routing it through the downspout outlet.

But if the gutters simply dump all the water on the ground next to your house, you're going to have real headaches. Your roof and siding may look nice, but your basement will soon be declared a disaster area, as all that water will find its way in there.

Imagine an inch of rain on a 2,000-square-foot roof. That calculates out to 1,250 gallons of water. If you collect all that from the four corners of a roof and dump it down onto little concrete splash blocks—*next to the foundation!*—where would you think that water would end up?

You see, the virgin soil that existed before your house was built and the soil was excavated had settled for thousands of years. It absorbed water slowly and the rest ran off. Once the soil is disturbed in the excavation, however, it becomes aerated and porous, and when it is replaced as backfill, it simply gulps water in and neatly delivers it right to your foundation. Since the backfill area is a perimeter of 4, 6, or 10 feet from the foundation walls, and a splash-block extends out only about 2 feet, your basement hasn't a prayer in a heavy downpour.

Therefore, a smarter way to go is to bury a 4-inch PVC pipe in the ground and reroute the water from the downspout to a low spot in the yard, a ditch, a culvert, or a storm sewer. It might have to be run 50 feet away from the house, but you'll sleep peacefully through the next downpour.

Another option developed by Basement Systems, Inc. (you'll meet its founder, Larry Janesky, in the next section) is known as the Underground Downspout Extensions (U-D-E). This is a buried PVC pipe that extends to a bubbler pot, a small plastic drywell that's covered with a small green grate flush with the lawn. This is a good solution if there's no low point on the property and the nearest culvert is in the next county. (To find a Basement Systems dealer near you, call 800-541-0487.)

Your gutter system needs to be checked and cleaned out twice a year: in May, after the trees have bloomed, and in the fall, after the leaves have dropped. Look in the Yellow Pages under "Gutters and Downspouts" for a cleaning service. If you have a lawn service cutting the grass, the workmen often take care of the gutters as part of the spring and fall cleanup. If you screen the gutters, you will only need to clean them with a hose every couple of years.

As Above, So Below: Basements

Ah, the basement. Admittedly my least favorite place in a house . . . but dark and spooky is a lot better than dark, *dank,* and spooky. And it's significantly better than dark, *wet,* and spooky.

The most common basement problem a homeowner faces is water (and wet basements have been troubling homeowners for over one hundred years). And not only is water in the basement a big problem for you, but real estate agents estimate that a wet basement can seriously handicap your chances of selling a house and that the market will penalize a seller at least 10 percent (sometimes 20 percent) of the sale price for a wet basement. But beyond that, it just doesn't make sense to pay a lot of money for a house and cordon off so much potentially usable square footage simply because it's prone to moisture problems. A wet basement can be cured, and you can use the space you're frantically paying for every month.

The first thing that should be examined is the slope of the soil around the foundation (the grading). It should slope 1 inch per foot away from the house. Soil around a house (particularly a new house) settles and can direct water toward a foundation instead of away. Adding soil and regrading will always help, but this is seldom a complete cure. More often a homeowner will need some kind of system inside the basement, also.

Basement Systems, Inc., has a good reputation around here because it is very state-of-the-art and is applying new technology to the age-old problem of water in the basement. I called the president, Larry Janesky, and we arranged to meet early one morning at his company's national headquarters in Stratford, Connecticut. Basements Systems is the largest waterproofing contractor in New England. It is also the parent company of a network of over eighty waterproofing companies throughout the United States, Canada, and Europe.

In his training classroom, and over coffee and danish, Larry Janesky launched into a four-hour lecture about water in the basement and its various cures. He started by saying, "Our job is to manage the water that falls from the sky and make sure it doesn't end up on your basement floor."

He then explained that this falling water travels through the ground and lands up next to the imperfect concrete structure of the foundation. "Imperfect" because concrete is portland cement, water, and an aggregate of stone and sand. Concrete may look solid to you, but it's actually full of a great many tiny pores. And these pores can draw water into the basement like tiny pumps.

Not only is the concrete imperfect, porous, and prone to cracking, but the physics at play in the house are guaranteed to bring water in. Since soil has almost 100 percent humidity and warm air is always rising to the top of the house and exhausting out the attic (the "stack" effect), the pressure in the basement is slightly reduced. This is perfectly natural and as it should be, but the situation makes it easy for the negatively pressured house to continuously suck moisture through the floor and walls into the basement.

Then there's **capillarity.** The tiny pores of the concrete pull water in like little suction pumps. You'll know whether capillarity is a player in your basement if you see a powdery white line of mineral deposits on your walls and floor. These mineral deposits are called **efflorescence.** (The good news is that these mineral deposits are basically harmless and can be brushed away with a stiff-bristled brush.)

So with an imperfect foundation, soil with almost 100 percent humidity, nonvirgin backfill soil that is very porous, capillarity, the physics of a house, cracks in concrete, and pounding rainstorms and torrents of melting snow, is there any chance for a dry basement in this all too imperfect world? (And I haven't even mentioned condensation yet!)

"Yes," says Larry Jenesky. "More innovations have been made in the last five years than in the last one hundred." I invited him to describe them for me.

"To fix water problems, you have to intercept the water along its path into the basement," he began. "Your first inclination probably would be to try to intercept it from the outside, before it has a chance to move into the basement. But to do this, a waterproofing contractor would have to excavate the entire perimeter of the house, down to the footings, sacrifice all the landscaping, and install a drainage system, waterproof the walls, and then restore all the soil and trees and bushes. This is a $10,000-to-15,000 proposition and a giant, disruptive mess. But the sad part is that silt and sediment can be dragged into the drainage system and clog it up, rendering it unserviceable. You're back to square one with the wet basement and the depleted bank account.

"A better way is to install an interior waterproofing system. These days we have some different types to choose from. The old-fashioned traditional system is a round pipe and gravel in trenches underneath the floor in the soil. But here again, you can have a clog because of the silt and sediment in the surrounding soil. Furthermore, if the soil washes out from beneath the foundation, it could cause settling problems. The foundation water could wash the soil from beneath the footing—the concrete base that the foundation is built on—causing air spaces under the foundation and thus causing settling of the house."

So, the system Larry recommends is set below the concrete floor, but it is not set in the soil, so it can never clog. Instead, the drainage system is set under the concrete but on top of the footing. If the walls are of concrete block, weep holes are drilled to allow water inside the blocks to drain continually into this drainage system. It also catches water from cracks or window wells. Any collected water is then routed to a sump pump.

If the conditions are right—the floor is in good condition and not currently leaking—a less expensive approach is a baseboard system. Hollow vinyl baseboard is epoxied to the surface of the floor and the water is channeled from the floor-wall joint and the walls around to the sump pump. This system is also less disruptive, because the floor does not have to be jackhammered and reconcreted.

Sump Pumps

Since I don't have a sump pump, and both these interior systems seem to have one at their heart, I asked Larry to spend some time talking about it.

"A sump is a hole in the floor that gathers water," he explained. "If you put a pump in this hole it's called a sump pump. As the water rises in the sump hole, the pump automatically turns on and pumps it through a PVC discharge pipe and out to the exterior, naturally directed away from the foundation. The pump runs in short, six-to-ten-second cycles. In a cold-climate region, an antifreeze device must be installed on the line outside, even if it's pitched, so the discharge line doesn't freeze when snow and ice cover the outlet of the pipe in the winter."

Larry went on to describe how important an airtight cover is to a sump pump. This prevents evaporation, keeps insects, radon, and odors at bay, and quiets the pump. But even more important, it safeguards a curious toddler from tumbling in.

Every sump pump should have an alarm that signals the homeowner of a pump failure before the floor gets wet. This sounds like a smoke detector with a continuous high pitch.

I asked Larry which sump pump he recommends, and he extolled the virtues of pumps manufactured by the Zoeller Company in Louisville, Kentucky. Why? "They have superior reliability, longevity, they're very quiet, and they are capable of pumping 2,600 gallons of water an hour—that's a lot of water," he answered.

Since we often have power failures, my next question concerned the storm that knocks out the electricity at just the time the rainwater is filling your basement. Is there a battery backup pump?

"Yes," said Larry, "but the best ones cost in the neighborhood of $1,000. Only 5 percent of my customers opt for it." We agreed that perhaps a homeowner should put that money toward a generator and be able to watch TV, work at the computer, and see the pump save the basement at the same time (see page 98 to read all about home generators).

So an interior waterproofing system with a good Zoeller sump pump (but without battery backup) costs in the $3,000–$4,000 range. (Try to remember that 10 percent you'll lose from the sale of the house if you have a wet basement.)

Just before we finished this part of the interview, I asked Larry about waterproofing with oil paints or coatings, because I kept reading about them. He told me, "Painting the inside to stop water leakage—negative-side waterproofing—is a Band-Aid approach. It rarely does anything. The water is already through the wall by the time it gets to the coated side of the wall, and it will blister the paint and push it right off the wall. Tell your readers not to spend their time or money this way."

Vertical Cracks

Larry and I then got up and walked through the showroom, and he showed me a demonstration wall with a vertical crack. Solid poured foundations routinely develop vertical cracks, and these are not generally from improper building practices and pose no structural threat. The biggest nuisance is that they leak.

In order to repair them, Larry's company injects a flexible polyurethane resin. This material flows all the way out to the soil, so it's a full-depth repair as opposed to a surface patch that can recrack. It's flexible, so that when the wall moves or the temperature changes, the resin moves with it.

The repair of one crack costs about $600, but it's a solution that unequivocally works. This technology is used to seal dams and subway tunnels and it is becoming the industry standard.

Summertime and the Basement's All Sweaty

While we haven't had any major wet spots on the lower level, come late spring and early summer, my office gets this musty, mildewy smell and there's a lot of dripping from the cold-water pipes in the boiler room. This is condensation. It is simply humid air condensing on cool surfaces such as cold-water pipes, concrete or masonry walls, and the concrete floor. Larry suggested several ways to deal with this.

"If you isolate the cold, dense surfaces—the cold pipes—from the warm, humid air, they can't clash and condense. Go to the hardware store and buy slotted foam pipe insulation. It's like a foam snake that comes in different diameters—1/2 or 3/4 inch—and in 3 foot lengths. You can just cut it with scissors and pop it right on. Target the cold-water pipes in the basement, and if you have a cold water storage tank because you have a well, buy an insulating blanket to stop condensation there.

"Next, keep all windows and doors and all other sources of air exchange to the outside closed and run a 30-to-40-pint dehumidifier that has been altered to run constantly. Every unit has a knockout on the tray where you can hook up a garden hose or a washing-machine hose and stick the other end in a sink, or you can even connect it with a Y where the washing machine hose goes in. This way it runs continuously and doesn't automatically shut off in four hours because the tray is full.

"And while we're in the laundry area, make sure your clothes dryer vents the moist air to the outside. I know it seems like an oxymoron, but your dryer is a major source of moisture."

Locating the Expert

Larry and I walked out of the demonstration room, and I looked out the window with alarm to see that the major winter storm that had been forecast for later that day had come upon us a bit earlier. The snow was coming down furiously, so I asked him my last question fast. How do you find a waterproofing contractor?

"It's always good to get strong recommendations from friends or a Realtor in your area, but the companies are listed in the Yellow Pages under 'Waterproofing Contractors.' Be sure that the company offers more than one kind of system, otherwise it is sure to be biased, and make sure the company's personnel are well trained and experienced in installing the type of system they recommend.

"Always ask for references, and call the other people for whom they've done work." And, he hastened to add, *"Never* let anyone inject a clay called bentonite into the ground outside your foundation run. It has a failure rate of 90 percent."

That said, I thanked this modern-day water wizard and drove ever so slowly home.

7. The Uninvited Guest, Part I: Insects and Other Pests

The Victorians had a thing about bugs. Insects figured prominently in their poetry, they catalogued and sketched them obsessively, and they were a favorite motif of the jewelry and accessories of that time. Realistic-looking beetles perched on hats and veils, wood lice and earwigs nestled on parasols, and artistic renderings of insects adorned brooches, necklaces, and earrings.

At the turn of the century, this insect craze culminated in the great jewelry of the Art Nouveau period. In her book *Art Nouveau Jewelry,* Vivienne Becker explains: "Insects became fantasy creatures, sometimes shocking, often exceptionally and sensuously beautiful. The innocuous butterfly, freed from its glass cage, was metamorphosed into a dragonfly with wings so real that the insect might at any moment flutter into life and fly away. The dragonfly's face often seemed to grin as if wearing a nightmarish mask, but on closer examination it was revealed to be that of a young girl. The images of fantasy and nightmare, and particularly metamorphosis (for example of chrysalis into butterfly), coincided with Freud's new theories of psychoanalysis which advocated probing into the subconscious to reveal rich or sinister imagery."

Where am I going with all of this? Well, I'm just hoping that this historical elevation and metaphorical romancing of the natural world will temper your shrieking when you realize you have an infestation of something in the insect family.

When I lived in the city, only cockroaches shared my space and exercised my killer instinct. Now, in the country, we have a whole new cast of characters which must be identified and dealt with.

Taking my clue from the great Victorians, I found that bugs are indeed fascinating and worthy of study. And, without a doubt, I would love a René Lalique brooch. But—I just can't help it—I still hold to the theory that the only good bug is a *dead* bug. Especially termites.

Termites: Know the Enemy

According to Dennis Devlin of Yale Pest Elimination in New Haven, Connecticut, there are two kinds of houses: those that have termites, and those that will get termites.

We're up against a formidable enemy. Apparently, for every human being on earth, there are fifteen hundred pounds of termites. There are some two thousand species worldwide. In the forest, termites perform the important function of clearing away dead trees and vegetation; in your house, they help clear away, well, your house.

The "stars" of the termite world live in Australia and Africa. The compass termites of the tropical north of Australia build huge wedge-shaped mounds that eventually reach a size of 12 feet high, 10 feet long, and 3 1/2 feet wide at the base. These termites actually construct their mounds on a north-south axis so that the nest receives the least sunlight at noon when the sun is directly over-head and terribly strong. This alignment also means that the tall, vertical sides of the mound that face east and west catch the great-est amount of sun at sunrise and sunset, when the air is cool. Thus, the nest stays at a comfortable temperature throughout the twenty-four-hour day.

There is a species of termites in South Africa that not only grow fungus gardens in the cellars of their nests but have somehow fig-ured out how to air-condition their mounds. This need for air-conditioning is acute. All those termite bodies breathing out carbon dioxide would poison the colony if there weren't proper ventilation, and the combination of the termite population and the growing fungus gives off so much heat and moisture that the insects would be cooked to death or drowned.

Incredibly, these insects have developed a nest design that renders the nest not only livable, but probably delightfully com-fortable. They hollow out the bottom of the nest and form a kind of a cellar. Pillars rising from the cellar floor support the actual floor of the nest, and air ducts are tunneled up through the sides of the mound. Through the network of ducts, the warm, moist air escapes to the ridges that surround the mound. Here the moisture is re-leased and the carbon dioxide exhausted. A current is established that brings cooled, purified air back down into the nest. No matter what the weather is outside, the nest temperature seldom varies more than a few degrees. Ingenious!

Well, the United States doesn't boast this "I. M. Pei" variety of termites, but we do have about forty species, which are divided into four major types: subterranean, Formosan, dry-wood, and damp-wood. Subterranean termites are the most common in many parts of the country, but Formosan (nasty little devils introduced from Asia during World War II) are spreading throughout the South. Dry-wood termites are found frequently in southern California and in Florida and other Southern states, and damp-wood termites are common in the Pacific Northwest. Texas has the dubious distinction of leading the nation with seventeen species of termites, but California is a close second with fifteen. Arizona and Florida have fourteen and thirteen respectively, but New York, Wisconsin, and North Dakota have only one.

Termites have quite a caste system going for themselves. The king and queen are endlessly busy procreating baby termites (one queen in Africa was observed laying 84,000 eggs in one day). The soldier termites protect the nest, and the blind, wingless workers administer to the constantly pregnant queen, gather the food, and build and repair the nest. Some of the termites are born with sight and wings. These are the reproductives, the princes and princesses who will one day swarm on a warm spring day and fly off to establish new colonies.

The menu of termites is primarily wood hors d'oeuvres, wood entrees, and wood desserts. It's the cellulose in the wood that they're after, and they'll vary the cellulose diet by eating cardboard boxes, newspapers, and books also. They can't, however, digest this practically indigestible carbohydrate by themselves. Not to worry. Termites carry around microscopic cellulose-consuming protozoa in their digestive tracts that do the trick for them. (The termites aren't born with these parasites in their tummies. The adult termites confer them upon the young through their saliva and feces.)

Subterranean termites need constant contact with a source of moisture. All except the winged reproductives are pale in color and would dry out if they were exposed to the air and sun. For protection, they construct tubes out of mud, feces, vomit, and saliva and travel through them; these mud tubes are often a sign of termite infestation. They will look for a bridge into the house that touches the damp soil at one end and a beguiling cellulose material on the other, so beware of attached planter boxes filled with nice damp earth and wood, or stacks of firewood or newspapers or even clumps of mulch leaning against the siding of your home. Avoid any soil-to-wood contact.

Formosan termites will sometimes sally forth without the protection of tubes, and dry-wood termites don't even need contact with soil or moisture. They'll let themselves into your house through any kind of opening, especially through attic vents or any cracks in the wood siding.

Seems a shame to ring the curtain down on such fascinating miracles of nature, but steel yourself—we're in the "eat or be eaten" arena now, and it's your nest egg, not their nest, we're out to protect.

How Do You Know If You Have Termites?

I thought we had a rosy bill of health from the termite inspector before we closed on the house. What we didn't understand was that all termite inspections are reports *only* on areas of a home that are accessible and can be seen with the naked eye. For instance, if your house is built on a concrete slab (and there is no basement or crawl space), or the basement is completely finished, there is little accessible to the examining eyes of the inspector. Could there be some very happy termites munching away behind those finished walls? You bet.

It turns out that based on a small section of basement on the far left side of the house, we were told we didn't have an infestation there. What's going on in the right side of the house, built on a slab of concrete with no basement or crawl space beneath it, is anyone's guess.

This means that homeowners have to be constantly alert to the clues that they might be playing host to a termite civilization. If you see a swarm of these insects on a warm spring day, suspect trouble. If you see termites on your tomato stakes when you pull them up, suspect trouble. If you see discarded wings—especially underneath doors and windows or under lights, to which they're attracted when they swarm—you can suspect that those prince and princess reproductives have made your home their castle and are honeymooning with fervor. Of course, mud tubes are incontrovertible evidence that you have roomies in your real estate. (The tubing looks like vines, without leaves, sculpted of dirt.) You'll know you have dry-wood termites if you see piles of tiny, seedlike feces pellets.

Some termite inspectors are experimenting with termite-sniffing beagles. At first this struck me as funny, but then I thought of the superior hearing and scent-tracking abilities of these dogs' counterparts on police bomb and narcotics squads. Apparently, the beagles can hear the rustle of the little critters and smell the gases they emit, and they can squeeze into places humans can't reach.

While the beagles don't have a 100 percent accuracy rate, they are thought to be a superior detection method and will probably become more available in the future. If you're interested in investigating this canine detection method, there are three companies you can call: Beacon Dogs Inc. in Annapolis, Maryland (410-757-4999); Industrial Narcotic Delivery Systems in Kenner, Louisiana (504-466-9964); and—the pioneers in this field—TADD Services Corp. in Belmont, California (800-345-TADD).

Help!

You have to call in the professionals to deal with termites, but don't panic. You won't be homeless in a week or two, since our very considerate kind of termites take years to destroy a house.

Up until 1988, termite specialists had the use of a powerful insecticide called chlordane. It made mincemeat of termites, but it was also toxic to humans, there was some speculation about a carcinogenic effect, and it was a vapor thought to be really bad for the ozone layer. It's been banned by the EPA.

Today, the termite-busters use other termiticides, but none of them are quite as good as chlordane, and they don't last as long. Plus, holes must be drilled every 12–15 inches through the concrete around the inside perimeter of the entire house and the chemicals have to be pumped in. (If your house is built on a slab, the wood must be removed first so that holes can be drilled through the concrete beneath it.)

These chemicals bond with the soil and create a barrier through which subterranean termites must pass on their trips to and from their underground nest. Termites need a dark, continuously damp environment in order to survive; they must return to the soil at least every forty-eight hours to replenish their source of moisture.) In the soil, they'll come into contact with the poison, and they'll carry it with them and kill off the rest of the colony. Any termites that stay inside the house will be cut off from the damp soil and will die in a few days.

Necessity *is* the mother of invention, and with the elimination of chlordane in the pest control operators' arsenal, a variety of new attack methods have taken its place. Some companies are experimenting with heat instead of chemicals to kill dry-wood termites as well as wood-boring beetles. They erect a huge tent around the house and place high-powered heaters, blowers, and ducts strategically in order to raise the temperature inside the house to approximately 160 degrees. Exposed wood surfaces reach a temperature of 145–150 degrees, and this temperature elevates the inside of the wood to 120 degrees—a temperature known to kill termites. (This may kill termites, but your candles will be history and I'm not sure I would leave my computer, fax machine, other electronic equipment, the piano, or Demitri's oil paintings in the house.)

Another new approach to the problem of dry-wood termites was developed by a company called Tallon Termite and Pest Control in California. Its system injects liquid nitrogen into the wall cavities to freeze the termites. It's aptly named the Blizzard System.

I'm pinning my hopes on an entirely new subterranean termite eradication method due out this year from DowElanco. If (or when) I do get termites, I'm praying this will save my wooden floors from all those drill holes. It's called the Sentricon Colony Elimination System, and it works as follows. About twenty-five or thirty plastic monitoring systems are placed around the *outside* perimeter of your house in the soil. There's wood inside the tubes, and a pest control operator comes once a month to check for signs of termite activity. Once there is evidence of active termites in the monitoring tube, the pest control operator replaces the tube with a bait that contains a chitin-synthesis inhibitor. Nothing appears untoward to the termites, and they continue to feed in this tube and invite other colony members to sup with them. However, come molting season, as the termites attempt to molt with the aid of the chitin molecule, the chitin molecule fails to kick in—it's been inhibited—and the termites die trying to shrug out of their old skin.

This system has low mammal toxicity—it wouldn't hurt a child, even if he or she could get to the formulation, and it doesn't leach into the soil, so it poses no danger to the environment. The cost seems to be working out to $10–$12 per linear foot—the perimeter of the house—for the first two-year attack. This includes the placement of the bait stations, the replacement with the chemical, and three to four visits per year for the twenty-four-month period. So a 50-by-60-foot house perimeter would run about $2,600. At the end of this two-year siege, a maintenance program costing about $260 a year is instituted. It's certainly not cheap, but a traditional termite extermination drills up all your floors and runs between $1,000 and $2,000 *before* you fix the floors. This new system is noninvasive to your home and nontoxic to you, your family, your pets, *and* the environment.

Right now everyone is hopeful that the Sentricon System will become the new Prozac of Pest Control, but only time will tell.

At any rate, the good news on our homefront is that we had to cut a hole through the closet wall to access the bathtub's drainpipe because it was leaking. The hole was still gaping when Dennis was here, and he was now able to see behind the walls. Blessedly, he found no termites. This time. But he suggested that we build a hatch door that would let us have a professional termite inspection in the part of the house built on slab every two to three years.

In the meantime, we're to conduct our own annual termite search by walking around the house and looking inside the crawl space for possible signs of termite infestation. If we see tunnels along the face of masonry walls and along pipes that enter the house, or if we see discarded wings, we're to place a call to a professional. The USDA Forest Service offers sound guidance regarding this search, and I reproduce it here with permission:

Termite Inspection Checklist

Check the following locations for termites visually and by probing with a pointed tool, such as an ice pick. Look for signs of moisture, damaged wood, and termite earthen tunnels and/or fecal pellets.

- **Cracks in the concrete foundation.** These give termites hidden access to house timbers.

- **Support posts set in concrete.** If these go all the way through the concrete to the soil, they invite termite attack.

- **Earth-filled porches.** The earth fill should be at least 8 inches below the level of any wooden members.

- **Leaking pipes or faucets.** These can keep the soil underneath continually moist.

- **Wooden form boards.** These are sometimes left in place after the concrete foundation is poured. They are tasty termite food.

- **Shrubbery near air vents.** Anything that blocks airflow causes the air underneath the house to remain warm and moist, an ideal climate for termites.

- **Debris under and around the house.** Pieces of wood can support a termite colony and permit it to grow to the point where the house itself is attacked.

- **Low foundation walls or footings.** These often permit wooden structural members to come in contact with the soil.

- **Brick veneer over the foundation.** If the bond between the brick surfacing and the foundation fails, termites have hidden entrances.

- **Flower planters.** If built against the house, these allow direct access to unprotected veneer, siding, and cracked stucco.

- **Wooden forms around drains.** As with wooden form boards, smaller forms left in holes in and around drains provide termites direct access to the wood within the walls above.

- **Porch steps that rest on the ground.** These literally offer termites a stairway into the house.

- **The area around the furnace.** The soil around and under the furnace unit is often kept moist year-round, accelerating termite development.

- **Paper collars around pipes.** Since paper is made from wood, it is very attractive to termites.

- **Trellises.** If a trellis touches the soil and is connected to the house, it provides a direct link for termites from soil to wood.

Mark your calendars and don't neglect your own yearly inspection.

And if you decide to do any construction or renovation to your home, make sure you call in a termite inspector as soon as the walls are opened so he or she can *really* inspect that formerly inaccessible area of your house.

Carpenter Ants

While people don't readily discuss their termite problems with me (termites seem to have all the social stigma of head lice), several people have talked energetically about their bouts with carpenter ants.

Carpenter ants are most commonly found in the moist, cooler regions of the United States. Unlike termites, they don't bur-

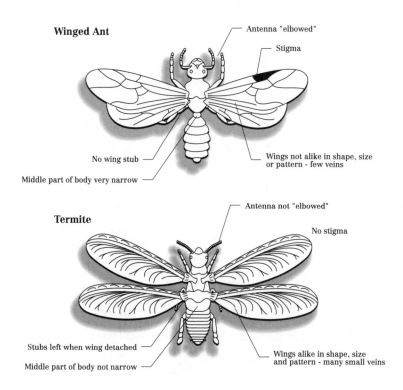

Winged Ant

Antenna "elbowed"

Stigma

No wing stub

Wings not alike in shape, size or pattern - few veins

Middle part of body very narrow

Termite

Antenna not "elbowed"

No stigma

Stubs left when wing detached

Middle part of body not narrow

Wings alike in shape, size and pattern - many small veins

row in wood to feed on the wood; they merely construct their nests within it. They're going to look for wood that is damp or decayed.

Most adult carpenter ants are black, but you may see some that are reddish to yellowish. They are piggish guests; it's not unusual to find piles of sawdust that they kick out of their galleries near their excavations.

People are rarely sure if they have termites or carpenter ants. The pictures above will help you make the diagnosis even before you call in an expert to confirm and destroy.

As you can see from the diagram, a termite has a broad, thick waist, while the carpenter ant's waist is pinched. The termite's wings are equal in size, but the carpenter ant's hind wings are smaller than the front wings. Finally, the termite has antennae that are concave, while the ant's antennae are elbowed.

Carpenter ants tend to show up in the spring. Dennis's company uses Ficam (Bendiocarb) as the chemical eviction notice for carpenter ants. It's a wettable powder suspended in water and is applied in a crack-and-crevice manner throughout the house. There are, however, about forty other kinds of chemicals that might be used for carpenter ants by other pest-control companies. Some are sprayed, some are pumped into drill holes which require patching. The degree of intrusiveness differs with each chemical, so call two or three companies and ask them how they go after carpenter ants.

Picnic Ants

The first February we were in our house, I began to see hundreds of little black ants foraging for crumbs in broad daylight. I went right out and bought a spray, but there were always more where they came from. My fingers were dialing a pest control company faster than you could say "carpenter ant," because I was sure that's what they were.

False alarm. These were just picnic ants that had come in for warmth and food. Dennis Devlin told me about a neat trick that he discovered in *Hints from Heloise* to get rid of a small colony of picnic ants: Make a thick mixture of sugar and water and put a large-pored sponge in the sugar solution. Then put the sponge on the floor and go away for thirty minutes or so. Upon your return you will find hundreds of picnic ants trapped in the sponge, and you can just transfer the sponge over to the kitchen sink and wash them down the drain. (Was she expecting us to pick up this mess with our bare hands?)

Anyway, Dennis's company treats picnic ants with a one-time treatment of a little Ficam and some ant baits. Sprays are useless—they kill only the worker ants that are out foraging for food. Baits, on the other hand, are taken back to the colony, where they can wipe out the entire infestation.

The Cockroach, the Flea, and the Silverfish

Now we're back to the old homey favorites. As I mentioned above, our New York apartment was often the gracious home to German cockroaches. Until I found Eleanor. She was an exterminator who didn't spray that smelly stuff that announces to all who visit that you're home is crawling with bugs. Instead, she blew an unnamed white powder all around, and in a few weeks we were the only apartment in the building that was cockroach-free. And this blissful condition lasted for an entire year!

Much as we coaxed, Eleanor would never reveal her magical secret ingredients. But while researching this chapter, I've come to believe that she was either using plain-old boric acid, or something with the tongue-twisting name "diatomaceous earth."

Diatomaceous earth is a white powder that is composed of the fossilized skeletons of marine and freshwater organisms that lived 20 million years ago. A protein in diatomaceous earth attracts the roaches, and the powder scratches up their waxy outer coating. Within a day or two, the bugs die of dehydration. And if you leave it in place and don't get it wet, it will continue working and working.

The powder is nontoxic and is apparently useful against ants, earwigs, fleas, sow bugs, silverfish, millipedes, and weevils. It's packaged by a company called Brookstone under the trade name Insectigone in an interesting place called Mexico, Missouri. Look for it in hardware stores, or call Brookstone at 800-926-7000.

So, this still leaves us with a question: Was Eleanor using boric acid powder or (it's just tripping off my tongue now) diatomaceous earth? Like diatomaceous earth, boric acid abrades the waxy coating of the insect, and it also poisons insects if ingested. Apply boric acid in areas not accessible to children or pets.

Sprinkle the boric acid lightly, the same way you would apply table salt, so that the roaches don't avoid it. Wear a mask when you apply either powder.

Dennis was very high on Combat Roach Traps. He told me that you should buy twice as many as the directions call for and place them carefully. He also told me something strange that's going on with the roaches in Florida. Apparently they will no longer eat sugar (glucose was an important attractant in the Combat bait). So the manufacturer recently reformulated the baits leaving the sugars out. Didn't I warn you we were up against a formidable enemy when you start to take on bugs?

Flea Alert

I was having my nails done two weeks ago when one of the owners of the business started complaining about her new dog and all the fleas he'd brought home with him. She was very agitated, and by the time we all had discussed it with her and given her all kinds of highly unscientific-sounding remedies, you could see at least three other dog owners itching to go home and do a flea check. Of course, I immediately got medical student's disease and began to feel itchy. And I didn't even own a dog then!

I mentioned all this flea hysteria to Dennis Devlin when he was here for the interview, and he passed on this ingenious flea-check recipe:

Fill a baking dish that has about 2-inch sides with water. Put in one drop of dishwashing liquid and swish it lightly around with your finger. Place this dish adjacent to your pooch's bed or in his favorite hangout area, and throw in two Alka-Seltzer tablets.

Come back in thirty minutes, and if you see a lot of drowned fleas, then—guess what?—you've got fleas. (Make sure you save two Alka-Seltzer tablets for your case of acid indigestion upon discovering this fact.)

Dennis went on to explain what's happening in this neat little trick. Fleas follow CO_2 trails, and the carbonation of Alka-Seltzer is carbon dioxide. If there were no soap in the water, the fleas would hop on and off supported by the surface tension of the water, but the dishwashing liquid destroys the surface tension of the water, so the fleas torpedo right through it and drown.

So, now that you've discovered that Fido has univited guests, you'll have to go to the vet or pet store and take care of him, and you've got to get rid of the fleas in your house and carpets. Steam-cleaning the carpets will kill most stages in the flea life cycle, and you should wash all throw rugs and vacuum regularly, throwing away the vacuum bag after each cleaning. Diatomaceous earth is effective for fleas, as I mentioned above, if you don't mind the powder around your carpet area.

Dennis said his company sometimes uses Drione, which is actually a silica gel. It's the rock dust that manufacturers pack into little bags and place next to cameras and electronics so that everything stays dry. The rock dust scratches the waxy shell of the flea and absorbs all its water, so it dies. But Drione contains 1 percent pyrethrin, which is extracted from chrysanthemums in Kenya, and—natural as this sounds—pyrethrins can provoke allergic reactions in some people and should never be used around people with asthma or other respiratory problems.

According to Jay Feldman, executive director of the National Coalition Against the Misuse of Pesticides, flea bombs are the last thing you ever want to use. When interviewed in an article for *Home* he stated: "The bomb approach is perhaps the least effective method and results in the highest level of potential contamination of the home."

Silverfish

The body of a silverfish resembles a flattened carrot, and its name comes from its metallic sheen and its wavy, fishlike turns. Yuch! The presence of silverfish is a sure sign that there's excess humidity in your home, so they're actually doing you a favor and acting as in-house weathermen. You'll often find them around bathtubs and basins, but the real reason you want them out of your house is that they eat books, papers, and pictures, as well as cereals. They love starch and will go through a book binding to sup on glue or eat the paste off the back of your wallpaper.

Silverfish are not that hard to get rid of. Correct the moist conditions that are attracting the bugs (check for leaks and employ a dehumidifier), and try a little boric acid, diatomaceous earth, or silica gel.

Perhaps the best piece of advice is to make sure you store all of your treasured photos in sealed plastic bags before placing them in boxes. Otherwise—eventually—they'll be ruined by silverfish.

The Itsy-Bitsy Spider

I am very ambivalent about spiders. I don't like to kill them. Remember the first song of our toddler years about waterspouts and sun and rain? Remember the big and oh-so-satisfying gestures of that song? Remember *Charlotte's Web*?

Any creature that can spin such beautiful webs is an artist in my mind, and destroying a web is like destroying a work of art. Plus, if you have spiders, they eat other insects in your home. (Of course, if you have spiders, it's a sure sign you *have* a lot of insects in your home.)

You say you're unmoved by my arguments and you want them out before your mother-in-law comes to visit and decides you live like pigs? All right. I'll do my job and tell you how to get rid of them.

First of all, the eggs are in the webs, so you need to destroy the webs. Dennis Devlin showed me the easiest way: Look everywhere for the webs—in every corner, under every shelf in your basement. Bring a flashlight with you on this reconnaissance mission. When you locate a web, take the bristle end of a broom and knock it down (webs are sticky and will adhere to the bristles). Then all you have to do is take the broom outside and hose it off with water. Your spider population will be greatly reduced and your house won't look like the set for Miss Havisham's room.

Carpenter Bees

Although they are similar in appearance to bumblebees, I had yet to make the acquaintance of any carpenter bees when my neighbors Ward and Marina asked me to look at the side of their carport. The fascia board—the horizontal trim attached to the outside end of the rafters—had all these surgically bored holes about half an inch in diameter, courtesy of a bunch of carpenter bees. I must say I was impressed.

I asked Dennis Devlin about all this, and he told me that the damage done by carpenter bees does not harm a home's structure but does affect its appearance. The bees use some of the holes as homes for themselves and others for little nurseries for their offspring. The galleries they bore don't extend more than a few inches into the wood, however. The males can behave aggressively but have no stingers, while the females possess a potent sting but use it infrequently. (Actually, it's an ovipositor—an egg-laying device—that has evolved into a defense weapon.)

Dennis said that the most effective repellent is to make sure the house is thoroughly painted or stained—including both sides of the fascia board—because the bees do not like chewing through paint.

If damage has already occurred, a homeowner can deal with it by replacing the damaged wood and painting or staining it on both sides, or by calling in a pest control company to inject a dust or liquid insecticide into the back of the galleries. Then the holes can be sealed with wood putty and the wood can be repainted.

Of Mice and Rats

The other home "companions" you may need to attend to are in the rodent division. Most likely you'll realize you have boarders in the fall, when field mice come inside for the warmth and food supply. Mice cause damage and carry disease. Undoubtedly, many fires "of unknown origin" are the result of mice gnawing through electrical wires in a home. In the opinion of William Olkowski, Sheila Darr, and Helga Olkowski, the authors of *Common-Sense Pest Control,* "One mouse in the house is one too many."

How will you know if your house is host to mice? You'll probably either see one streaking across an open space, or you'll see droppings (they look like caraway seeds), nest material, or gnawing damage. What can you do about them? You have two choices: traps and poison.

Trapping requires a strong stomach, because the successful result is a dead or dying animal that you have to confront and see through to the finish. Traps provide physical evidence of capture (poisons don't), but it's quite a job baiting them and checking them every day and dealing with the captured animals. Also, you don't want to use traps if you have children or pets around.

If you decide to go with snap traps, look for expanded-trigger bait traps and make sure you handle them with rubber-gloved hands only so that you don't impart human smells to the traps. Place the traps every 10 feet along the perimeter walls of your basement, attic, and kitchen. The traps should be perpendicular to the wall with the triggers facing the wall.

Through the years, people have experimented with all kinds of baits to lure the animals to the traps. A bait should be sticky to ensure that the mouse will disturb the trigger mechanism even if it touches the bait only lightly. A tiny dab of peanut butter applied with a paper match works well, as do gum drops. (Remember to bait first and set the trap second or you may have very sore fingers.)

Even better is to pull off the cotton head of a Q-Tip stick, dip the cotton in anise extract (look in the spice shelf of your grocery store), and wrap it thoroughly around the unset trigger and then set the trap. This "nest material" will be very attractive to the mice, but won't attract other insects, as peanut butter will, and you can go away for a day or so without leaving rotting food around.

Because mice are suspicious about new objects, place the traps baited, but unset, for a few days. If you see the bait disappearing, you'll know the mice approve of your culinary or nest-building choices and you've placed the traps in the proper place. The authors of *Common-Sense Pest Control* suggest that you plan more than one trapping event in case you missed any during the first trapping. (The gestation period of a mouse is twenty days. Once born, the mouse matures and mates at six to ten weeks of age. A mother mouse produces a litter of about six babies ten times a year. Considering all this, there are probably quite a few Mickeys and Minnies running around turning your house into a virtual maternity ward!)

Now the big question becomes: What the hell do you do with this dead or dying animal besides scream or jump around in a panic?

Get hold of yourself! Put on rubber gloves and get a shovel. If the unfortunate animal is still alive, shovel it up and drop it into a bucket of sudsy water so that it mercifully passes into mouse heaven. If the animal is dead when you come upon it, ventilate the room and spray it and any droppings with a bleach solution of 3 tablespoons of bleach mixed with 1 gallon of water, or use a commercial disinfectant like Lysol. Do not use any disinfectant with a propellant, which will push fecal matter up into the air, where you will breathe it in. Then, (only with gloved hands) deposit the carcass in a plastic bag, double-bag it, and dispose of it in the garbage.

Nests, droppings, tainted food, and any other affected material should also be sprayed with the bleach solution, double-bagged, and disposed of. All traps should be bathed in bleach to disinfect them. Because a deadly hantavirus has been associated with rodents in isolated parts of the United States, it may be better for pest control operators—people with know-how and respirators—to handle and dispose of the mice.

Glue traps and sticky box traps are also effective, but they are not the most humane way to rid yourself of a rodent problem, because the trapped animal suffers for a long time. My cousin Scott told me of his experience with glue traps in his Maryland home:

"I walked in and saw one of the mice in a glue trap that it had dragged to the other side of the room, and it was doing this sort of 'silent scream' with its jaws pulling apart in what I took to be absolute terror. Now, I had to quickly decide how to put the fellow out of his misery. All I could think to do was to suffocate it in a plastic bag or smack it with a shovel. I went with the bag. I don't love mice, but this is no way to start a day. Glue traps are for the strong of stomach. I've got to find a better mouse trap."

If that story doesn't make you squeamish and you do decide to use glue traps, make sure the glue traps don't get dusty, as dust renders them totally ineffective. Also, don't place them on any carpeted areas, because the trapped animal will turn them over and the glue is very difficult to remove from the carpet fibers. An animal can be released from a glue trap by smearing some oil into the glue, but I don't know if you want to get that close to a very agitated rodent.

You and Scott should know about Havahart mouse traps. They're plastic boxes that sit on a fulcrum and the door snaps shut as the mouse comes over to investigate. Then you put on rubber gloves and transfer the box to your car and take it out to the country somewhere and release the animal. Just remember that there are usually more than one or two mice in the house, and you will soon be running a shuttle service—Mice on Wheels—between your house and the woods or field.

Yale Pest Elimination uses tamper-resistant bait stations. These are a hardened structure with a *block* poison inside. They can only be gnawed onsite, and—for the safety of your children and other animals—they can be opened only with a key. Dennis advises against using pellet poisons, which resemble fat ice cream sprinkles, because they can shake out or be stashed away by a rodent and a child or a much-loved pet could come across them and be very unprotected.

Not only are these hardened bait stations safer for little ones, but your life does not begin to revolve around dying animals; you are not always baiting and setting and watching and finishing off rodents. True, with poisons the mice die in the walls of your house (an unpleasant thought), but 99 percent of the mice in your house die in your walls from natural causes anyway (mice live only about one year), and within three days the dead animals desiccate and there is no odor. If there are any odors because of a hole or break in the wall, stick a cotton ball with oil of wintergreen in that area and it will take care of the problem until the three days pass.

Better to avoid dealing with mice all together. Make sure that all the doors in your house fit securely and leave no room at the bottom for shivering field mice to squeeze inside where it's warm and toasty. Their bodies are mostly cartilage, and they can flatten down to fit into incredibly small places. A fully grown mouse can squeeze through an opening the size of a dime! A door sweep—a metal strip lined with rubber with holes for screws—or a saddle can be installed to eliminate space under the door; either will keep mice on the outside where they belong. And you must take a careful look to see if there are any gaps or holes where pipes or wires enter a house. Fill such holes with steel wool, caulk, or plaster.

You Dirty Rat

How can you tell if your mouse is a rat? Well, your typical field mouse is much smaller than a rat. A mouse's head and feet are small, but its ears are large and its nose is pointed. A rat has small ears and a blunt nose (I doubt we're going to get a chance to study one and make comparisons until the postmortem period).

Rats found in the home are probably the large Norway rat (also called the sewer rat) or the smaller roof rat.

Probably because of the "Disney influence," people are less afraid of mice than of rats, and until the recent outbreaks of hantavirus carried by mice, rats were far more likely to be the vector of plague and other pathogens. Also, rats are more likely to bite and be aggressive, and they are better gnawers and cause more damage to your home. Don't try to deal with rats by yourself. Call a pest control company immediately.

Raccoons

Guess whose coming for dinner? Every night we have a nocturnal visitor with a bandit black eye mask and a ringed bushy tail. And every morning we find our garbage strewn all over the lawn.

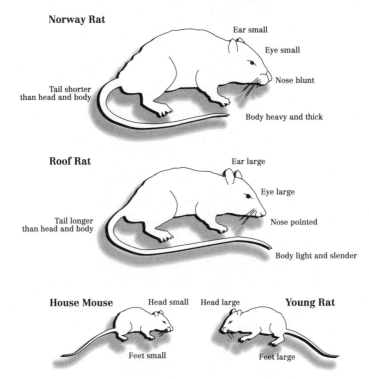

Reprinted with permission from *Common-Sense Pest Control* by William Olkowski, Sheila Daar, and Helga Olkowski. Newtown, Conn.: Taunton Press, 1991.

We have one persistent, dexterous raccoon who finds our throw-aways absolutely compelling and will do anything to get at them.

I've always liked raccoons, but now that rabies has reached epidemic proportions in some raccoon populations, this is not a "guest" you want to have as a regular.

Be particularly cautious of any animal that does not seem frightened by you, as this fearlessness may indicate a rabid animal. Don't send your dog out to deal with the animal either, as raccoons can be quite ferocious if cornered or attacked.

Just about the only thing you can do to eliminate raccoons from your property is to practice exclusion techniques or to have them live-trapped by a pest control company. In this state, a live-trapped raccoon must be destroyed, but each state has its own laws concerning this.

Try the exclusion techniques first. Replace your garbage cans with ones that have spring-loaded top bars that secure the lids to the cans (just ask for them at the hardware store), and make sure that the screening in your louver vents is in good repair so that raccoons can't climb up the side of the house and nest in your attic.

I was getting extremely tired of spending the first part of my day cleaning up garbage, and I wondered if we needed to invest in some expensive bunker for the garbage pails, but Dennis Devlin said no, we just needed to replace the garbage pails.

My son Alex came up with a solution. Our four new pails are lined up on the side of the garage, and he suggested we attach screws just to the side of the two end pails and string bungee cords across the pails so they couldn't be knocked over. That and the spring-loaded top bars have discouraged our guest. He is supping elsewhere tonight.

How Do You Find a Pest Control Company and How Often Should You Call It?

Before I can really point you in the right direction, we should discuss the different philosophies of companies. Yale Pest Elimination takes care of most nontermite problems with a one-time application and a ninety-day warranty (carpenter ants have a one-year guarantee). Many other companies do a one-time big job and ask you to sign a one-year contract for twelve subsequent monthly treatments. They'll tell you that the problem can be dealt with only by follow-up treatment—especially since the EPA has eliminated so much of their arsenal that has a residual effect. It's hard to know whether a company is overselling or being forthright with you.

Certainly, for my little picnic ant problem, a one-year contract was not a smart decision on my part. If I'd known better, I would have had a pest control company use ant baits and waited three weeks for the problem to abate.

Very few pest control operators wanted to comment on the practices of their competitors, but I sensed a whiff of disdain—maybe even a bit of envy?—for companies that have pest control operators busy on their routes twelve months a year.

One pest control operator told me that with a few exceptions, the only times he could see there being cause for a twelve-month contract would be:

- If you have carpenter ants every spring and mice every fall and winter, or if you constantly have yellow jackets and bees.
- If you live in a multifamily dwelling and are at the mercy of your neighbors' possibly sloppy living habits.
- If you have absolutely *no* tolerance for centipedes, millipedes, sow bugs, and pill bugs (the dampness bugs found in every basement).
- If your middle name is "I'm phobic about insects." In this case the approximately-$42-a-month charge is cheaper than seeing a psychiatrist.

All others should ask for recommendations from friends, and interview two or three companies after reading this chapter and becoming familiar with the techniques and chemicals used in pest elimination. Think very carefully about signing any long-term agreements, and understand that a general contract will not include termites or carpenter ants, because they are harder to eliminate.

Try to look for a company that practices a kind of pest control called **Integrated Pest Management (IPM).** This is a philosophy that takes people's health and the health of the environment into consideration and attempts to use a less toxic insect control program.

A company that uses IPM will integrate a chemical approach with a nonchemical system: the pest control operator analyzes what attracts the insects to which places in the home, and teaches the homeowner what he or she can do to detour these pests, with changes in homeowner habits, physical barriers, and the use of the least toxic chemicals.

A good company will always ask if there are infants or young children in the household, if anyone has asthma or respiratory problems, or if anyone is pregnant, and modify its strategy for pest control.

You should know about a nonprofit corporation in Berkeley, California called the Bio-Integral Resource Center. BIRC was formed to provide practical information on the least toxic methods for managing pests. It publishes journals and numerous educational materials and will consult with you about your problem over the phone. Write for information about membership at PO Box 7414, Berkeley, CA 94707, or call 510-524-2567.

Meantime, you can do a lot to prevent your house from turning into Bug Central:

Critter Control Inside

- Use tightly woven screens and keep them in good repair.
- Don't leave your doors open as you unpack cars or talk to people standing outside.
- Caulk openings around doors and windows, cracks and crevices around pipes, fixtures, and cabinetry.
- Repair all leaking pipes or faucets immediately.
- Vacuum frequently.
- Put food away in pestproof containers and keep counters, cabinets, garbage cans, and ovens scrupulously clean. At least once a year, empty the pantries, vacuum all the crumbs, throw

away all old foodstuffs, and wash the shelves down with bleach. If you do find a foodstuff crawling with some kind of pest, wrap it in plastic, put it in the freezer overnight (this will kill the bugs), and toss it in the garbage the next morning.

- Inspect grocery bags and boxes for infestation.
- Don't allow recyclables or newspapers and magazines to pile up.
- Don't use your sofa as a dining table. Bugs will settle in its comforts too, assured of frequent snack times.
- Use dehumidifiers and keep every area dry. It's dampness that attracts bugs.
- Install door sweeps so that bugs and rodents don't have easy access to your house.
- Dry-clean all your woolens and natural-fiber clothing before the summer so that the larvae of the webbing clothes moths are destroyed. It's the larvae that pick holes, not the adult moths, and the mother moth lays her larvae in woolens with the scent of human perspiration. Store cleaned sweaters in sweater bags or even zip-lock plastic bags. Cedar closets help.

Outside
- Make sure your gutters are cleaned and in good working order and that the grading of the house diverts rainwater away from the foundation.
- Trim tree branches that can serve as insect "bridges" into your home.
- Do not stack firewood against the house and on the ground. Instead, build a pedestal with two concrete blocks and cross these with two steel bars. Pile your wood on this and the air will circulate and the wood will stay dry.
- Think about placing an apron of gravel or bluestone around

basement door areas so that mossy decay is kept to a minimum and insects are not attracted to this potential access area.

- Try to avoid placing trellises against the house (they provide a direct link from the soil to wood).

- Planter boxes built next to a house are another direct link from soil to wood, siding, or cracked stucco. The BIRC group recommends that you pour a 2-to-3-inch protective concrete wall between the planter and the house. An air space several inches wide must separate the planter wall from the house and must be kept free of dirt and debris.

- You know that ivy that's so beautiful growing up the masonry of the house? Think about getting rid of it; it's also providing a direct link from soil to wood.

- Check your garage-door jambs and make sure they don't go right into the ground (termites can move right in and begin their work). Cut the doors above ground level and fill in with concrete.

- Don't position sprinklers so that they soak the house.

The Bug Salute

There are literally billions of bugs on the earth, so I guess we really have to change our attitudes about them and broker a peace. After all, they are a very important part of the ecosystem. Without them, we would have no apples or grapes or honey no cotton, no oranges, and far fewer songbirds. The rich wildlife and plant life on this planet are brought to you by insects.

Now understanding all of this, I'm eyeballing insects differently. While not quite as gaga about them as the Victorians were, I'm willing to let bugs be bugs. (Just let them do whatever it is they do *outside* my personal living space!) But—as all of the above demonstrates—there's a lot we can do to flash a "No Vacancy" sign to our insect brethren. With common sense, physical barriers, dehumidifiers, the discouragement of repellents, and the occasional supplementation of chemical controls, we should coexist quite amiably, and appreciate each other—however warily—from a nice, comfortable distance.

8. The Uninvited Guest, Part II: Physical and Electronic Security

Focusing on home security frightens me. I have this childish belief that whatever I concentrate on tends to happen, and if I get very concerned about burglary, I'm going to come home one day soon and find my door ripped off its hinges by something creepier than a subterranean termite. I guess one side of me thinks that the more cavalier I am, the less likely anything is to happen. Besides, I don't think we're in New York City anymore, Toto. Didn't we move to a nice, safe suburb?

Well, burglary is a fact of life, here and everywhere, but I've learned you can be prudent without being paranoid. Because a new homeowner is drowning in a sea of complicated and time-consuming tasks—finding the house, securing a mortgage, moving, and building a life—doodads on doors and windows don't rank high as a priority. In fact, statistics show that most homeowners don't do anything about security until they've lived in a house for approximately two years. People tend to spend any available funds on furnishing the empty house and almost never get a kick out of saying: "Oh, look, Mary, I've got brand-new deadbolt locks and this terrific-looking charley bar!"

But you have to move security issues to the front burner, sooner rather than later. Otherwise, you're living with a, well, *false* sense of security and you're unconsciously issuing invitations that could procure unhappy results. And somewhere, underneath all the tumult, you already recognize this.

All the pamphlets and books try to scare you with the ever-growing crime statistics, but the truth is, burglary's been with us since before the pyramids, and each generation has made attempts to keep what it owns. In the Old South there was something called the "false step" built into a stairway. One of the risers was an inch or two different in height from the others, so anyone with mischief on his mind would stumble and break his leg on the way up. Today, you have the option of a very sophisticated electronic security system to safekeep you and your belongings, but before we delve into all that, there is a lot you can do in a low-tech way *for very little money* that will significantly reduce your chance of becoming a victim.

Oh Joy, Oh Rapture

Every single book I read and the video I reviewed on the subject of home security advised me to think like a burglar and look at my house through his (yes, "his": burglars are predominantly male) eyes. And once I worked my way into this little acting exercise, I started jumping up and down with glee. This house was such an easy target it was like Christmas and my birthday rolled into one. So many rich choices of entry, such nice high bushes to hide behind, a glass side door close to a puny lock, windows left open during little trips to the supermarket . . .

Suddenly my eyes hardened derisively and I thought: "Who are the *fools* who live here?"

Well, I couldn't stand the idea of being looked down on by a common criminal, so once I got done with my Method acting (being sociopathic is easier than you realize), I began to make a big effort to remove us from the "fool" casting call. I called in a locksmith and security expert to walk through the entire house and educate me as to its vulnerabilities and decide how we were going to "target-harden" my house. "Target-hardening" is the phrase the security experts use for making a house more resistant to any type of forced entry.

The Walk-Through: Doors

Paul Peterson, a security consultant, came over on a Friday evening to take a look at what I described to him over the phone as our zero percent security problem. We started at the front door, and I'll pass on what he taught me and define things as we go along. A lot of it is complicated, but I think it should be a lot easier if you picture it all in context. So, welcome to Chez Papolos *before* the Reformation.

Actually, Paul approved of the front door: It's solid-clad. This means that hardwood blocks are laminated together and covered with veneer. Don't consider anything but a solid-clad or metal door. There are hollow-core doors with nothing but a honeycomb of cardboard on the inside, and a burglar can kick his foot right through them. Your solid-clad or metal door should be hung in metal or hardwood framing, and the door should fit closely and swing smoothly on strong hinges.

I felt I was earning brownie points from Paul because the hinges on the door were on the inside. If there are hinges on the outside, the burglar simply removes the pins and lifts the door off.

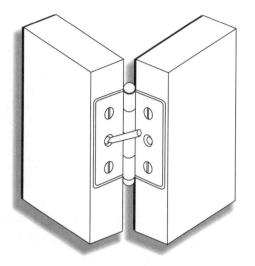

You have two choices here: Either change the door, or drill holes into the center of both leaves of each hinge and then install two headless screws, leaving 1/2 inch exposed. This way, when the door closes, the screws go into the other leaf and hold the door in place even if the pins are removed from the outside.

My front-door lock is a Schlage **deadbolt** with a 1-inch throw. A deadbolt lock gets its name from the fact that the bolt doesn't spring back—it's "dead." A burglar can't pry it back with a piece of plastic the way he could a spring bolt. The **throw** is the total length of the rectangular bolt that shoots out when you twist the thumb turn and lock the door. A 1-inch throw makes it difficult for a burglar to use a crowbar or car jack to pry the door from the doorjamb.

My Schlage lock is rated a Grade 2 by the American National Standards Institute (ANSI). Grade 1 is overkill for a home, Grade 3 just doesn't make the grade in the safety department, and Grade 2 is excellent for light commercial and residential use. (Kwikset, Master Lock Co., and Andrews make an excellent Grade 2 deadbolt lock also.)

Deadbolt

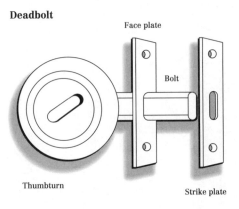

Face plate

Bolt

Thumbturn

Strike plate

But we're not home free yet. A good solid-core door with the hinges on the inside secured by an excellent deadbolt lock is easily defeated if the strike plate has any vulnerability. And most strike plates are completely vulnerable.

A **strike plate** is the metal socket affixed to the doorjamb into which the deadbolt slides. The doorjamb is the vertical piece that forms the side of the door opening. Most strike plates come from the factory packaged with 3/4-inch screws that can easily be ripped from the doorjamb with a couple of kicks.

Consumer Reports, in its May 1994 issue, reported on locks and security systems. Its technicians set up a test doorway typical of better home construction and placed a mechanical kicker that repeatedly bashed the door, upping the force with every second blow. They found that no lock withstood more than five kicks before it failed, usually when the strike plate ripped from the doorjamb.

When they replaced the 3/4-inch screws in the strike plate with 3 1/2-inch screws that penetrated not only the jamb but the house's studding beyond it and installed a high-security, reinforced strike plate (they used the Dexter Guardex 550), the door survived all eight test kicks intact.

We now have a solid-clad door, a Grade 2 Schlage deadbolt

with a 1-inch throw, and a reinforced strike plate with 3 1/2-inch screws. Of course, I'm still wondering why the factories are packaging the strike plates with 3/4-inch screws.

Paul and I next moved over to the nightmare called my side door. It has a glass pane very close to the door handle, and glass anywhere within 40 inches of the doorknob is a big security problem. (The 40-inch rule is taken from the maximum length of an adult male's arm reaching through a broken window pane to unlock the door from inside.)

We had two choices: We could install a **double-cylinder deadbolt,** or we could replace the door. A double-cylinder deadbolt requires a key to unlock it not only from the outside but from the inside as well. This thwarts the grasping hand of a burglar. But such locks are a real fire hazard. What if you (or a child) can't locate or operate the key in such an emergency?

We replaced the door with one whose glass is placed high above the thumbturn of the single-cylinder deadbolt (naturally it has a reinforced strike plate with 3 1/2-inch screws). Plus, we made sure the door had a wide-angle viewer in it so we could see anyone on the outside (chains are worthless and can be forced with very little effort).

The laundry room on the ground level has a double door with a metal hasp. Not only had I never come across the word "hasp" before, it took me a while to realize that I had to supply the case-hardened steel padlock to secure it. A **hasp** is a hinged metal strap that fits over a staple and is secured by a pin or padlock.

Paul Peterson approved Demitri's choice of padlock and reminded us to show everyone in the house—the children, the babysitters—where the key to the padlock is, so they can get out quickly in the event of a fire or other emergency. Make sure the screws of a hasp are not on the outside of your structure where they can be removed easily.

I have to tell you about the fiasco over the office door downstairs. It's a Dutch door: the top and bottom halves of the door swing open independently. About a month after we moved in, we noticed the lock was faulty, so I gathered a bit of energy and let my fingers do the walking through the Yellow Pages and landed on a locksmith who shall remain nameless. He came right over and, for a tidy sum, installed a double-cylinder deadbolt *on the bottom half of the door.* This was to prevent the grasping hand of Benny the Burglar from tapping out the glass from the top half of the dutch door and turning the thumbscrew. So, here I am worried about everyone finding the key in the event of a fire, when Paul and I notice that the top half of the door has a flimsy latch that the Big Bad Wolf could blow open without so much as a huff and a puff. Paul just stared and noted dryly: "I guess that locksmith didn't spend a lot of time examining this door."

So, the Papoloses are spending a lot of time in the door department of Home Depot.

Just about the only problem I don't have in the door department is sliding glass doors. But many, many houses have them, and

Glass Door with Charley Bar

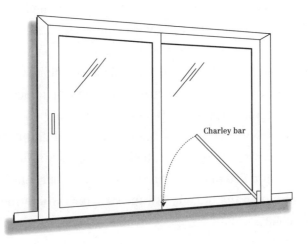

Charley bar

if they're not dealt with, then you are not safe in that home. The frames and locks are weak and can be forced open by prying the sliding panel away from the doorframe. You need to do two things: Screw a row of sheet-metal screws into the top track, leaving them protruding so they just clear the door but leave no room for jostling, and put a wood dowel or metal rod in the bottom track to prevent an intruder from sliding the door open. For even greater safety, insert a bar horizontally in the middle of the glass door. These **charley bars** and other kinds of sliding glass door barriers are sold in hardware stores or home improvement centers, and they are inexpensive. For instance, for less than $5 you can purchase a package of antilift plates for the top of the sliding glass to resist someone using a crowbar to lift the sliding sash out of its lower track.

On a Clear Day: Windows

Windows are the eyes of the home. They are also another form of entry for Benny the Burglar. I think one of the reasons we were a little lax about all the other entrances was that we have two walls of floor-to-ceiling Andersen casement windows on the side of the house that overlooks the property, and I assumed that anyone could break them and walk right in. Well, Paul told me I was wrong. Thermal windows, when locked from the inside, are very difficult to jimmy, and they are very tough to break. Most burglars walk on by these locked thermal windows. Easier to kick in a door, I guess. Amazing what a bit of information does for you—I'm feeling much cozier about these beautiful windows.

The rest of the windows are the extremely common double-hung variety. Again, these are built with very flimsy locks. The simplest and most effective way to thwart an intruder is to drill a small hole in the top corner of each bottom sash and put a headless nail in it. (Eye bolts and cotter pins can also be used.) It's called "the pin-

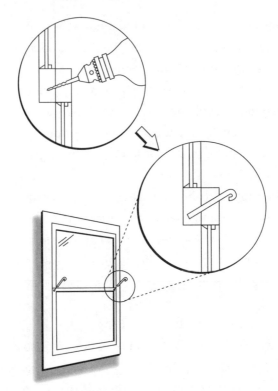

in-the-sash trick" and prevents a window from being lifted from the outside. For pennies, you've secured these possible entryways. You should also know that there are keyless locks for these and other types of windows available in the hardware store or at Home Depot. Mount them in the corners or sides so the window can be locked even in a partly open position.

Paul asked me if people in Florida would be reading this book. Well, I certainly hope so, I replied. "Tell them to replace all jalousie windows, as quickly as possible," he said. These are glass-slatted and are often found in doors and windows in warmer climates and beachside locales. All a thief has to do is slide out the glass slats and—presto!—he's in. You can make them immediately safer by mixing a two-part epoxy glue, smearing it on the sides of the glass panels, and sliding them back in, but make replacing them a priority for safety and peace of mind.

And while we're on the subject of hot climates, Paul told me that window-unit air conditioners pose a security problem. If the unit is not locked down, a thief can shove it right back into the room and climb in through its now-vacated space.

Shrubbery and Bushes

Paul was a bit concerned by the shrubbery that was placed by the bedroom windows. We like it for the privacy and the beauty it lends the house; Benny the Burglar likes it even better, because he can hide behind it while he does his devil's work. For the present, I'm counting on my security system to act as a deterrent in this area, but you should seriously consider cutting down all shrubbery close to windows and tree branches that might be used to climb into a house. A lot of experts advise planting thorny bushes near windows and doorways. Burglars don't like to bleed or get scratched up any more than the rest of us do.

Let There Be Light

Shadows and darkened areas are like mother's milk to thieves, so good lighting acts as a great deterrent. It doesn't have to look as if the Fourth of July is being celebrated on your property, but any security lighting plan should include well-lit walkway and entrance doors, an illuminated driveway and garage, and a focus of light on any small structures on the property, such as a tool shed.

Take a good look at your property at sundown with your present lighting system turned on full throttle. Do you see any areas that might hide an intruder? A dark corner by the back porch? A dense group of shrubs next to the front entrance? It's quite probable that a few carefully placed floodlights and some well-thought-out landscape lighting will erase these hiding places.

I was working on this chapter near the end of October, so, naturally, as we trick-or-treated, I couldn't help but focus on all the outdoor-lighting systems in my neighborhood. A delight to us stumbling in the dark with a little Ninja and the Grim Reaper were the motion detectors which activated lighting as we moved across the sensor's path. These sensors are used in conjunction with floodlights, and they are anathema to would-be burglars. It throws them off guard—they wonder what other tricks you might have up your sleeve—and they respond to them like Dracula to a crucifix. They are best placed on driveways, all entrances to the house, the garage, terraces and decks, and any dark thickets I mentioned above.

People, animals, and cars radiate heat waves, and motion detectors are electronic eyes that detect and respond to the infrared waves these warm objects emit as they move. When motion is detected, the sensor automatically turns the light on. You can program the lights to remain on anywhere from one to twenty minutes, and then they will automatically shut off. (In case you were wondering why they don't light up during the daytime, a photoelectric cell registers daylight and prevents the motion detectors from being activated during that time.)

A motion detector's field of view is limited, however. It will turn on the lights when motion is detected up to about 50 feet away within an arc of about 110 degrees, so you need to adjust it strategically.

In between all the candy grabbing, I asked my neighbors where they got those great lights. Home Depot and the hardware store are the answers that came back to me, at a price point of about $50 for the floods equipped with motion sensors.

You can install them yourselves if you are of the do-it-yourself temperament, but since I'm hopeless about these things, I asked my electrician, John Krozer, to do the honors. It took about two hours one Saturday for him to install them, and I couldn't wait till dark so I could go out and trigger the sensors. It's so welcoming to come home and have the lights go on—no more fumbling in the dark for packages in the car, and when guests leave at night, we see them off in good light. I love these lights!

The only disadvantage to sensor lighting is that the lights may come on and it may only be Bambi chomping his way through your shrubbery, and you're inside thinking you've scared off a prowler for the rest of the evening.

To illuminate walkways and stairs, think about low-level, low-voltage tier lights. I'm told they are inexpensive to install and operate.

Locating a Security Consultant

You, like us, may also want a security consultant to walk through your home and point out vulnerabilities and remedy any security lapses in your home. Bill Phillips, the president of the International Association of Home Safety and Security Professionals (IAHSSP) and the author of *Home Mechanix Guide to Security,* advises you to look for someone with extensive training and experience in two or more of the following areas: criminology, law enforcement, locksmithing, alarm systems installation, safe servicing, and fire fighting. For instance, Paul Peterson is a locksmith with twenty-five years of experience as an electronic alarm installer. He is also a member of ALOA, the Association of Locksmiths of America. Headquartered in Texas, it's one of the most advanced associations for locksmiths, and members must pass a very difficult proficiency test.

Another indication that a security consultant is qualified is certification by a security trade association. The most prominent associations are the American Society for Industrial Security (ASIS), the International Association of Home Safety and Security Professionals (IAHSSP), and the International Association of Professional Security Consultants (IAPSC). Each of these organizations certifies members who meet certain guidelines and who pass a rigorous test, but the IAHSSP is the only organization that specializes in training security professionals who service homeowners and apartment dwellers.

Another possibility is to contact the police department detective bureau in your town and see if it has a burglary squad. Many departments send over a detective—free of charge—to do a security survey. He or she will walk through the house and offer you valuable advice about its vulnerabilities and how you can best target-harden your home. The detective can also tell you if the police department has a Neighborhood Watch Program and help you organize one so that your neighborhood puts the bad guys on notice. Such programs have caused as much as a 50 percent reduction in crime in neighborhoods that implement them.

The Westport Police Department offers such a program and referred me to Detective Michael Barrett. Detective Barrett told me that 90 percent of arrests for burglary are made because of an alert neighbor's phone call to the police.

He then went on to describe the program. "Let's say you decide to organize a Neighborhood Watch. You call us and we schedule an evening to do a presentation and answer questions. Then you inform the neighbors and gather everyone at your house.

"We lecture about security elements and often show a videotape that teaches homeowners how to target-harden their houses as well as how to be alert to things happening in their neighborhood. For instance, do they observe people who look like they don't belong in the neighborhood? Are these people asking vague questions about their neighbors and their whereabouts? Does someone ring the doorbell and try to sell them something that just doesn't look or sound convincing? While we want neighbors to use a certain amount of common sense, we never want them to hesitate to pick up the phone and call the police. Also, if a homeowner sees someone hanging around a neighbor's yard and something doesn't look right, we suggest that he or she call that neighbor and check it out. If that neighbor is not at home, we want him or her to call the police and let them check it out."

Apparently people always bring up the subject of dogs at these meetings. Are they really a deterrent? Mike Barrett repeated to me something he'd been told by a longtime burglar who stole to feed a drug habit. "We don't like barking dogs," the burglar said. "They attract too much attention. And if it's a German shepherd, a rottweiler, a Doberman, a pit bull, or anything like those kind of dogs, there's no way I'm goin' in."

Detective Barrett also told me that dogs serve as an early-warning system for a homeowner—the barking may mean something is amiss. "A wake-up call from an alert dog can buy you the time you need to check things out and call for help, as well as perhaps change the mind of the criminal about to enter the scene," he said.

Checking It Twice

How gratifying would your house be to Benny the Burglar? Take a good look at the list below and check off the "yes" or "no" boxes. Then make careful notes and plan the remedies that will place all your answers in the "yes" category. When that happens, you'll have a target-hardened home.

Doors

yes   no

o   o   Are all the exterior doors constructed of metal or solid wood construction and at least 1 3/4 inches thick? Don't forget to check that the door leading from the garage to the living quarters is metal or solid-clad. Burglars have a predilection for these doors.

o   o   Do all exterior doors close tightly?

o   o   Are the hinges of the doors either on the inside or protected from outside removal?

o   o   Do all the exterior doors (including the door from the garage to the living quarters) have deadbolts with 1-inch throws? Are the strike plates the high-security type, and anchored with 3 1/2-inch screws?

o   o   Is there glass within 40 inches of the lock? If so, do you have a double-cylinder deadbolt lock to secure the door? Is the key readily available to adults and children in the house?

o   o   If there are no windows in the door at eye level, do you have a wide-angle viewer?

o   o   Have you made sure that the door locks cannot be reached through a mail slot or pet entrance?

o   o   Are sliding glass doors secured from being lifted out of their track? Is a charley bar or key-operated auxiliary lock in place?

o   o   Have you replaced any jalousie windows or doors?

o   o   Have you replaced or sufficiently secured both parts of a Dutch door?

o   o   Are the garage doors kept closed and locked at all times?

Problems: ....

....

....

....

Windows

yes   no

o   o   Have you made sure that all your windows have key-operated locks or a "pin-in-the-sash" trick in addition to the regular
locks?

o   o   If you keep windows in an open position for ventilation, have
you made sure that they be locked in that open position?

o   o   Are window air conditioning units bolted to prevent removal
from the outside?

o   o   Have you made sure that no one could enter the house through
the basement windows?

o   o   Are the skylights well-secured?

Problems: ....

....

....

....

Home Exterior

yes   no

o   o   Have you trimmed shrubs and trees low, below window level?

o   o   Is your outdoor lighting sufficient? Do you have motion sensors
and floodlights?

o   o   Are your house numbers clearly visible from the street so that
the police or fire or emergency personnel can easily identify the
house?

o   o   Did you take down the sign that proclaims that the so-and-so live here? Signs allow a burglar to look you up in the phone book and call to find out if anyone's home or not.

o   o   Are all ladders put away and secured with a chain in the garage or toolshed?

o   o   Are your tools or barbecue equipment lying around? They can be used to gain entrance to your house.

o   o   Did you take your spare key out of the prefab rock you were "hiding" it in? Thieves are always delighted to see them.

Problems: ....

....

....

....

Your Role in the Safety Plan

yes   no

o   o   Do you lock all the doors and windows when you leave the house, even for a short time?

o   o   Do you require proper identification from everyone before opening the door, even if he or she is wearing a uniform and looks official? Also, it is not unusual for thieves to carry books or pamphlets and case out a place by ringing the front door to see if anyone is home.

o   o   Do you have a video inventory, room by room, with an oral commentary of the make and model numbers of all appliances and electronic devices and other valuables? Make a copy of it, and put both tapes in other, safe places.

o   o   Did you tell your baby-sitter or mother-in-law about all of these safety measures?

Well, we failed this quiz abysmally the first-time around, but we're getting our act together and we're landing right on column "yes."

Leaving the Lived-In Look Behind You

Do you know how aware you are when your neighbor's not home? The car hasn't pulled into the driveway, the lights haven't been flicked on, the packages are stacked by the door. Well, burglars are avidly looking for the visual cues that someone's not home also. Stymie them by providing clues of your presence and removing the evidence that says you're not around.

Nothing says "We're home" more than lights going on randomly throughout a house, so the first device you need to purchase is an automatic timer that allows you to set timings on different lamps, the television or radio, and on outdoor lighting. The X-10 Corporation in Closter, New Jersey, manufactures the largest selection of these automatic timers. No home should be without them. You can buy them at Sears or Radio Shack or at home centers. They are modules that plug into lamps and appliances like TVs, radios, or even coffeepots, and they transmit radio signals over all your existing house wiring.

Each one of these modules has a number on it. For instance, the porch light is #1, the kitchen light is #2, the bedroom is #3, etc. You set the alarm clock component for a time and then punch "random," and it staggers the timing of the light-up some forty minutes plus or minus a day, giving a very realistic feeling to your plan-of-action. One of the modules even takes daylight savings hours into consideration—I recently learned that those two transition weeks of the year are peered at closely by some of your more intelligent, methodical burglars. You should program some outside lights and four to six inside lights, and the outdoor lights should come on at dusk and go off at bedtime.

But there are other preparations you should make and checks you should do before you leave home. If you think it would be helpful, photocopy this list, put the sheaf of papers away in a folder, and pull one out each time you prepare for a trip.

Much to Do Before I Leave

yes   no

○   ○   Did you stop the delivery of the paper and mail?

○   ○   Did you arrange to have the grass mowed or the snow shoveled during the period you'll be away? Virgin snow is a big giveaway.

○   ○   Did you ask a neighbor to watch the house while you're away? Does he or she have your vacation number and address in case of an emergency? Is he or she a keyholder to your alarm system and familiar with its workings? Will he or she check the house daily and remove any unexpected packages or mailers or flyers?

○   ○   Is the answer machine to your phone turned on, or did you turn off the bell of the phone? Long and insistent ringing is a clue that the house is empty.

○   ○   Did you park a car in the driveway, but ask a neighbor to move it periodically so it appears that you're really using the driveway and not just setting the stage?

○   ○   Did you set the automatic timers on your lights and TV?

○   ○   Did you store your valuables in the vault?

○   ○   Did you leave the shades and curtains in their normal positions? Closed curtains or blinds are a clue that you're away.

o   o   Did you unplug appliances such as air conditioners, irons, toasters, and coffeepots?

o   o   Did you put any outdoor umbrellas in a collapsed position in case of storms?

o   o   Did you turn down the thermostat?

o   o   Did you check to see that all windows and doors are locked?

o   o   Is the alarm system armed and in working order?

The Whole Nine Yards: Electronic Security Systems

I have to admit, I took a deep breath when I typed the head above. We're in complicated territory now, and the options are dazzling. So are the price tags, so let's first discuss why you might choose to investigate this subject and go the whole nine yards. While I can't quite get to the Letterman Top Ten List, the following reasons are compelling enough:

1. Electronic security systems are definitely a deterrent to burglary.

A 1988 study done by Figgie International, a security firm in Willoughby, Ohio, asked 589 people imprisoned for property crimes to rate the effectiveness of various security measures. The responses were tabulated on a scale of 0 (not effective) to 2 (very effective).

Alarm systems that were linked directly to police stations ranked the highest at 1.5. Electronic sensors in windows ranked second at 1.35. (Exterior lights were rated at 1.2, and barking dogs at 1.1.)

A study conducted at Temple University concluded that homes without alarm systems were three times as likely to be burgled.

Closer to home, and even more compelling, was one of the conversations I had with Detective Michael Barrett of the Westport Police Burglary Squad. He waved his hand over the 1994 Westport burglary files on his desk and told me that out of the more than a hundred successful burglaries that year, only two or three of the homes had alarm systems.

2. You, your family, and your home are physically safer with a security system.

Electronic systems offer you the option of "panic buttons." These are often placed next to your bed or in a downstairs office, and with a touch of your finger, they summon the police to your home.

In the awful event that you encounter an intruder outside your house and you are forced to turn off the alarm as the two of you enter the house, there is a Distress Disarm Feature on the keypad that silently summons the police.

A system can also include smoke detection and call the fire department, so even if you're away and unable to hear the smoke alarms and call the fire department, the firemen can get to your house in time to limit the damage.

If there's a monitor on the furnace and the furnace shuts off while you're in the Caribbean, someone will know about it before your pipes freeze and burst in the middle of winter.

If your $5,000 goldfish is especially meaningful to you, a sensor that measures the water temperature could alert someone that Goldy is in danger.

3. You get a 5 to 20 percent reduction on your homeowner's insurance if you have a monitored security system.

I checked in with two insurance companies and found that Allstate and Prudential offer a 10 percent reduction to all homeowners with monitored electronic security systems. Prudential also offers a 10 percent reduction if homeowners have a fire detection device as part of their monitored system. Thus, 20 percent off a policy might pay most of the yearly monitoring fees. (Allstate also offers a 5 percent discount if you have deadbolt locks on all exterior doors and smoke detectors and fire extinguishers in the house, so don't forget to ask for this after your Reformation.)

4. Peace of mind.

There's an unpleasant rule of the jungle implicit in what *should* be number five: If your neighbors have alarm systems, you almost have to have one.

You know that story of the two hunters being chased in the woods by a ferocious grizzly bear? In the middle of a clearing, one of the hunters sits down on a tree stump and changes into his Nike running shoes.

The other hunter stares at him in disbelief and says, "What are you doing? You'll never outrun that bear."

"I know," the runner replies. "I don't have to outrun the bear. I only have to outrun you."

The moral? If your neighbors all have alarm systems, and you don't, it's your door the burglar's going to come knocking on.

Although there are significant advantages to owning a security system, you need to note the disadvantages going in:

1. Having a security system is a commitment. It's like a new member of the family who requires thought and work.
2. False alarms can be a heart-stopping and money-consuming event. (More about this later.)
3. If you are considering getting a pet after your system is in-

stalled, discuss this with your salesperson in advance or false alarms may be generated by Fido the leaping dog or Fifi the pouncing Persian.

4.   A good system can have a pretty hefty price tag, and there's usually a monthly monitoring fee of approximately $20.

You say you're allergic to animals, or that Fido hasn't lifted his snout off the floor in years, and the advantages outweigh the disadvantages? Read on.

Wired or Wireless?

There are basically two kinds of systems that fall under the category of electronic security: wired and wireless.

Hardwired systems use wire to connect the control panel to each sensor and the siren. **Wireless** systems rely on radio waves instead of wires for communication between the control panel and its sensing components.

Wired systems have always been the alarm of choice among professional installers because they provide maximum reliability and are often cosmetically superior.

Wireless systems are improving, but are still a developing technology. Any radio technology can suffer interference, and situations can develop where the signals may not always get to the control panel. For example, a police car driving close to a home with a wireless system could trip a false alarm as its strong police band radio interferes with the radio waves of the wireless system.

There are two other disadvantages to a wireless system: The transmitters run on batteries, so there is the maintenance and expense of changing them; and the aesthetics leave something to be desired. You will have doodads that look like little plastic cigarette packs screwed to your walls in "random" places.

But wireless systems from an alarm company and do-it-yourself wireless systems that can be purchased at home centers or Radio Shacks can be less expensive than wired ones and may well be better than no system at all. If you decide to go the wireless route, you must get a supervised system. This is one that regularly checks the transmitters/sensors to confirm that they're communicating properly with the control panel. Otherwise, you won't know if a transmitter/sensor is in place and functioning properly.

Some companies are beginning to use a hybrid system which combines hard-wired and wireless installation. You should make sure you understand what percentage of the installation is to be hard-wired and what percentage of the job is to use transmitters before you make any decisions.

Selecting a Security Provider

There's a lot a homeowner needs to understand and to be on the lookout for when he or she ventures into the area of alarm companies and security options, and I needed someone inside the industry to explain it as comprehensively as possible. On the very strong recommendation of a friend, I called Ken Swain of Phoenix Security, here in Westport. I am glad I did.

At the time of the call, I was reading Tracy Kidder's excellent book *House,* in which he chronicles the building of a Greek Revival house by the Apple Corps Builders of Amherst, Massachusetts. By the time I finished that book, I not only understood a great deal more about the process of building a house, I only wanted Apple Corps— master craftsmen who do things the *right* way—to build one for me. Throughout the hours of interviews I conducted with Ken Swain, I was so impressed by the philosophy of Phoenix Security and the integrity of its principals I kept wishing that it had put in my security system. "My God," I thought to myself, "I've found the Apple Corps of the alarm industry."

Ken Swain is an extremely articulate thirty-seven-year-old who's worked in the alarm business for over eighteen years. In a way, he sort of grew up with the industry. Though I was chafing to talk about all those electronic gizmos, Ken first wanted to stress that there's a lot a homeowner can do before he or she ever speaks to an alarm company. Like Paul Peterson, earlier in this chapter, he spoke of low-tech target-hardening and enhanced lighting as a deterrent against break-ins.

But once a homeowner decides to investigate the subject of electronic security, he or she can quickly become confused by all the different alarm companies, their promises and sales pitches, their technology, and especially their contracts. And Ken Swain was anxious to shed some light on those subjects first. Ken's feeling is that you focus on the *company* initially, because the right company is going to specify and explain the right technology, and will "do the right thing" if a problem arises.

"Before the salesperson even gets to your house, you can assess something about the company," Ken said. "When you call the company on the phone, pay close attention to the person who answers it. Is the person bright, responsive, and efficient? Do you feel good talking to that person? It's a sign that the owners care about this 'front-door-of-the-company' position. That they have chosen this staff person well, trained him or her, and explained the importance of the position. They care about the image of their company and how you feel when you call. It travels down from the top."

He then went on to explain: "There are basically three kinds of companies: large national ones, mid-sized companies, and the solo practitioner—the owner who typically works out of his home.

"You are looking for a mid-sized company, because they are usually more state-of-the-art and more businesslike and professional. You want a company with overhead and staff who can respond quickly, 365 days a year, twenty-four hours a day, with an inventory of parts and equipment so you don't have to wait three weeks for a part to be ordered. You also want a company that is concerned about its reputation in your community and that doesn't specify proprietary equipment, as many of the large national companies do."

Call me stupid, but I needed to make sure I understood the phrase "proprietary equipment." It seems that several big companies use equipment manufactured by them and solely for their use, so if you don't like the service the company is providing, you're rather stuck, because no one else can monitor and service their system. If you decide to change companies, many of the most expensive components in the system might have to be ripped out and you'd have to start from scratch.

"Big national companies have designed systems and contracts that lock the customer to the company for a long period of time," said Ken Swain. "They 'give' you the system in order to lock you into long-term monitoring and service commitments. If a consumer proceeds thoughtfully and with a certain amount of knowledge, however, he or she can own a quality security system, enjoy a good relationship with a local business, and be free to take his or her business elsewhere if a serious problem develops."

On the Dotted Line
Ken told me that there are four things a consumer should look for in a contract that will speak volumes about the company's philosophy and style:

1.   Under "Term," you want to see "One year." Get skeptical if you see a three- or five-year contract. "Factor this into your assessment of the company," said Ken. "You want a one-year contract only. Why commit yourself for such a long time with a company when you have no previous track record with it?"

2.   Under "Warranty" you want to see one or two years (a ninety-day warranty is unacceptable) with the option to extend that on an annual basis for about 3 to 6 percent of the installation of the system. Seven-day-a-week service would be wonderful, but it is not the industry standard. More likely you'll be offered Monday–Friday, 9:00 A.M. to 5:00 P.M., with a surcharge for any other times.

3.   Most contracts read that companies have the unilateral right to sell your contract to another company without your knowledge and consent. You want it written in that you must be notified and given the choice of going with the new company or selecting your own.

4.   The fourth clue requires a bit of explanation. It concerns your system's master control panel. Control panels are "downloadable," meaning that they can be programmed over the telephone line. This can be an advantage to you. If you leave for the airport and realize that you've failed to turn the alarm system on, you can call your security company, give it your authorization code, and it can arm the system remotely—over the telephone. Also, the company can diagnose a problem with the system by retrieving information from the master control panel over the phone line.

But in order to protect you, there is a combination code that only your installing company knows. The panel cannot be programmed without that code. It is electronically locked.

That's great, unless you decide to switch alarm companies. For all intents and purposes, the panel has become proprietary to the company that installed it.

You need to make sure the company is contractually obligated to unlock the panel at your say-so. Insist that your salesperson amend the contract with the following: "Company agrees to restore downloadable master control panel to factory default code on twenty-four-hour notice, no questions asked."

This request is absolutely reasonable. It also signals the alarm company that you are an extremely savvy consumer. You are well within your rights to ask for *all* of the above, or continue your search until you find it. Otherwise, for your security investment, you're a virtual prisoner of the alarm company. (You should understand, however, that these concessions will not be available on the "special deal" packages that are advertised on the radio or in the newspaper.)

Once you've squared away that the contract reflects a company you'd like to do business with, you want to note if a company is taking the time to understand you psychologically and question you about your fears (which may be allayed or exacerbated by certain options in a security system) and your family life (are children or pets likely to produce a problem of false alarms?).

Then you want to question how the installer is going to get the wires to the doors and windows. You want to hear that they will be snaked through the walls, not tacked up and visible the way the phone company or cable companies run wire. You are seeking an aesthetically inoffensive installation.

Finally, you want to find out the agenda of the job-start and finish. Will the salesperson show up for the installation job-start and train you and your family to use the system after the work is completed? You do not want the installer to pinch-hit as teacher.

When you receive two or three written recommendations, compare them, using the factors of price, service, warranty, and credibility and credentials of owners and employees. Intangibles such as your gut instincts about the company's personnel and philosophies, as well as references, should also be considered.

It's a red flag if a salesperson urges you to sign a contract the day of the sales presentation. This is a company that wants to make a quick sale and will probably care little for your problems after the deal is locked up.

This happened to my new neighbor Marina. Her salesman wanted her to sign a $2,500 contract for a wireless system whose monitoring station was in Texas. The salesman left no written memo or security plan after Marina said she needed to think about it. And he was never heard from again. A word to the wise. . . .

Send in the Gizmos

In my second interview with Ken Swain, he hauled in a huge box of components and carefully explained them and all of the options a system offers.

Ken broadly outlined that the **master control panel** is the "brain" of an electronic security system, and detection devices called **sensors** are its eyes and ears. When the sensors sense the presence of an intruder, they relay the information to the system's control panel and trigger the siren.

Detection devices generally fit into one of two categories: **perimeter** or **interior.** Perimeter devices protect the doors, windows, skylights, or walls. They detect an intruder *before* he can enter your home. The three most common perimeter devices are **magnetic switches, alarm screens,** and **glassbreak detectors.**

Interior devices detect an intruder *after* he has entered the protected area. The most common interior devices are **passive in-**

frareds (PIRs), microwaves, and dual techs, which combine two detection technologies into one sensor.

Ken first explained perimeter technology. Doors, windows, and skylights—perimeter entry points—will most likely be protected by magnetic contact switches. The sensor is usually composed of a magnetic switch and a magnet. The magnet is installed on the opening surface (the movable window or door) and the switch is installed in the stationary surface (the window frame or doorjamb). When a homeowner shuts the window or door, the two units oppose each other. As long as they stay in this position, a continuous electrical current is maintained. But if someone should open the window or door and disrupt this flow of current, the sensors triggers the alarm. For the best look, these magnetic contacts should be recessed—embedded into the window and doorjamb.

A company that cares about its installation and your security will be reluctant to answer your needs for ventilation by placing the magnets up on the sides of a window, thus allowing the window to be opened a few inches. A savvy burglar can simply tape his own magnet on the switch with electrical tape, the switch will be "content," and he could have access to your house with no alarms ringing until he's ready to open the door and leave.

If you want ventilation, you're best advised to purchase alarm screens. These are made of fine, hard-drawn breakwire that is capable of supporting electricity. If any part of the hard-drawn wire is cut, or disturbed in any way, the alarm is triggered. Most people purchase screens for the bathroom and bedroom windows, but they would be especially wonderful to someone like me who has a slight claustrophobic tendency and likes windows open, but worries about someone walking in to the house when I'm downstairs in my office. They're quite expensive, however. A high-quality screen will run $140–$190, installed.

Ken told me that he has known couples to give them to each other as gifts ("Oh, darling, an alarm screen. Just what I've always wanted!"). Nonetheless, to some of us, they're more precious than rubies.

He then went on to explain glassbreak technology. This usually involves the use of such devices as audio discriminators (sound detectors) and shock sensors. "The best units marry these two technologies into one unit for added stability—fewer false alarms," Ken explained. "Otherwise, the sound of your keys jingling or dropping on the floor can set off an audio discriminator, or the rumble of thunder or a bird smacking into the window can trip a shock sensor."

Ken cautioned, "Beware the salesperson who promises 'whole room' stable glassbreak detection from one centrally located device. It can be done, but requires skill in placement and calibration to balance detection with stability."

When discussing glassbreak detection, let the salesperson know up front that you want reliability and are willing to pay for the extra glass sensor if it's necessary. You don't want the salesperson "pushing the limits" of the device's specifications in order to turn in a lower bid. You also want the technology tested with a device that digitally simulates the sound of shattering glass before you hand over the final check.

Making Sense of Space Sensors

As I mentioned earlier, interior or "space" sensors detect an intruder only *after* he's entered the room. There are several options on the sensor front, but the most commonly used and most cost-effective are known as PIR—passive infrared. PIRs sense rapid changes in temperature by monitoring energy in the form of heat—infrared radiation. They detect changes in the pattern of thermal energy in a protected space.

The word "passive" refers to the fact that this detector is not transmitting anything, it's simply looking at the environment. The lens focuses an image of the room onto a small sensing element inside the unit and is set at a neutral baseline of thermal energy. When it senses a heat change, such as a person or animal entering that protected space, it triggers the alarm.

One problem with PIRs is that they don't "see" everything in a room. The fanlike "fingers of protection" allow for unprotected spaces between and outside the beams. The number, length, and direction of the fingers, as well as the positioning of the device, determine how much of an area is protected.

Many PIR models have interchangeable lenses that can be reconfigured and so can offer a variety of pattern alternatives. This is particularly useful for homes that house pets, because a "pet alley" can be created which is several feet above the floor, allowing Fido and Fifi to roam freely. The problem comes when one of them decides to leap up. Ken says: "Don't use a pet alley unless Fido is old, decrepit, or very small."

Because PIRs are so frequently specified, any good company will question you as to your future plans of pet purchase. I told Ken he

PIR Beam Patterns

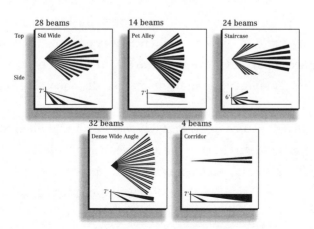

should travel with a psychic so people would know whether a furry friend was in their future, but it should be discussed, at any rate.

(Ken just called and told me that a new technology has come on the market. It's called a Pet-Resistant PIR. This sensor ignores infrared sources of heat of any body up to 50 pounds. This means that your small-to-mid-sized dog or a cat can leap around the house without triggering the alarm. It also means that you have better security, as a PIR with a pet alley could allow a burglar to crawl across your home undetected.)

Conceivably, a mouse could trigger an alarm with a PIR, so there is an option called a **quad** PIR (in the industry simply referred to as a **quad**) which is actually two PIR sensors in one unit. A quad cuts down on false alarms because to trigger the siren, both sensors must detect an intruder at the same time. The mouse might be noticed by the fanlike beams of one PIR, but would be too small to be detected by the other, and would thus scurry away, with no alarm accompanying its intrusion.

In a very stable environment—someplace with no skylights, windows, or heaters, such as a stairway or foyer—the single technology of a high-quality PIR might make sense. In an unstable environment, dual-technology devices—called **dual techs** in the industry—should be specified. This is a sensor that incorporates two different types of sensor technology in one housing: frequently passive infrared and microwave, which senses motion. Therefore, unless it senses heat and movement the alarm will not be triggered by a space heater suddenly coming on or even the oncoming headlights of a car.

I held a dual tech in my hand. It was heavy and filled with coils and complicated circuitry. This is a very sophisticated unit with much more false-alarm-rejection circuitry built in, thus it is a more expensive device. In 1996, one of these dual-techs costs three-to-eight times what cheap, low-end single PIRs do. But, when you think of how much you are going to spend on Clairol and Grecian Formula to cover the gray in your hair caused by false alarms and the money you're going to pay in fines to the town's police force for those false alarms (see page 262), you will appreciate anything that eliminates their occurrence.

So, a basic burglar alarm system, without the options, might include:

- **Multizone master control panel and keypad(s).** The master control panel is the "brain" of the system. It should be installed out of sight, in the basement or a closet. The keypad, however, is installed inside the front door, and often another is installed on the second floor. The homeowner interacts with the system at the keypad. Here the system is armed and disabled and its status is displayed. A four-bedroom house might need eight zones (each sensor or group of sensors is referred to as a zone). But Ken suggests that if you do a basic system of doors and an interior sensor or two, you should still purchase a sixteen-zone panel so you can expand the surveillance zones without having to put in and pay for a new control panel. The Napco panel is a very good one and is often specified. All master control panels have a battery backup in the event of a power failure, a power monitor, and the ability to bypass zones. This means that you can bypass interior sensors, but still arm the alarm for protection on the perimeter of the house. You merely bypass the appropriate zone(s).

- **Two alarm sirens.** One inside and one out. These should be programmed with a timer so that after fifteen minutes, the siren stops and the system rearms itself.

- **Magnetic contacts.** For perimeter doors as a minimum, and, better, for windows and skylights as well.

- **One or two PIRs.**

- **One backup battery.** It should be 4.0 amp-hour or more.

- **One transformer.** This brings the voltage down to 16 volts. Alarm systems are low-voltage systems.

- **One yard sign.** An inoffensive one, if possible. It warns of an electronic security system.

- **Window stickers.** These too should be placed inoffensively but visibly.

There are several options that can be added to your package that cost more money, but I don't think you or your home are secure without some of them.

- **Panic buttons.** These are commonly located next to beds or alongside doorways, or under a desk, and they can be manually activated if you suspect an intruder. They immediately alert the police, and their signals are given a priority by the police. These are twenty-four-hour manual-activation points—the system does not have to be on for the panic buttons to work.

- **Heat/smoke detectors.** In my mind, smoke detectors are not optional and should be in every hallway, inside every bedroom, and protecting every staircase (see Chapter 12, "The

Great Escape"). Heat detectors are supplements to this system and are often placed in areas where the environment is harsh—too cold, too hot, or too dusty for smoke detectors, as in attics, garages, furnace rooms, and kitchens. Heat detectors are never a substitute for smoke detectors, because most people are killed by smoke, not by the flames of a fire. If a smoldering fire has broken out and is producing poisonous gases and fumes, a heat detector will not sound in time to warn you of the deadly danger. Only a smoke detector will buy you the time you need to escape.

- **Furnace- failure monitor.**

- **Personal duress alarm.** You appear to be complying with a criminal's demand that you disarm the alarm, but you are really sending a message that you're in big trouble.

- **Strobe light.** A flashing light outside the house that indicates that the system had been previously triggered and rearmed. This cautions the newly returning homeowner, who may find it wisest to go to a neighbor's house and call the monitoring service and find out what happened. The homeowner may then decide to have the police come out again and go through the interior of the house.

- **Telephone-line protection.** In case anyone cuts the phone line, a radio backup system goes into play.

- **Power-surge protection.** Any kind of microprocessor-based device—and an alarm system is one of them—is harmed by transient voltages that enter the house for a number of reasons: lightning, problems with the power company, accidents, etc.—and should be protected with a power-surge protector.

From there on, security can be customized to meet your special needs or interests; art, wine caves, Goldy the Goldfish tank protection, etc.

Saved by the Bell

But what exactly is the typical scenario after an alarm is triggered? Ken talked me through the process:

1. When the alarm is triggered, sirens should sound inside and outside the house as the digital communicator dials the central monitoring company.
2. The message "Break-in at 1313 Mockingbird Lane" comes up on a computer screen at the central monitoring company.
3. The operator from central monitoring calls your home. If you accidentally triggered the alarm, you answer the phone and give your password, such as "Zordon" or whatever you've previously told the company. (If you are under duress of any kind, you make up a false password.) If there is no answer at the house or an incorrect password is given, the company calls the police and dispatches them to your home. The operator also makes a phone call to a designated keyholder.
4. The police arrive and generally check the perimeter doors and look to see if any windows have been broken.

We need to back up and discuss that phone call the operator is making to the designated keyholder. I am a keyholder for two different neighbors (and about to be appointed by a third), but I get a lot of vague instructions from my neighbors. I've had neighbors tell me to meet the police over at their house and open the door for them, or just to go in and shut off what they are sure is a false alarm. Ken's eyes widened when I told him that.

"There's a life-threatening sequencing problem inherent in this situation," Ken said. "The police are across town, and the neighbor is twenty seconds away from the house with a shrieking alarm. No matter what anyone tells you, stay in your own house and wait until the police check everything out."

I brought this up with Detective Mike Barrett, and he advised: "Let the police come over to *you* and get the key. You don't want to be in the middle of a hypothetical shoot-out on the lawn."

Keyholders are really responsible neighbors or friends who will follow up in the aftermath of a break-in or problem. For instance, if your neighbor is away when a break-in occurs, you might arrange to have the door fixed or a window reglazed. Or if the furnace monitor announces a problem, you might arrange for the service person to fix it. Never risk your physical well-being for a piece of stereo equipment, Mike and Ken concurred.

False Alarms: The Greatest Bugaboo

Before you vote on an alarm system with your pocketbook, think what a second-rate system can do to you and your family. An alarm that goes off in the middle of the night is a heart-stopping event. You never stop to think that it's only the wind or some lightning. You begin to imagine the worst possible scenario, and you grab your children up out of sleep and huddle with them in your bedroom, waiting the interminable moments until the police arrive. People who've experienced this scenario tell me their sleep is disturbed for weeks and that they can only guess the toll this "ersatz emergency" has taken on their children. Two women told me they're afraid to even put on the alarm system at night. They simply couldn't go through the experience again.

False alarms may be caused by lightning, the wind, a dense fog, a door that doesn't close quite as tightly as it should, and—too frequently—by operator error. But while all the books seem to blame the homeowner for false alarms, Ken Swain takes a different point of view. "We feel that most of the time, false alarms are caused by the person who designed, installed, specified, or applied equipment improperly," he said.

After that broad comment, he got very specific. "Very often," he explained, "a salesperson is trying to keep the bid in the running, so he or she specifies single-technology sensors, which are considerably cheaper. But single-technoogy glassbreak sensors can go off if your keys drop and make a high pitched sound, or if they measure vibration, a distant roll of thunder or a bird flying into the window will trigger the alarm. Yes, you want a good price that you can afford, but not at the expense of your psychological well-being.

"And let's stop bringing the police out to your house fifty times and making your neighbors crazy," Ken added.

I checked the ordinances of a few of the towns around here. New Canaan fines a homeowner $100 for every false alarm after the first one, and Westport has an escalating rate of fines that begins at $35 and tops out at $100. This is a strong motivator to discuss this problem of false alarms with your salesperson.

False alarms are dangerous, because they breed a cavalier attitude in everyone. It's so natural (and probably so comforting) to think that it's just another false alarm that people *and* the police get careless. A few years ago a policeman in Weston was shot in the chest by an intruder. He entered a house with a ringing alarm without his firearm drawn because he was sure that it was a false one.

So, if we all play "the boy who cried wolf" because we don't want to pay for better systems, everyone in society is harmed, and we all foot the bill anyway—whether it be because our police are tied up investigating false alarms, or because we have to listen to each other's sirens all the time, or because we're opening the mail and staring at big fines from the police department.

Think about all of this when you decide to trust your money and home security to a company.

Okay. I've said enough about all this, and I'm ready to move on to more comfortable subjects—like radon and ventilation. I wish we could all sing Porgy's song: "I got plenty of nothin' and nothin's plenty for me. I got no lock on the door, that's the way to be." But last time I looked, my town was neither in Kansas nor on Catfish Row.

Anyway, I hope all of this information stirs you into taking the necessary steps to safeguard your home and family. I noticed we felt generally better about the house after we applied some of our newly acquired security savvy and replaced doors and locks and lights and lazy ways. I'm betting you will too.

9. The Healthy House

It's a toss-up as to whether I got more paranoid researching this chapter or the one on home security. Now that I've hard-targeted the house and locked a potential danger out, I've got time to think: *What am I locked in with?* What is the quality of the air within these walls? What toxic chemicals are we breathing in or drinking every day?

While I was not particularly picky about what paint we used or the chemical composition of the furniture we bought (I was just happy to *have* that paint and furniture), lately I've noticed that I have an uneasy feeling every time I turn on the tap to drink some water or to fill the coffeepot. Could there be lead leaching from the pipes? I reach for the Poland Spring, but begin to wonder if I'm kidding myself: Who's checking the quality of that water before it's topped off in the jug? And my New Year's resolution this year was to get two carbon monoxide detectors in place before the clock struck twelve.

The only thing I knew about "green and healthy" homes was

that my brother and sister-in-law, Rob and Dianna, had built one at considerable expense and effort. I remember them talking about "outgassing" and particle board and special stains for their all-wood floors at a family dinner, but—it has to be said—they *are* from L.A. It kind of goes with the territory.

Now I'm wondering if they weren't on to something. Perhaps we shouldn't have rolled our eyes; perhaps we should all be a bit more concerned about our home environment.

You will hear about a healthy home directly from Rob and Dianna, as well as from a designer who helps create environmentally safe living spaces, later in this chapter, but even if you don't go totally "green" with your house, there are some environmental risks that must be dealt with by every homeowner in the country. Topping the list are radon, lead, asbestos, carbon monoxide, and poor-quality drinking water. Following these are the toxic chemicals that are entering the house with such seemingly benign articles as kitchen cabinets, carpeting, and furniture, cleaning supplies—even dry-cleaned clothes.

Because we are now in the realm of science and statistics, it's all a lot to gather in, so I've decided to divide these environmental concerns into the time frames in which you need to confront them: What possible hazards do you need to check out *before* you buy the house? What possible hazards do you need to investigate *after* you move in and set up the home? And then how do you *maintain* the house so that it is a safe and healthy sanctuary for you and your family and friends?

Stage I: Environmental Concerns Before You Buy the House

Before you sign your life away on a thirty-year mortgage, you're going to need to know all about radon, asbestos, and lead.

Radon

The bank requested that our house be tested for radon before the mortgage approval, but I remember little about the process except that the home inspector put some kind of canister in the basement and the office and it was a three-day test. I guess there wasn't a problem, and we proceeded with whatever was next on the agenda in the moving process.

And that was the last time I thought of radon. Until this chapter, when I rolled up my sleeves, read everything I could get my hands on, spoke to countless people at the EPA, interviewed mitigation contractors, and attended a seminar sponsored by the board of health about the dangers of radon.

Radon 222 is a colorless, odorless, radioactive gas that has been present in the earth's crust for billions of years. It is found in rock and bedrock and soils. In a succession of radioactive decay, uranium produces radium, and radium then releases the gas known as radon.

As the gas is released from the ground, it moves into buildings where the air pressure is lower than the pressure around the building's foundation. This "basement depressurization" can be caused by exhaust fans, combustion appliances, clothes dryers that expel air from a house, temperature differences inside and outside the house—even the velocity of the wind swirling around the house. And if there's a significant pressure differential, the basement can begin to act like a chimney, sucking in the radon gas through cracks in the foundation, dirt floors, sump pumps, and joints, and even through the tiny pores in hollow block basement walls. Depending on how porous the soil is, a negatively pressured basement can pull radon in from long distances away.

Outside, radon is diluted, so it doesn't pose much of a threat.

In an enclosed space like a house, radon can accumulate and build to high and unhealthy levels.

We now know that radon increases the risk of developing lung cancer. When you breathe in radon, it releases small bursts of energy and particles that can bombard and damage lung tissue. The alpha particles released by the nuclei of radon atoms and radon progeny as they decay are thought to damage DNA molecules. If those damaged DNA molecules don't repair themselves but suffer a permanent mutation and go on to replicate, the danger of cancer arises. When exposure to radon is combined with smoking or inhaling someone else's smoke, the risk of lung cancer increases dramatically.

The Surgeon General and the EPA warn that radon is the leading cause of lung cancer deaths in nonsmokers and the second-leading cause of death in smokers. The EPA estimates that radon is responsible for anywhere between 7,000 and 30,000 lung cancer deaths each year, and though there is some dispute about these figures, the Centers for Disease Control, the American Lung Association, and the American medical Association concur that radon is indeed a health hazard.

The bad news is that the EPA estimates that as many as one out of fifteen houses in this country has radon levels above the recommended action level of 4 picocuries per liter of air. (A picocurie is a trillionth of a curie, a unit of radioactivity named in honor of Madame Curie. Picocuries per liter are abbreviated as pCi/L.)

Take a look at the map on page 268 and determine if you are living in a state with high radon levels.

The good news is that radon is a very controllable environmental hazard and there is no reason not to buy a house because the radon levels are high. There are many techniques that will prevent radon from entering your home or effectively dilute the inte-

Map of Radon Zones

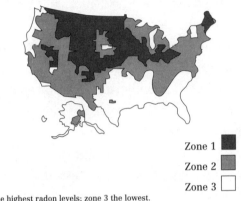

Zone 1 ■
Zone 2 ■
Zone 3 □

Note: Zone 1 has the highest radon levels; zone 3 the lowest.
Source: The Environmental Protection Agency

rior radon concentrations, which we'll discuss shortly. But first you have to know what the radon levels are, so the seller can mitigate the problem before the transfer of property. At this writing, some fifteen states mandate that radon tests be conducted during real estate transactions, but mandates or not, it behooves all home buyers to ascertain the levels of radon entering the home.

Testing for Radon

Ideally a test for radon should be conducted sometime between November and March, when windows are likely to be closed and radon levels will register higher. A 1988 study at the University of Pittsburgh found that radon levels measured 60 percent higher in winter and 40 percent higher in the spring and fall than in the summer when windows are thrown open and the house is thoroughly ventilated. Thus, summer measurements may be highly misleading and offer you a false sense of comfort. Our test was performed in May, but the house was closed for the duration of the test.

We complied with the EPA's initial recommendation: An activated charcoal canister was placed in the lowest livable level of the house. Test canisters can be purchased at the hardware store, or a

professional diagnostic service will provide them. Often, two charcoal canisters are placed side by side as a reference check to make
sure the readings make sense and to screen out possible lab errors.
There are two-to-seven-day tests.

Our test was done by our home inspector, and it was a three-
day version. I haven't a clue as to the level or what it meant. As I
said earlier, it seemed to be okay, so we wiped it off our mental register (if it was even there to begin with).

But what should you do if you're considering buying a house
whose radon levels in a similar screening test are higher than 4.0
pCi/L? Because radon levels can vary by a factor of five or more from
week to week, the EPA recommends a longer-term test with a more
accurate testing device such as an alpha-track detector, an electret
ion chamber detector, or a continuous radon monitor.

At this point, definitely hire the services of a qualified tester.
Call your local board of health and ask for recommendations, or call
your state's radon office. You want a company that is listed in the
EPA's Radon Measurement Proficiency Program, or your state's certification program if it has one. Don't choose a tester whose company does radon reduction work as well as testing, because this
situation might compromise test results and recommendations.

Once you get your test results, make sure you don't panic. You
have to take action, but you're not in mortal danger within the next
few months. It's long-term exposure (ten to fifteen years) to radon
that can be devastating.

Gauging Radon Levels

The Radon Program of the state of Connecticut issued the following guidelines to help a homeowner decide how quickly to take
action to reduce the radon levels in the home after the results of a
long-term follow-up test have been received:

1.   If the follow-up test results are greater than 50 pCi/L. Take ac-
      tion to reduce levels as soon as possible. These results are
      among the highest observed in homes.
2.   If the follow-up test results are from 20 to 50 pCi/L: Take ac-
      tion to reduce levels within six months. These levels are greatly
      above average for homes.
3.   If the follow-up test results are from 4 to 20 pCi/L: Take action
      to reduce levels within one year. These results are above av-
      erage.
4.   If the follow-up test results are less than 4 pCi/L: You might
      not want to take any action except to open a window or crawl-
      space vent, which reduces radon levels by a factor of 2.5.

You should know about the current debate in the field. Although the EPA has set a recommended level for remedial action
at 4 pCi/L and above, studies show that four to five people out of a
hundred exposed to that level during their lifetimes will die of
radon-induced lung cancer. The level of 4 pCi/L is the equivalent of
receiving 200 chest X-rays per year. The American Society of Heating, Refrigeration, and Air-Conditioning Engineers (ASHRAE) sets
standards for indoor air quality, and it recommends a 2 pCi/L guide-
line; most people who understand the radon issue will champion
that point of view.

Lowering Radon Levels

Should you verify that the radon levels are above 4 pCi/L, your
best bet is to hire a professional diagnostic service to figure out
where the radon is seeping in from. Once you have some answers,
the most effective remediation method can be put in place. Again,
check with your local board of health or the regional EPA for a list

of qualified contractors, and have two or three come over and give you a written scenario of what they plan to do and how much it will cost.

There are three common radon reduction techniques that may be employed:

1. Sealing off any radon-entry routes. Cracks and crevices, and any spaces around pipes and utility penetrations can be sealed with caulks. Sump pumps and drains can be covered with air-tight covers, and any open dirt areas in crawlspaces or floors can be covered with a polymeric vapor barrier or concrete.

2. Reducing basement depressurization so that less radon can be sucked into the house. This can be done by installing fresh-air-makeup systems next to clothes dryers, furnaces, and gas heaters. If fresh air is routed from the outdoors via metal ventilation ducts, the appliances do not draw combustion air from the basement, causing a negative air situation. And if negative pressure is minimized, so is the suction that the house places on the soil.

3. Employing a method called **subslab depressurization (SSD).** When radon levels are high, this very effective method is most often used. Typically, the system consists of one or more pipes which are embedded in the soil below the basement floor. The pipe then rises vertically and exits through the roof of the house. A small fan enclosed near the top of the pipe creates a suction that literally pulls the radon from the soil beneath the basement slab and vents it out above the roof to the atmosphere. An SSD system can reduce your radon levels by about 99 percent and costs in the neighborhood of $1,200 to $1,800.

Comparison of Radon Reduction Methods

Method	Typical Range of a Contractor's Installation Costs	Typical Range of Fan and Electricity Operating Costs and Costs for Heating or Cooling Air	Typical Range of Radon Reduction
Natural ventilation of the house.	None. ($200-$500 if additional vents are installed)	There may be an increase in energy costs.	Up to 50%.
Heat recovery ventilation.	$1,200-$2,500	$75-$500 for continuous operation.	25%-50% if used for entire house; 25%-75% if used for a basement.
Sealing radon entry points.	$100-$2,000	None, but there may be some costs for periodic caulking.	Up to 50%.
Subslab suction.	$800-$2,500 (active) $550-$2,250 (passive)	$75-$175 There may be an increase in energy costs.	80%-99% (active) 30%-70% (passive)
Drain tile suction.	$800-$1,700	$75-$175	90%-99%

Comparison of Radon Reduction Methods (continued)

Method	Typical Range of a Contractor's Installation Costs	Typical Range of Fan and Electricity Operating Costs and Costs for Heating or Cooling Air	Typical Range of Radon Reduction
Sump hole suction.	$800-$2,500	$100-$225	90%-99%
Blockwall suction.	$1,500-$3,000	$150-$300	50%-99%
Natural ventilation of the crawl space.	None. ($200-$500 if additional vents are installed)	$150-$500 There may be an increase in energy costs.	Up to 50%.
House (basement) pressurization.	$500-$1,500		50%-99%
Water systems.	$3,000-$4,500 (aeration) $1,000-$2,000 (activated carbon)	$40-$90 (aeration) None (activated carbon)	95%-99%

Source: U. S. EPA (1992c)

After the mitigation work is completed, you should follow up with another test to determine if the mitigation techniques have been successful.

A few weeks ago I was panting away on the StairMaster at the Y and overheard a man mention that he'd just sold his house after dealing with a radon problem. I couldn't resist turning to him and asking him what had happened. In short, breathless sentences he told me:

"The buyers tested the house and the reading came back at 8.2. We agreed to take care of the mitigation, and I called a highly reputable company here. After surveying the building, the contractors installed two pipes below the slab—the basement is very long. Actually, they drilled a hole about a foot square in the basement floor, then they stood a 4-inch PVC pipe, joined the pipes, and ran the piping outside the house and along and up the chimney. Then they installed the fan outside. This all took about a morning to accomplish. A week later, we retested, and the radon reading was 2.2. End of story, except for the $1,200 bill."

The Radon Program of the state of Connecticut prepared a booklet called *Radon and You* which includes an impressive flow chart as to plans of action for radon reduction in different levels of a home. I reproduce it here with permission.

If your levels are good, you should still test every five years or so, because as the ground moves and topography changes over time, small amounts of gas can reach the surface and diffuse into your house, elevating the radon level. If you do any renovation and make structural changes or alterations in the home, you should test before and after the changes are made. It is much easier and cheaper to install a radon reduction system before or during renovations than afterward.

For those of you live in high radon areas and who are about

Radon Reduction Decisions during Real Estate Transactions

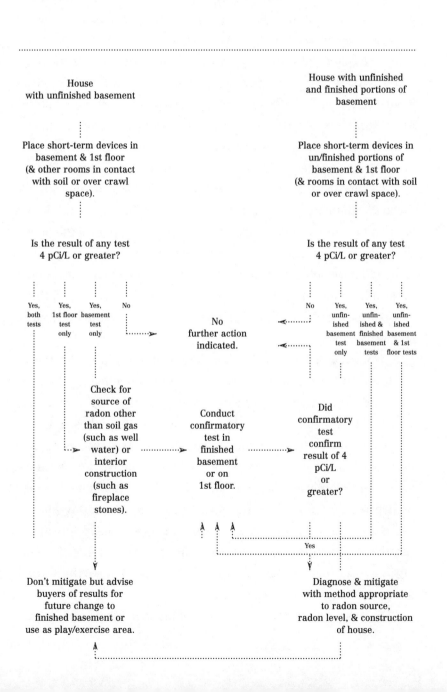

to break ground on a new house, talk with your builder now and find out if radon-resistant construction techniques will be used. This consists of a 6-inch layer of crushed stone placed underneath the slab and subslab depressurization piping coming up through the slab and going right up through the ceiling. Because it's incorporated at the time of construction, it's simple to accomplish and costs in the range of $300–$400, not the $1,200–$1,800 we spoke of above. Builders in areas that have radon problems typically have a radon clause in their contracts that calls for them to mitigate the problem if your test and their test average 4.0 or above.

During the writing of this chapter, I decided to walk myself through another screening test to see how difficult it was. I also wanted to know what the radon levels were in the part of the house that was built on slab (the bedroom/living room section) and was directly above soil (the real estate transaction test was positioned in the office downstairs on the other side of the house). What if there was bedrock underneath my pillow, so to speak, with higher radon levels?

I spent about $25 for an EPA-approved test that my friends at the hardware store recommended. At home, I opened up the canister and placed it on a shelf in the baby's room, away from an exterior wall, at head level (it should be at least 30 inches from the floor), and left it with the windows closed for seven days (it was January, so I wasn't tempted to open any windows anyway). Seven days later, I dutifully closed the canister, secured it with the tape the company provided, and mailed it from the post office Next Day Air.

Exactly a week later, I saw the envelope from the radon analysis lab in my mailbox and opened it to find we had a 1.4 pCi/L reading in the bedroom. I was so proud of that reading you'd think I had done something to achieve it.

Before we move on to the subject of radon in water, understand that your neighbor in a seemingly identical house could have a high level of radon and you have a clean bill of health, or vice versa. There are small construction differences and different underlying soils in every house that effect the entry of radon. Have a good test conducted and you'll know exactly what your situation is.

Radon in Water: How Well Is Your Well?

If you have city water, you don't have to be concerned about radon levels in water because the problem, if any, is treated by the municipality. Besides, water from municipal systems releases most of its radon before it ever gets piped into individual homes. But those who draw daily from wells are at greater risk. Radon gas released from bedrock or soil can dissolve in the well water. And then, as water—especially hot water—pours into sinks, tubs, and appliances such as dishwashers and washing machines, large amounts of radon can volatilize into the air. Every 10,000 pCi/L of radon in water contributes about 1 pCi/L of radon to the radon level that already exists in the household air.

So if the indoor level is high, you need to know what the level of radon in the water is, because radon in well water can contribute to the indoor air levels of radon in the house. If your test reveals that the radon levels in your water are below 10,000 pCi/L, then you can reduce your exposure to airborne radon, very cheaply, by simply ventilating your bathrooms, kitchen, and laundry room.

The most widely used method for reducing moderate levels of radon in water is to filter the water through a bed of granular activated carbon (GAC). This system costs about $800–$1,200. Readings higher than 20,000 picocuries demand a different kind of remediation: An aerator should be installed that blasts the radon out of the water and exhausts it through a vent that rises above the roof. This costs about $5,000. The GAC and the aerator systems need to be in-

stalled at the point the water line enters the house, and both require
cleaning by a professional once a year. This could cost anywhere
from $175 to $250, depending on labor and parts replacement.

The EPA estimates that some 8 million people have undesir-
ably high radon levels in their water supply. Preliminary studies indicate that drinking water infused with radon may perhaps lead to
stomach or intestinal cancer and possibly leukemia, so it behooves
all well owners to test the water.

Asbestos

A woman I met at an (adult) Barbie Tea Party yesterday told
me that she remembers her real estate agent pointing out pipes
wrapped in asbestos in the basement of the home she was considering buying. The realtor noted that the insulation was intact and
told her it was safe to leave alone. Indeed, most houses that were
built between 1900 and the early 1970s contain asbestos, a seemingly "miraculous mineral" that was used to insulate walls and
heating pipes and as soundproofing and fireproofing, as well as to
strengthen vinyl floors. It even helped gave many paints their texture. Remember those pebbly "popcorn" ceiling textures? That texture is thanks to asbestos. In fact, so useful was asbestos that some
30 million tons of it was used in the building industry from the turn
of the century on.

Unfortunately the rose hid thorns. Very ugly thorns. We now
know that microscopic particles of asbestos can be released into the
air and inhaled and can cause asbestosis (a serious lung disease),
lung cancer, and mesothelioma, a cancer of the lining of the lungs
or lining of the stomach. These illnesses typically develop fifteen to
twenty-five years after exposure to the mineral.

Only a small percentage of banks require an asbestos inspection before the real estate transaction, but your home inspector

should be on the alert for the presence of asbestos anywhere in the home. Make sure you talk with him or her about it. It might also be advisable to hire the services of a certified asbestos testing company so that you know exactly what the situation in the house is. The local board of health or the EPA asbestos office in your region can recommend a testing company.

Most inspectors "knows it when they sees it," but areas like vinyl floors or the mastic used to glue the vinyl down or asbestos-containing soundproofing may require testing to confirm the presence of asbestos. The most common technique used to identify asbestos is known as **polarized light microscopy (PLM),** but a more accurate test is done with a **transmission electron microscope (TEM).** However, a single sample analysis with a TEM can cost between $200 and $600.

The real estate agent who told that Barbie-party attendee that it was okay to leave the pipe wrapped in asbestos gave her advice she'd be unlikely to hear today. The thinking has changed on the subject: It's probably best to get it all out of the house right from the get-go.

The removal of asbestos-containing material is going to be something the lawyers on both sides argue about. There is currently no requirement for a seller to provide a buyer with an asbestos-free environment. Although sometimes the seller pays for the abatement before he or she puts the house on the market, in many cases the buyer foots the bill and makes all the arrangements. However you resolve the question of payment, make sure the abatement is done before you move into the house. There are two reasons for this: You don't want to move in only to have to pack up the kitchen or basement and then move your family out so that the abatement can take place; and if there's mastic that must be removed, the mastic remover smell can last for weeks. (Let me not be so ladylike; if there's

Possible Sources and Control Methods for Asbestos in the Home

Possible Sources	Activities That Release Fibers	Control Methods
Vinyl floor tiles, floor cements, and vinyl sheet flooring.	Sanding, dry scraping, and cutting.	Cover old vinyl tiles or sheets with new flooring material.
Patching and spackling compounds used before 1977 in patched walls and ceiling joints.	Sanding and scraping.	Leave alone if in good condition; remove if damaged.
Textured paints used before 1978.	Sanding, scraping, and cutting.	Leave alone if in good condition; remove if damaged.
Troweled-on or sprayed-on ceilings and walls constructed or remodeled between 1945 and 1978.	Sanding, scraping, drilling, and impacting.	Leave alone if in good condition; remove if damaged.
Stove insulation and cement sheets, millboard, and paper used to insulate the floors and walls around woodstoves.	Normal wear, sanding, scraping, drilling, and sawing.	Leave alone if in good condition; remove if damaged.
Furnace insulation: oil, coal, or wood furnaces wrapped with asbestos-containing cement and insulation.	Normal aging and wear, updating systems, and impacting.	Leave alone if in good condition; remove or remove if damaged.

Possible Sources and Control Methods for Asbestos in the Home (continued)

Possible Sources	Activities That Release Fibers	Control Methods
Door gaskets in furnaces, ovens, and wood and coal stoves.	Normal aging and wear.	Remove.
Hot water and steam pipes installed or insulated between 1920 and 1972 and wrapped in asbestos paper tape or asbestos blanket.	Normal aging and wear and impacting.	Leave alone if in good condition; repair or remove if damaged.
Ceiling and wall insulation installed between 1930 and 1950.	Renovations and home improvements.	Remove.
Appliances, especially hair dryers (recalled in 1979) with asbestos containing heat shields.	Appliances are unlikely to release fibers (except for pre-1980 hair dryers, which release fibers during normal use),	Hire a qualified technician for repair.
Roofing, shingles, and siding.	Scraping, drilling, and cutting.	Leave alone if in good condition; repair or remove if damaged.

mastic that must be removed, the mastic remover *stink* can last for weeks.)

Study the accompanying chart to get an idea where asbestos may be present in a home and what kind of activities would cause asbestos fibers to become airborne. You need to be thoroughly informed, because any renovation project in the future, even the pulling up of a linoleum floor, could cause asbestos fibers to become airborne and put everyone in the household at risk.

Often, people have the option to entomb or encase asbestos as well as pull it out, but Gary Stone, president of Homeguard Environmental Company of Stamford, Connecticut, told me that there's a federal law that says if 3 feet of asbestos are to be touched in any manner, it must be done by an asbestos abatement contractor in full regalia under full containment conditions. This means that your house will look like those final scenes in the movie *E.T.,* where the scientists are in space suits with respirators and there's a lot of plastic around.

In fact, two layers of 4-mil plastic will be placed on the floors and walls and all the seams will be taped. A microtrap/negative air machine that filters the air in the work space and exhausts it to the outside will be put into use, and at the entrance of the work area a decontamination area will be created, which will consist of a supply room, a changing room, and a portable shower. At the end of the project, an independent company comes in to test the air.

Because all of the above must be put into play even to spray a sealant on an asbestos-containing object, or to entomb it, it's Gary Stone's (as well as that of other professionals I spoke with) opinion that you shouldn't merely seal or entomb the asbestos. It's still there, and its presence leaves you vulnerable when you go to sell the house down the line. If the money and effort is going into full containment, make sure the asbestos problem is permanently removed.

How much does all of this cost? Well, a 200-square-foot kitchen floor abatement where the subfloor and linoleum would be ripped up would cost about $2,200. While a typical asbestos removal project in the basement would run about $2,000, an abatement of a "popcorn" ceiling could cost tens of thousands of dollars. This is a terribly important environmental issue as well as a costly one, so make sure you check it out and have full facts and figures.

In most states, asbestos companies must be licensed. Call the Department of Environmental Protection in your state and it will supply you with a list.

Lead

Demitri remembers our Realtor, Jill, handing us a paper to sign stating that we understood that there was a possibility of lead in our walls because of lead-based paint. She also gave us a pamphlet stating the dangers of lead-based paint. (I can't remember any of this, but I've definitely come to believe that there's a disease called "new homeowner's amnesia." Never has so much been blocked out in so little time.)

Of course, Jill remembers our lead discussion. Prior to 1950, paint that contained high levels of lead was widely used. The lead made the paint shinier, it fixed the colors better, and it made the paint more durable. It also had superb covering qualities and ease of application. In fact, lead paint was a selling point from the early years of this century right up until the 1970s. According to a study completed in 1990 by the Department of Housing and Urban Development, of the 77 million privately owned homes built in this country before 1980, lead-based paint has been applied in 57 million of them, or 75 percent. Of these, 11 million homes have lead paint indoors, 18 million have it outside, and 28 million have it both inside and outside.

After 1950, and especially after the advent of latex, the lead content of paint decreased and the use of lead paint declined, but both interior and exterior lead-based paint continued to be available until the mid-1970s. In 1978, the Consumer Product Safety Commission finally banned the manufacture of paint containing more than 0.06 percent lead by weight for use on interior and exterior residential surfaces, toys, and furniture.

Young children, especially those under the age of six, are at greatest risk of lead poisoning, because they stick everything in their mouths (paint chips as well as toys that may have paint dust on them), and because their lungs are bigger in relation to their bodies. Thirty percent of the lead they absorb ends up in the brain and other soft tissues of the body, as opposed to the 10 percent of absorbed lead that will end up in the brain and soft tissues of an adult.

Most lead poisoning begins slowly and results from a gradual build-up of lead in the body. Although early lead poisoning may not be accompanied by any symptoms, early symptoms may mimic the flu and could include headache, tiredness, irritability, constipation, diarrhea, appetite loss, stomach pain, and occasional vomiting. A parent may notice behavioral changes—the child may exhibit restlessness, a short attention span, impulsiveness, and difficulties with hand-eye coordination. Children who are becoming severely poisoned may have persistent vomiting, clumsiness, muscle and joint pains, weakness, and convulsions.

At present many pediatricians test for lead between the ages of one and two, and then at yearly intervals until the age of five or six. But if you know that your child was recently around a renovation or even a window replacement in a house containing lead-based paint, you may want to have him or her tested. The Centers for Disease Control states that blood levels in children of 10 micro-

grams per deciliter are elevated and require monitoring. If a child
tests at 20 micrograms per deciliter, the local health department
sends out investigators. (There is a process called chelation which
washes lead out of a human body. It used to require hospitalization
and painful injections, but it's an oral treatment now.)

The only way you will know for sure about lead in the house
is to have a lead inspection by a certified person. Your real estate
agent can recommend a service, or the local board of health will
give you a list of qualified laboratories that use EPA methods to test
for lead.

Basically, there are two ways to measure the amount of lead
in painted surfaces. The first is to hire a testing company, which will
come to the house for several hours with a portable **X-ray fluores-
cence analyzer (XRF).** This looks like a bullhorn and it shoots X-
rays at a surface, analyzes the echo, and in a matter of seconds gives
a reading of the amount of lead present, both on the surface layer
and in the layers underneath. The analysis does not disturb paint
surfaces and costs in the neighborhood of $300 to $500 for a 2,500-
square-foot house. However, the results of this test may be unreli-
able in some cases and should be verified by another testing
method.

The second method is for a technician or a homeowner to collect paint chip samples which will be sent to a testing laboratory for
an analysis by **anatomic absorption spectrometry (AA) test** or an **in-
ductively coupled plasma-atomic emission (ICP-AE) spectrometry
test.** A positive test for lead is 0.5 percent or more by weight or 1.0
mg/cm. The average cost of a lead assessment is $25–$40 per chip.
Companies also check for lead by doing wipe tests: A technician uses
moistened nonalcoholic baby wipes and covers a precise square area
with each, and then analyzes the wipes for lead. Again we're talking
in the neighborhood of $25–$40 per dust wipe analysis.

What if the assessment reveals that there is a high level of lead in the walls? If the walls are intact and there is no chipping, peeling, or flaking, it's quite possible that you don't have to do anything. If, however, you have a surface problem, or you plan on doing renovating and remodeling which would involve the sanding or scraping of lead-based paint, then the danger of there being lead-contaminated dust in the air becomes acute. It's time to bring in a professional who is trained in the removal and repair of lead-containing materials.

I think that was the point Jill was trying to get across to us: She was warning us to do no renovation (even changing windows) with our then one-year-old child anywhere near the house and without full lead-containment procedures (these resemble those we talked about for asbestos containment). She also warned us that pregnant women should never be anywhere near a renovation project where lead dust is kicked up, because fetuses are extremely vulnerable to lead.

Even if all surfaces are intact and there is no chipping or peeling, and you've planned no renovations, your windows and doors (the friction surfaces that are opened and closed) are a continual source of lead dust. It's common to find considerable amounts of lead dust in the window wells (the depression behind the sill where the window fits when it's closed). Some homeowners choose to replace the doors and all the windows (an enormously expensive proposition).

Another prudent course is to wash the sills and nearby surfaces once a week with a lead-specific detergent called Ledizolv. (It's quite interesting: The EPA's pamphlets tell you to use trisodium phosphate, but—because of environmental concerns about phosphates—TSP is outlawed in several states.)

Ledizolv has the advantage over TSP because it has no phosphates and has a neutral pH, so it causes less irritation (common household dishwashing detergents are harsher on the skin). It is biodegradable and thus easily disposed of without hurting the environment. According to substantial independent data, Ledizolv does a superior job of removing the lead. It is used exclusively by many lead poisoning prevention programs and professionals in their lead abatement and lead-contaminated-dust cleanups.

Ledizolv can be purchased through its manufacturer, Hin-Cor Industries in Charlotte, North Carolina, by calling 704-587-0744. The product is highly concentrated; each quart mixes 50:1 with water. Put 1 ounce in a quart spray bottle for cleaning window wells, sashes, and sills, and 2 1/2 ounces in a gallon of water for cleaning floors, walls, and other flat surfaces. A quart costs about $18.55.

Vacuuming the area with a HEPA (high-efficiency particulate air) filter vacuum which will not spit the lead dust out the back of the canister is another option. But a HEPA vacuum costs about $1,000. Call your local board of health and see if you can rent one, or talk to your neighbors and see who's willing to chip in for a neighborhood HEPA for periodic cleaning.

Another rational way of dealing with the possibility of lead dust is to have your children frequently wash their hands—all through the day, but especially before mealtimes, naps, and bedtimes. Keep their nails trimmed short so that lead dust cannot accumulate under them. If you can't replace the windows right away, open them only from the top so that the child has no access to the window wells where most of the friction dust accumulates. Feed your children a well-balanced diet high in calcium and iron (beans, milk, cheese, and cooked greens). When these minerals are present, a child absorbs less lead. Limit greasy foods, as fat slows down the body's ability to get rid of lead.

If you do plan on abating the lead, the internal walls can be plasterboarded or paneled, and, as we said above, the windows can be replaced and the doors sent out to be stripped. Look at woodwork with a cautious eye: Because woodwork required tougher coatings than ordinary walls, it is likely that lead-based paint will be found on windows, windowsills, doors, baseboards, wainscoting, mantels, and wood trim. Never strip these surfaces yourself. They should be removed or restored to the original wood onsite *only* by professionals using full lead containment.

Few people can afford to do total lead abatement of a house. If the walls and ceilings are intact, Gary Stone recommends prioritizing the following way: Replace the windows first, because they have the tightest friction points and thus produce the most dust. The doors are the next components to attend to, because people go in and out, knocking bags, boxes, and furniture into the door casings. Then the wood trim should receive attention, because the baseboards are constantly being whacked by vacuum cleaners, tricycles, toy trucks, furniture, etc.

Naturally, if there is any water damage on the ceilings, they would have to be plasterboarded in order to prevent dry and crumbly lead dust from escaping. And the nursery, where a toddler spends the most time and might do a lot of damage to baseboards and walls, is where you absolutely want to spend a part of your lead-abatement budget.

If there is lead paint on the exterior of the house, vinyl siding or clapboard will effectively encapsulate it.

Gary Stone asked me to remind you again that "the existence of lead paint itself is not a disaster; but the existence of lead paint in *poor condition* or in places like windows could well be a dangerous proposition to children and pregnant women."

The soil around your house may have become contaminated by peeling lead-based exterior paint that has leached into the soil. If you suspect that the soil may be contaminated, you should have it tested. Lead levels in soil are usually reported in parts per million (ppm), and levels greater than 500 ppm are cause for concern.

If the soil has indeed been contaminated, it will remain there posing a threat for over 2,000 years unless the soil is dug up and removed. This should be done by a certified lead removal contractor, because the disposal of lead-contaminated soil must be done according to federal, state, and local regulations. Because most of the lead is on the top 1/2 inch of the soil, you can probably remove the lead hazard by removing that layer and replacing it with a fresh topsoil.

The Residential Lead-Based Paint Hazard Reduction Act of 1992 (Title X) requires sellers and landlords to disclose the presence of lead-based paint to prospective buyers or renters of pre-1978 housing. This means that eventually all real estate agents will have a discussion similar to the one Jill had with us and give new homeowners a pamphlet to read about the dangers of lead-based paint, before they sign a paper stating that they understand the risks. The regulations will require home sellers to disclose whether any lead tests were done and what the results were. Buyers would then have ten days to conduct their own tests for lead, at their own expense.

All of the above is more than ample reason to check out the levels of lead in a house before buying it. Then proceed cautiously with all renovation projects, with the benefit of professional advice.

A critical resource on the subject of lead and a child's health is *Lead Is a Silent Hazard* by Richard M. Stapleton.

The Case of the Aging Oil Tank

I was taking the train into the city one morning and was pleased to run into my neighbor Rusty. After we had settled ourselves with coffee and the papers and caught up on things, our conversation drifted to—what else?—our houses. Rusty told me how worried he was that he might have a leaking oil tank. If it was leaking and contaminating the water table, the EPA could hand him a cleanup bill with a lot of zeros tacked onto it (tens of thousands of dollars). He was going to have it dug up, but he was regretful because it lay peacefully (or so he hoped) under his front patio and rock garden. All that work and beauty would be dug up in the process.

I shook my head in commiseration and said: "Rusty, I love your house, but I couldn't afford your house."

He looked at me somewhat quizzically and said: "But Janice your house was built the same year, and you've got the same 1953 oil tank."

I do? Oh, God, I do. (Tell me. Is it fair that I should have to worry about an aging oil tank as well as an aging septic system?)

This issue gnawed at me for a few days, and then, almost miraculously, I received a pamphlet from my fuel company inviting me to purchase insurance for the tank and an environmental cleanup for up to $100,000. The insurance was $76 for the year. *Never* was a check drafted so fast.

The insurance saves us from insolvency, but no responsible person can afford to let the chips fall where they may. Most oil tanks were buried in the ground during the building boom of the 1950s and 1960s (and many were buried even in the 1970s and 1980s), and since the life span of an oil tank is about thirty years, quite a few of them are reaching or have already reached the outer limits.

However, based on soil conditions and the extent to which water has been accumulating within the tank, a fifty-year-old tank could still be going strong (I hold on to this fantasy whenever the anxiety level gets too high). But soon—very soon—we've got to excavate that tank and put it out of service.

How is this done? "There are slight variations in the actual tank removal, depending on the local jurisdiction in which the project is taking place," says Gary Stone, "but generally, the removal process is as follows.

"The soil above the tank is removed and placed aside. The tank is then pumped out by a special pump truck and the contents are disposed of in accordance with EPA regulations, or transferred to the new, aboveground tank. The tank is then opened and cleaned on-site.

"After the tank is removed, the opening or hole is checked for contamination. In some locales, a fire marshal comes in and checks; in others, soil samples are taken and tested by the EPA. If there is no contamination, the hole is backfilled with gravel and then covered over with the original soil. It's a good idea to schedule the project in the spring or summer, after the heating season and when the ground is soft."

Gary continued, "If a leak has occurred, then regulations require that it be cleaned up. This generally consists of excavating down to the point where there is no more soil contamination. Once this is done and tested, the work is backfilled. If the underground water tables have been compromised, however, remediation can be frightfully expensive."

A home buyer would be wise to ask the seller the age of the tank and decide how both are going to handle the excavation and placement of a new steel tank in the basement or furnace room. I asked Gary how this is usually handled, and while every real estate transaction is a unique proposition, in some cases the buyer pays for the tank removal while the seller pays for the new tank and any soil contamination. (Naturally, if the house is well priced and there are four backup offers, the seller need not negotiate this at all.)

Whatever you decide, Gary Stone advises you not to put the tank out of service by simply abandoning it. This process consists of cleaning out the tank in the ground and cutting a hole in the bottom in order to take a soil sample and determine if there's been any contamination. If everything checks out okay, the tank is filled with sand or cement and then covered over with the original soil. These "abandonment" steps are pretty much the same as tank removal, so the costs are about the same. The problem is, one day down the line, you may try to sell the house and you'll have to disclose that there is an abandoned oil tank on the property. A potential buyer may suspect it wasn't abandoned legally, or may develop anxiety about sinkholes, and it leaves you open to a lot of questions. If, however, the tank is gone, it's gone, and that's the end of the story.

For about $400 you can have an existing underground tank tested, and I advise you to do so during the time of the home inspection so that you do not inherit a leaking and contaminating oil tank. The only test that should be used is **volumetric testing** as it does not exert pressure on the tank and crack it during the test. This is typically done in one of two ways: In the underfill method, sonar equipment and a portable computer are used to determine the volume of oil in the tank, and in the overfill method, the tank is topped off and a fill pipe is inserted. Allowing for adjustments in temperature that affect the volume of petroleum, the pipe is monitored. If the volume decreases, a leak is no doubt taking place. Both tests cost around $400.

Volumetric testing is accurate, but it will tell you only how the tank is doing that day. A week later a leak could develop.

Just to put this all in perspective: Peter Zack, an environmental analyst with the Leaking Underground Storage Tank Program at the Connecticut Department of Environmental Protection, was interviewed in a *Connecticut Magazine* article about the problem of oil tank leakage, and he reported six catastrophic leaks a year and seventy other kinds of leaks. The leaks are not pandemic—yet—but the clock is ticking, and each year will bring more of them. Get the insurance policy in place the day you take title to the house and plan on getting that older tank yanked.

Stage II: Environmental Concerns Once the Van's Pulled Away

I still can't get over that there's no honeymoon with a house. The movers have gathered up their quilts and wraps, you've paid them more than the original estimate, but you dig in trying to put things away and create a semblance of order. All that hard work has made you thirsty. You (somehow) find a glass and fill it with water, turning to survey all you now own and have to pay for . . . and I'm standing over your shoulder, hectoring you about the quality of your drinking water and asking you when you're going to go out and buy those smoke and carbon monoxide detectors?

Let's tackle the staff of life first. If you bought a house with a well, you'll no doubt have had testing done before the closing, but those of us who have municipal water figure the house is receiving good, filtered H_2O that we don't have to worry about. Right?

Wrong. Besides H_2O, there's a frightening number of toxic chemicals that could be pouring into your drinking glass or coffee cup.

Lead in Water

The first thing you should assume is that there's probably lead in your water. In 1986, the EPA estimated that approximately 40

million Americans were using drinking water containing potentially hazardous levels of lead. That translates to one out of five
households.

Very little lead occurs naturally in water. Primarily, lead enters your drinking water from the corrosion of plumbing that contains lead. Houses built from about 1910 to 1940 have service pipes
built of lead, and many houses built between 1940 and 1986 have
galvanized steel or copper pipes that are connected by solder that
is half lead and half tin. Brass faucets also contain lead, as do submersible brass well pumps. A 1986 federal law banned further use
of leaded solder on pipes that carry drinking water.

Chronic low-level exposure to lead in adults is associated with
high blood pressure, anemia, and nerve damage. Pregnant women
have to be especially careful, as lead may cause problems for the
fetus—it may impair mental development as well as increase the
risk of low birth weight. And, as I pointed out in the lead paint discussion, children are at considerable risk. Recent studies show that
lead exposure at an early age can cause permanent learning dis-
abilities and hyperactive behavior.

I spoke to Jo-Ann Anglace, the director of the Water Quality
and Environmental Information Management division at the Bridgeport Hydraulic Company in Bridgeport, Connecticut—the company
that supplies the water to our town—and she told me that while
most of us have lead somewhere in our plumbing systems, there are
two high-risk groups: those who have all-lead plumbing, and those
with newer homes built between 1983 and 1986 before the use of
lead solder was banned.

This surprised me, because I thought that homes built in the
1980s would have been in better lead shape than a house like ours,
built in the 1950s (the Dark Ages of Environmental Concern). "No,"
she responded. "Houses built twenty, thirty, or forty years ago have

leached much of their lead already. It's the houses built with lead solder closer to the present day that are more actively leaching their lead, and thus have higher levels."

Even though I'm greatly relieved to hear that our chances of very high lead levels are far lower because of the age of the house, I'm having the water tested. A contractor pointed out all the silver bands of lead that fuse the pipes going into our hot water heater. Because *Consumer Reports* recommended National Testing Laboratories, Inc., in Cleveland, Ohio, I called the company at 800-458-3330 and charged a lead test to my credit card. It cost all of $35, which included the postage for dropping the test bottles in the mail box. Note: This company offers a seventy-four-contaminant analysis which represents all of the common contaminants that the EPA has found in U.S. drinking water and identified as unhealthy or unpleasant. If you live in a rural area, order the "Watercheck with Pesticide Option," which tests for some twenty additional pesticides, herbicides, and PCB contaminants that may be present in agricultural areas (thus, this tests for a total of ninety-four contaminants). The seventy-four-contaminant test costs $94, and the Watercheck with Pesticide Option costs $139. In a week or two, you receive a complete printout of contaminant levels, together with explanations of which contaminants—if any—are above recommended levels, and advice on what action you should take to correct levels that exceed EPA recommendations.

A few days after I requested a test kit over the phone, it arrived in the mail, with instructions that I was to fill one bottle with the first water to be drawn from the tap after the night, and I was to fill the other bottle with water after the pipes had flushed out. I then put the bottles and my paperwork in the cardboard tube provided and dropped it in a mailbox.

But Jo-Ann Anglace at Bridgeport Hydraulic suggested that

until I had it in writing that my lead levels do not exceed 0.015 ppb
(parts per billion), my family and every homeowner who is unsure
about lead levels take the following precautions:

- Don't drink the first water out of the tap in the morning, because the water that sits overnight has a nice period of time to
  accumulate lead. Allow the cold water to run from the tap until
  it gets as cold as it will get (this means you've now flushed out
  the tepid water that's been sitting in the pipes all night and are
  now drawing from outside the house). Apparently this eliminates the water with the highest lead level, but you should understand that taking a shower does not flush out your water at
  the tap; this has to be done with each faucet you plan on drinking from. Also, if you've been away at the office all day, or out
  for over six hours and no one's been using the tap water, allow
  the water to run cold before drinking it or using it for cooking.
- Never use the hot tap for cooking or drinking, and especially
  never for making baby formula. Heat increases the corrosion
  of lead substantially, so hot water will have much higher lead
  levels than cold.
- Use bottled water for drinking and making coffee, and as much
  as possible for cooking, until the report arrives in the mail.

One week later I got a report that graded both samples "ND."
I quickly scanned the code and was ecstatic to realize that ND indicates that "none of this contaminant was detected at or above
our detection level." I guess our 1953 pipes have leached their
lead.

If your test results contain lead levels at more than 20 parts per
billion, you should probably install a treatment device (see page 299).

Home Alone: Well Owners and Well-Testing

Except for lead which joins up with water inside the home, people on municipal water systems are protected, because their water is tested and treated by their municipality. Homeowners with wells are on their own, however—the responsibility for testing the water and treating possible contaminants lies solely with them. While the well will have been tested before the closing to make sure the water is potable (and you should also have asked the home inspector to check for radon in the water), there are periods throughout a year when it is important to run tests.

There are differences of opinion on how frequently to test the water, but Ingrid Ritchie, Ph.D, an associate professor in the School of Public and Environmental Affairs at Indiana University, and Stephen J. Martin, the executive director of the National Association of Environmental Risk Auditors, offer some guidelines in their book, *The Healthy Home Kit:*

- **Bacteria.** Test at least once a year and anytime you notice a change in the taste, odor, or color of the water. Also test after periods of significant rainfall, after flooding, and after the spring snowmelt.

- **Nitrates.** Test at least once a year. Test whenever there are nearby potential sources of contamination such as farming, gardening, and livestock. Whenever bacterial contamination exists, always test for nitrates, since the two contaminants can come from the same source.

- **Lead and other heavy metals.** At least once, test each tap that supplies water for drinking or cooking, and repeat tests until any problems are corrected. If you have a submersible brass pump it's especially important to test for lead.

- **Synthetic organic chemicals.** Fertilizer and pesticide runoff from agricultural areas, golf courses, yards, and gardens is a large source of these chemicals. Other important sources include industrial discharges, leaking underground storage tanks, urban runoff, chemical spills, and improperly managed solid and hazardous wastes. Routine tests are not needed unless you live in an area that has groundwater contamination (let's hope you'll read about it in the newspaper or the department of health will notify the community).

- **Readily apparent taste, odor, color, or staining problems.** Test whenever you see clothing or fixtures stained red or brown, or green or blue, or when you see cloudy or off-color water, or note unusual taste and odor (for instance, a rotten-egg smell is caused by hydrogen sulfide, a gas formed by sulfite-reducing bacteria; a metallic taste could come from metals such as iron and zinc). Hard water occurs when dissolved minerals such as calcium and magnesium are present in the water. Test for these and inquire about a water softener for your water supply.

Chlorine

Lead was our main concern, but I noticed the highly chlorinated taste of the water when we moved, and it bothered me.

Chlorine is effective in eliminating waterborne diseases such as typhoid, cholera, and diphtheria, but we're also discovering that chlorination seems to spawn new contaminants called tri-

halomethanes (THMs). They are created when chlorine reacts with
organic matter such as rotted leaves. Chloroform, one of the four
major THMs, is known to cause cancer in laboratory animals and
is suspected of causing bladder cancer in humans.

Am I being an alarmist? Not according to some scientists. In
June 1988, the National Cancer Institute released the results of a
10,000-person study: It found that people who drink chlorinated
surface water for long periods of time have twice the risk of bladder cancer as those who don't drink chlorinated water. The more
chlorinated water you drink, the higher the risk. Fortunately, installing a water filter at the pump takes care of this.

Buying a Water Treatment System

But before a water treatment system can be specified and put
in place, a homeowner has to know what problems or contaminants
are present in the water spilling from the tap. It's best to have the
water tested either by a national laboratory such as I mentioned
above, or by a company in your area, which would no doubt be
aware of certain problems in the local water (look in the Yellow
Pages under "Laboratories—Testing"). Try not to rely on the company that provides the treatment device to test the water as well.
It's an independent, unbiased opinion you're after.

Once you find out what the problems with your water are, you
have two choices: You can drink bottled water, or you can have a
filtering device installed in your home.

Unfortunately, no one filtering device is a cure-all. They each
do their own thing, so to speak, and you may need a multiple system for the treatment of multiple problems. Once you have the
water tested, you can call a dealer to install a device to remedy the
problem or problems. Look in the Yellow Pages under "Water Purification and Filtration Equipment."

How do you know which company to call? One way is to see if the company displays the logo shown below in its advertising. This symbol means that the company's personnel have been educated, tested, and certified by the Water Quality Association (WQA) and thus are very proficient in the specification, installation, and service of water quality improvement devices. WQA members also have to adhere to a strict code of ethics.

 Water Quality

In addition, the WQA operates a "Gold Seal Product Testing Program": the gold seal is given to a water quality improvement or treatment system that has passed a strict battery of tests for performance, capacity, and longevity. So, if a water treatment device bears the gold seal, it indicates that a production model of the equipment was tested and found to meet industry performance standards. For general information on water treatment equipment call the WQA at 1-800-749-0234.

The National Sanitation Foundation International (NSF) is another agency that tests and certifies the performance of filtering devices. If you see its seal of approval on a device and its packaging, you can be sure the product will perform as promised. If you write or call at P.O. Box 130140, Ann Arbor, MI 48113-0140 (800-NSF-8010), the NSF will provide you with an information packet that includes a list of the units that have been certified for specific contaminant-reduction claims and also information about its testing program.

There are three basic methods of water purification used in devices for in-home treatment of water. They are activated carbon (in granular or block form), distillation, and reverse osmosis. Below are brief explanations of each of the three methods: what each is, what each can and can't do, and special considerations, if any:

Activated Carbon Filter

What is it? A device that removes impurities by passing water through a honeycomb of very small channels in a carbon cartridge. Block filters and granular filters are more effective than powdered filters.

What's it do? Removes chlorine, pesticides, herbicides, radon, industrial solvents, gasoline compounds, and trihalomethanes.

What can't it do? Doesn't remove microorganisms, or dissolved minerals such as nitrates, calcium, magnesium, iron, sulfates, or hydrogen sulfide.

What's it cost? $20 to over $500 for the under-the sink model, which is most effective.

Drawbacks: If filters are not changed in a timely manner, bacteria can multiply many times over. Also, testing done by Rodale Product Testing Labs demonstrated that the contaminant removal process diminished after about 75 percent of the rated life on all the filters tested. Therefore, Rodale suggested changing the filters more frequently than the manufacturers recommend.

Distillation

What is it? A system that produces high-quality water by boiling it to form steam that then condenses it back into water as it cools.

What's it do? Removes impurities from water. Bacteria, minerals, and other substances are left behind as the water turns to steam.

What can't it do? These units are not as effective on chlorine compounds and volatile organics such as chloroform and benzine. As the water vapor cools, these chemicals tend to reenter the water. (Fractional distillers can remedy the chloroform problem.)

What's it cost? From around $150 to over $500.

Drawbacks: Slow, difficult to keep clean, water tastes flat because there are no minerals in the water. Expensive to operate—it takes about a dollar's worth of electricity to produce 5 gallons of water, and it wastes water because it takes 6–7 gallons of water to make a gallon of distilled product. Major drawback: Stainless-steel distillers seem to add traces of aluminum to the finished water, and since aluminum has been linked with Alzheimer's disease and other diseases of the nervous system, it would be best to choose a glass distiller.

Reverse Osmosis Systems

What is it? A three-canister system that passes impure water under pressure through a presediment filter, a cellophane-like membrane, and finally through a carbon filter.

What's it do? Removes lead, nitrates, organic chemicals, particulates, bacteria, asbestos, and inorganic chemicals (lead, arsenic, cadmium, barium, magnesium, etc.).

What can't it do? Does not remove microorganisms and only filters volatile organic chemicals such as solvents and gasoline by-products.

What's it cost? Ranges from $350 to $1,000.

Drawbacks: This system wastes an incredible amount of water. About 20 gallons a day are wasted by being flushed through the unit, even if you don't use any water. Also, some membranes need chlorinated water and some are destroyed by chlorine, so check into this carefully.

In-Home Water Treatment Techniques

Containment	Reverse Osmosis	Activated Carbon	Distillation	Aeration	Chlorine
Asbestos	•	•			
Bacteria	•		•		•
Inorganic chemicals	•		•		

Lead	•		•	
Nitrates	•		•	
Organic chemicals	•	•	•	
Particulates	•		•	
Pesticides		•	•	
Radon		•		•
THMs		•		•
VOCs		•		•

(Volatile organic chemicals)

From: *The Healthy Home: An Attic-to-Basement Guide to Toxin-Free Living* by Linda Mason Hunter (Pocket Books, 1990).

Are Bottled Waters a Good Bet?

Several books I read about healthy homes and a recent article in *New York Magazine* about the potential dangers to the city's water supply system all inevitably turn to the discussion of bottled waters. All mention how little monitoring is done and make a point of stating that bottlers can bottle and sell plain tap water. They delight in pointing out that bottled water is about 1,000 times as expensive as tap water.

Being extremely math-deficient, I haven't quite figured out the exact bottle-to-tap costing ratios, but I did spend quite a bit of time finding out just who's watching the bottled water industry and what kind of testing is required, and I found out something that's— well—positively refreshing: Bottled water is a very highly regulated industry.

Apparently, 85 percent of all bottled water producers and distributors are members of an organization called the International Bottled Water Association (IBWA), and this organization imposes very strict testing guidelines on every phase of the process. There are numerous tests at the source, during the bottling process, and of the finished product.

Members of the IBWA must also submit to an annual unannounced plant inspection administered by an independent inspection organization which audits quality and testing records and checks compliance with the Food and Drug Administration Quality Standards as well as any state regulations.

You should know that the filtration of this water is done with ozone and not chlorine, so you are not subject to the health risks of chlorine.

Call the IBWA at 703-683-5213 to find out which bottled water distributors in your region are members of the organization and abide by its guidelines. Then cross this worry off your list.

Carbon Monoxide

The dangers of carbon monoxide were made tragically apparent to the public in 1994 when tennis star Vitas Gerulitas died in a small cottage because of a faulty pool-heating system that emitted carbon monoxide and asphyxiated him as he slept. Some 10,000 people each year seek medical attention because of some degree of carbon monoxide inhalation, and according to the January 5, 1994, issue of the *Journal of the American Medical Association,* carbon monoxide is the number one cause of poisoning deaths in the United States.

Carbon monoxide is produced by the incomplete combustion of natural gas, wood, coal, oil, gasoline, kerosene, and tobacco. So woodstoves, fireplaces, candles, kerosene heaters and lamps, gas ranges, furnaces, water heaters, dryers, pool filters, space heaters, and cigarettes can emanate carbon monoxide.

Carbon monoxide is colorless and odorless. It is especially deadly because once it enters the lungs, it latches on to hemoglobin, the main component of red blood cells that normally shuttles oxygen to the cells of the body, and refuses to let go. Carbon monoxide is over 200 times more attracted to hemoglobin than oxygen is. (Talk about a fatal attraction: The resulting oxygen deficiency can initially cause headaches, nausea, and drowsiness—typical flulike symptoms—followed by respiratory failure, irregular heartbeat, convulsions, and, eventually, death by asphyxiation.) Unborn babies, infants, the elderly and those with cardiovascular or lung disease are at greatest risk.

According to home safety experts, all homeowners should take the following precautions to ensure carbon monoxide levels are kept to the absolute minimum in the house:

- A forced-air furnace is frequently the source of leaks and should be carefully inspected every year.
- The furnace connections to flue pipes and venting systems to outside the home should be inspected annually for signs of corrosion, gaps, or holes.
- The furnace filters and filtering systems should be checked annually for dirt or blockages.
- The forced-air fans must be inspected annually for proper installation and correct airflow of flue gases. Improper furnace blower installation can result in carbon monoxide buildup, because toxic gas is blown into rather than out of the house.
- The combustion chamber and internal heat exchanger should be checked annually for cracks, metal fatigue, or corrosion. They must be clean and free of debris.
- The burners and ignition system have to be inspected annually. A predominantly yellow, flat, lazy-looking flame in a natural gas furnace indicates fuel is not burning efficiently and

thus is releasing higher than usual levels of carbon monoxide. Oil furnaces with similar problems can give off an "oily" odor.

- All venting systems to the outside, including flues and chimneys, should be checked annually for cracks, corrosion, holes, debris, or blockages. Fireplaces and wood and coal stoves should be cleaned and inspected before each heating season. A chimney cap should be installed as quickly as possible if you don't have one. Animals and birds can build nests in chimneys, preventing gases from escaping. (See page 162 in Chapter 5, "Creosote Is a Dirty Word," for the importance of chimney caps.)

- Have all other appliances that use flammable fuels such as natural gas, oil, wood, or kerosene inspected annually. These include water heaters, clothes dryers, kitchen ranges, ovens or cooktops, wood-burning stoves, and gas refrigerators.

- Be sure space heaters are vented properly. Unvented space heaters that use a flammable fuel such as kerosene can release carbon monoxide into the home.

- Never warm up your car in an attached garage. Carbon monoxide will build up and travel through the walls and into the home.

- Never barbecue inside. Charcoal emits high levels of carbon monoxide.

- Never use your gas oven to heat a room.

I can't stress enough the importance of having a yearly inspection of your furnace or boiler and water heater, as well as having your chimneys inspected and cleaned. If a crack occurs in the heat exchanger of the furnace (the metal drum which collects the combustion gases) or fissures appear in the flue pipes that are attached to the walls, or the vents corrode and are not corrected, carbon monoxide can begin to disperse in the house in high levels.

There are two other dangerous scenarios that can unfold with the terrible consequences of carbon monoxide and other pollutants entering the living space. They both have to do with air pressure changes and ventilation in and around a home and are known as **backdrafting** and **reverse stacking**.

Normally, carbon monoxide and other by-products of combustion exit the house through the chimney or flue. But it's dangerously true that what goes up *can* come down.

Thanks to today's very tight, energy-efficient houses, the leaky windowsills, door gaps, and drafts that let outside air mingle with the warmer air inside are a thing of the past. Also, a modern house is chock-a-block with exhaust fans that vent bathrooms, clothes dryers, kitchen ranges, furnaces, and water heaters. The fans and the tight construction help create negative air pressure inside the house.

And when outside air pressure levels are higher than those inside the house, a downdraft can occur that sends combustion gases right back inside: Carbon monoxide, instead of being sucked up and out of the house, flows back down the flue and into the air you breathe. This is called **backdrafting**.

If the problem is backdrafting of a woodstove or fireplace, you would typically see the smoke spilling into the living space and know that there was a problem. However, your only hope in a backdrafting situation with a furnace or water heater would be a carbon monoxide detector, which I will discuss shortly.

Reverse stacking occurs when two or more combustion appliances—for example, a gas furnace and a gas water heater—sit in the same basement and share the air available to them in that space. When one device is operating and the other is not, a reverse stacking condition can occur.

It could happen as follows. When the burner of the gas furnace turns on, it needs combustion air to burn its fuel. This combustion air normally comes from the furnace room or the basement, but the burner is not picky about where the air comes from. If the house is sealed tightly enough and there is no air coming in through cracks in the basement, the furnace may begin drawing air down the stack of the now-passive water heater. And the pollutants that are idling inside the water heater's stack will be sucked down and forced into the house.

How can you prevent this from happening? A good solution is to duct outside air directly to the burner of the furnace. Today you can buy a high-efficiency furnace that is either a sealed-combustion or an induced-draft unit (see page 74 in Chapter 2). Sealed-combustion furnaces do not use the air inside a house; instead they draw air from *outside* the house. Induced-draft furnaces employ a small fan to force combustion gases right up the chimney. If there is no proper draft, the furnace burner will not operate, thus avoiding the dangers of reverse stacking.

Fortunately for all of us, we can buy peace of mind and insurance against carbon monoxide poisoning by purchasing carbon monoxide detectors for the home.

I have to admit that it took me over a year to get around to buying them and placing them on both floors, but they really should be on that first list you take to the hardware store with you. We were terribly remiss in not squaring this away immediately.

There seems to be a lot of confusion as to where to place the detectors, so I spent some time on the phone with two of the major manufacturers of these devices.

First of all, never place a detector on the furnace or in the furnace room. It's tantamount to placing a smoke detector over your stove. Of course it will go off and scare you out of your wits. One detector should be placed in the hallway of each sleeping area, and another outside the furnace room. All should be positioned up near the ceiling, near your smoke detector if possible.

The reason for placing it high is not that carbon monoxide rises (its molecular weight is similar to that of air, so it disperses pretty evenly in air), but to let it remain undisturbed by children, pets, furniture moving, etc. This point was driven home to me when I proudly went to point out my plug-in detector to someone and was shocked to find it missing from the outlet. Behind me, my two year-old, Jordy, piped up in an awfully knowing voice: "It's gone. It's not dere." (He'd pulled the plug and tossed it in a toy box.)

Another reason for placing it near the smoke detector is so you are reminded to test both devices. Although the carbon monoxide detector and the smoke detector will chirp when the battery is running low, you should push the buttons on both devices once a month in order to hear the beeps and test all detector functions. The batteries on most carbon monoxide detectors need to be changed about every two years, but check your instruction booklet to be sure.

I have a First Alert battery-operated unit near the bedroom wings, and, as you know, I *did* have a plug-in-the-socket unit near my office, but when we lost power the other day in a winter storm, I thought it might be better for people not to depend on electric power—especially since its during power failures that homeowners tend to use fireplaces.

One final note: I just replaced my electric stove with a gas one (how do you cook with electric? I couldn't get the hang of it) and then I read how much safer electric was than gas. Newer studies, however, conclude that if a range is operating properly, the pollution emissions are minimal. Pilot lights were the highest source of emissions, but today's models bypass that problem with spark ignition—a device for electrical ignition. This not only cuts fuel consumption and thus reduces your gas bill, but reduces the amount of combustion gases by a third. If you have an older model that employs pilot lights, make sure you adjust the flames so that they burn blue instead of orange, and if you're like me, and really want to cook with gas, earmark some money for a new model that employs electronic ignition.

Stage III: Furnishing and Maintaining a Healthy Home

Now that you've squared away any problems with radon, asbestos, lead, carbon monoxide, and the quality of the water, you're probably starting to think about furnishing the house and really making it into a home. But here too you need information, because without knowing it, you may be filling the house with furniture, cabinets, carpets, and other home furnishings that are actually adding to the chemical cauldron in the house and contributing to a very unhealthy and even toxic home.

Formaldehyde

Formaldehyde wins "Most Ubiquitous Chemical" in households today. It is an important industrial chemical used to make other chemicals, building materials, and household products. Billions of pounds of formaldehyde are used in making plywood and particleboard, medium-density fiberboard, and other pressed-wood products, and so it finds its way into our homes through cabinets, doors, paneling, flooring, countertops, and furniture. These pressed-wood products are manufactured using adhesives that contain urea-formaldehyde (UF) resins. In fact, medium-density fiberboard contains a higher resin-to-wood ratio than any other UF pressed-wood product and is generally recognized as being the highest formaldehyde-emitting pressed-wood product.

The list goes on. Formaldehyde is also used in treating textiles such as those used for many draperies, upholstery, and carpets. It is found in lipstick and shampoo, toothpaste, milk cartons, paper bags, wax paper, paper towels, car bodies, household disinfectants, sheets, clothing, and a kind of insulation not used anymore but still present in over 400,000 homes, urea-formaldehyde foam insulation (UFFI). According to the Consumer Federation of America in Washington, D.C., products containing formaldehyde account for 8 percent of the gross national product of the United States.

There's a reason for all this use: Formaldehyde is highly esteemed in industry for its qualities as a preservative and as a bonding agent in the manufacturing of glue. But formaldehyde belongs to a large family of chemicals called **volatile organic compounds (VOCs).** The term "volatile" means that the compounds vaporize, or become a gas, at normal room temperatures. When formaldehyde is used in the manufacturing process of a product, the chemical may not always bond or be completely transformed in the mixture. In the early life of the product, then, this "free formaldehyde" can be released into the air—the famous "outgassing" you'll hear so much about. Another problem exists. Pressed-wood materials (particleboard, medium-density fiberboard, waferboard, flakeboard, and hardwood plywood) or UFFI can combine with water or water vapor, and the chemical reaction can cause a continuous but declining emission of formaldehyde gas—especially in warm or humid weather. These formaldehyde fumes are associated with adverse health effects.

What are those adverse health effects? Formaldehyde irritates the eyes and throat, causes runny noses and other respiratory symptoms such as coughing, chest tightening, and wheezing. Some people report nosebleeds, fatigue, headache, skin rashes, memory problems, nausea, and dizziness. The National Research Council estimates that approximately 10–12 percent of Americans may have some degree of formaldehyde sensitivity.

In the laboratory, formaldehyde has also been shown to cause cancer in animals exposed to high levels of fumes, but one can't extrapolate reliably from animal data, so it's not certain what this means to human beings. According to the Consumer Product Safety Commission and several other scientific panels, exposure to formaldehyde is likely to pose a risk of cancer to humans, particularly after long-term exposure.

If you suspect that there may be a high level of formaldehyde in your home, causing problems for you or your cohabitants, there are testing devices. Again, look in the Yellow Pages under "Laboratories—Testing" or "Environmental and Ecological Services." This test should be done by professionals. You want to ensure that the level of formaldehyde in your home is below 0.1 part per million (ppm). If your levels are higher, you will no doubt be told to ventilate more or use an insulating paint or coats of polyurethane varnish to seal bare pressed-wood surfaces (just make sure these contain no formaldehyde).

If you keep the humidity level of the house low by running the air-conditioning system or dehumidifiers, you can help reduce formaldehyde emissions. Also, bear in mind that studies demonstrate that formaldehyde levels typically drop by half about every four and a half years, and even UFFI installed five to ten years ago is unlikely to still release formaldehyde. However, some people exhibit sensitivity at levels of 0.03 ppm.

So, all those nice and expensive things we're building into our homes and accepting delivery of from stores and manufacturers may not be so good for our health. (Great. There's a new "F" word in our vocabulary.)

Designing a Nontoxic Home

Few of us can accurately assess which products are toxic and contributing to an unhealthy air quality within a house, so I turned to Susan Pedersen, president of SPI Design, Inc., in New York City, a firm that specializes in creating healthy homes for its clients. First of all, I was curious to know how she got into this niche in the design field.

"I noticed that the more time I spent on site during renovations and construction, the more chemically sensitive I became," she told me. "The allergic reactions I was having to a lot of the grouts and adhesives and paints began to concern me, and I began to investigate other resources that were less toxic. This interest prompted me to return to school. I attended Harvard University's Graduate School of Design, where I studied environmentally sound architecture and new technologies for healthful and efficient buildings. My background allows me to think always of the health consequences of the furnishings in my clients' homes."

This led me to wonder how she begins working with clients who might want a healthy home but might not be sure which of the paint or furnishings ingredients or components were troublesome for them.

"When I first sit down with a client, I interview him or her or them," Susan Pedersen explained, "and I find out which allergies or chemical sensitivities they have, if any. I conduct sniff tests with every product I'll use. For instance, I'll put small amounts of glue or adhesive or paint in clean glass jars for a few days and ask my client to sniff each one. We'll note reactions such as headaches, dizziness, or respiratory difficulties to each and eliminate those that are problematic.

"Even if they have no known sensitivities," she continued, "I tell them that I will always keep the quality of the indoor air in mind, and that I will use the least toxic products I can find, as well as furnish in the most healthful way."

When I asked her what this means, she answered, "Well, let's start in the kitchen and bathroom, favorite renovation rooms. I like to use Corian or marble or stainless steel, because it requires little grout, and if possible, I make sure the cabinets are solid wood—not constructed of particleboard that will off-gas formaldehyde—and we use a water-based finish on them. I pay particular attention to the ventilation in these rooms so that mold and mildew and carbon monoxide are kept to absolute minimums."

She then told me that she installs hardwood floors throughout the home and finishes them with a water-based polyurethane.

On the walls, she likes to use latex—a water-based paint. Apparently oil-based paints contain thirty to forty chemicals, whereas water-based paints contain only twelve to fifteen. "For those with chemical sensitivities, I order Auro or AFM paints and products, which are specially formulated for the chemically sensitive and have only nontoxic components. They do not off-gas and have very little odor," she said.

"When I use wallpapers, I use the hand-painted paper ones and affix them with a clay-based adhesive I discovered from the Allergy Resource Company in Palmer Lake, Colorado. I never put fabric on the walls."

I was beginning to feel there might be some merit to my sparsely furnished living room that I never stop complaining about, and I asked Susan Pedersen how she creates a healthy environment in that space.

"I use as few fleecy materials—fabrics, carpets, and draperies—as possible, because these absorb the outgassing of other products and trap pollutants and dust mites and molds," she began. "I use a lot of cotton for upholstery and slipcovers, and a mixture of antiques. Antiques are considered environmentally safe because all the outgassing has already taken place. I also scatter antique area rugs on the floor, but I first conduct a sniff test to make sure there's no mildew."

She laughed and went on to say: "People think that an environmentally friendly home means simply white cheerless walls and unbleached cotton. But there are many materials which used creatively can add texture, color, and glamour while helping to keep your home efficient and healthy. Some of these materials are glass, metal, wood, marble, and cottons. An example of combining these elements would be a window treatment made by installing a brass-trimmed glass screen covered with a shirred, beautifully colored gauze fabric in a living-room bay window, thus combining traditional and modern at the same time using three of the above elements."

She told me that in rooms that really require window treatments for privacy, she tries to use mini-blinds, wooden shutters, or minimal draperies such as Roman shades.

I was anxious to discuss wall-to-wall carpeting, because I kept hearing bad things about the chemicals in the backing of the carpets. When I asked Susan Pedersen if they were really all that bad, she pointed to a story—now a classic in the design world—about the new carpet installed in the offices and hallways of the EPA several years ago.

Apparently, many of the people who worked in the offices had severe problems when new carpeting was installed. Ten percent of the workers there got sick and experienced symptoms; some even required hospitalization.

It turned out that a chemical with the daunting name 4-phenylcyclohexene (4PC) was the suspected culprit. It's a by-product of the process used to make the latex backing of carpets. This is only one of a number of potentially harmful substances found in carpeting. A new carpet direct from the factory can emit as many as twenty-five to thirty different chemicals into the air. Many of these chemicals are chlorinated hydrocarbons that control fungi, molds, insects, and rodents. The adhesives used to lay some carpeting can release even more toxic chemicals than the carpeting itself.

Susan was quick to tell me how she deals with this problem: "About four days after installation, the levels of 4PC and other chemicals produced in the manufacturing process begin to fall, so if someone insists on wall-to-wall carpeting, we try to unroll it and air it out in a garage or mudroom for a few days before the installation. Then we keep all the windows open and I set up fans around the room. I want those chemicals out of the carpet and out of the house. Fortunately, much of the outgassing occurs in the first three months or so."

Susan mentioned some good news for those of us who are still going to purchase commercial carpets. The carpet industry is aware of the problem and has made great efforts to reduce the emissions of carpet and to minimize the impact of carpet on indoor air quality. It has developed a program called IAQ (Indoor Air Quality), and the manufacturers who use this logo on their carpets participate in a research program which tests for certain chemicals and makes a concerted effort to lower the emission levels.

"Of course, I prefer to use natural-fiber carpeting only," said Susan. "For example, wool that has not been mothproofed, with nontoxic pads and adhesives. But I'm unhappy about wall-to-wall carpeting in general because it's a sinkhole for dust and mold and other pollutants."

I was beginning to get an idea of the elements of healthy home design, but I knew there were colonies of dust mites and molds floating around everywhere that cause allergy problems for people who are not particularly chemically sensitive, so I asked Susan Pedersen about this.

"Dust mites and mold and mildew flourish when the humidity climbs in a house, so I always investigate ways to lower the moisture in the air," she answered. "Since mite colonies thrive at 70 percent humidity, the summer months are a problem. Air-conditioning will control the humidity, but often one or more dehumidifiers also need to be running during these humid months.

"Good ventilation is a must in any home, but, when needed, many types of air filters can be used to clean the air of dust particles and chemicals. I often use the Allermed HEPA filter, but I ask people to check with their allergists for other recommendations also."

She then went on to tell me that she has concerns about something as seemingly benign as a person bringing home dry cleaning, removing the plastic bag, and sticking it in the bedroom closet. Clothes that are dry-cleaned are immersed in a chemical called perchloroethylene, a volatile organic chemical that is a known carcinogenic. (While the spinning removes some of the chemicals, it doesn't remove all of them.)

"Now my client is breathing in these chemicals all night long, as they emanate from the newly cleaned clothes and disperse into the bedroom," said Susan. "In order to avoid this, I install a rack in a client's mudroom and ask him or her to unbag and hang the newly cleaned clothes there so that the chemical disperses in a well-ventilated area, away from the sleeping or living space.

"And while we're on the subject of clothes," she added, "I tell my clients to build cedar closets if they can, but never to use mothballs, which are also toxic, especially to children."

I told her that I liked all this concern for health, but I was wondering how much extra it costs to use all the special paints and grouts and sealants and non-particleboard cabinetry. She explained that a person furnishing a home this way can expect to spend 10 percent more than when doing it with commercial products.

Just before the tape recorder clicked off and Susan got ready to rush off to another meeting, I asked: "Do many people really opt to do this?"

"Yes," she answered. "People are becoming more and more aware of the unhealthy quality of indoor air and are seeking advice about less toxic solutions for comfort and beauty in their homes."

After talking with Susan Pedersen, I couldn't wait to get on the phone with my sister-in-law Dianna and ask her about the healthy house she and Rob built up near the Nevada border. Dianna does have multiple chemical sensitivities, and I realized how uncomfortable she had been for a long time. I was really curious how a totally healthy house would change things for her. First I asked her to describe the symptoms she experiences.

"I've always had allergies," she said, "but after working on some renovation projects in my twenties, I began to experience troubling, flulike symptoms whenever I was around new carpeting, paint, paint thinners, and anything heavily scented. I would feel this tightness in the throat and a kind of itchiness on the roof of my mouth, and I noticed that I developed headaches, laryngitis, and rashes soon after some exposure to any of these chemicals. I knew I was going to have to be very careful when we built this house or I would have real problems."

When I asked her how difficult it was to build and design a house with nontoxic products and health foremost in mind, she told me: "Products for the chemically sensitive were not talked about in our circles, so I had to do a lot of research to seek them out. I ordered nontoxic paints and finishes and building supplies from Livos in Santa Fe, New Mexico, Auro in West Germany, and AFM Building Supplies in Riverside, California, but my real problem came when I had to persuade workmen to use products that were new and handled a bit differently. One tile man walked off the job, one painter did things *his* way and didn't apply the paint right—building isn't stressful enough, right?" She laughed.

"But I pressed on and the house eventually was finished with few if any items that could outgas and cause difficulties for me. Plus, I felt good that I'd created a nontoxic environment for my husband and son.

"Interestingly, a few of the workmen came to me afterward and reported that they didn't have the headaches and fatigue they were used to experiencing at the end of the day. They generally felt better while working on this house."

I expected my brother to be a bit more skeptical, and—at first—he didn't disappoint me:

"I watched her do all this research and order products from Germany and New Mexico, and I was willing to pay for it, but didn't really think the end result would be worth all the effort. Remember, it's easier to get products today than it was six years ago."*

But then he added: "It was funny, though. After a few weeks in the new house, I began to notice that I could be inside all day without feeling logy, and my 'stress' headaches disappeared. The most surprising thing was that I began to taste food more acutely. There is something to this after all."

This doesn't mean that you have to go rip up every shred of carpet in your house and throw out all your draperies and new fur-

---

*Dianna would not have so much trouble today. A new company called Healthy Home Designs™ offers architect-designed home plans that promote the wellness of their occupants while using building materials that are, for the most part, environmentally benign. The plans emphasize ventilation and energy-efficiency, as well as specify low-tox materials that don't outgas or pollute the environment. The company also directs the homeowner to suppliers of environmentally-friendly, resource-conserving products. Call Healthy Home Designs™ in Des Moines, Iowa at (515) 255-1425.

niture. Unless you are a chemically sensitive person or have an asthmatic family member, you might want to study more about ways of improving the indoor air quality in your home and make gradual changes.

First of all, *open your windows!* Ventilation forgives a multitude of sins. In fact, good ventilation could reduce up to 75 percent of all home air problems. But if there's only one change you're going to make, examine the products you're using to clean your house. They are among the most toxic products you'll find in your home.

Healthy Products for Maintaining the Healthy House

My mind likes things in neat categories: This can is for the furniture dusting, this bottle is the window and glass cleaner, and this can of bathroom cleaner has really strong fumes, so it must be powerful. A spritz of this, a capful of that, and I have an impressively clean and antiseptic house.

But while researching this section, I actually had names of all the chemicals I was unleashing in my home, and I'm no longer quite so sanguine about the products I pull out of the basket at the checkout aisle. I decided to be open to trying other products that wouldn't be harmful to our respiratory systems, wouldn't damage the environment, and wouldn't hurt the septic system (and you all know from Chapter 4 how concerned I am about my frail and aging septic system).

It seems that vinegar, borax, and baking soda are the great triumvirate of nontoxic house cleaning. You can clean almost anything—bathrooms, kitchens, windows, glass tables—with one of these substances. It's cheaper, it doesn't irritate anybody's nasal passages, and you don't have a cache of poisons sitting around your house posing a danger to curious little ones.

While this is hardly scientific, I experimented with different nontoxic cleaners that I either mixed myself or bought at the health food store or ordered from catalogs. Things seemed pretty clean after I applied the new cleansers. (Maybe cleaning is more a matter of the universal solvent, water, and some good elbow grease, and there really isn't as big a need for extremely harsh, burning and odorous chemicals as we've been led to believe?) I will admit, though, it took me a while to adjust to the absence of that harsh chemical "clean" smell.

I'm including some possible substitutions for cleaning supplies and some recipes to help get you started in your new life as the Nontoxic Hausfrau or Hausmann. Of course, your local health food store will stock environmentally friendly, nontoxic cleaning supplies, and you can order others from Allergy Resources in Colorado (719-488-3630) or the Janice Corporation (no relationship to author) in New Jersey (800-JANICES).

But you should definitely read Debra Lynn Dadd's book, *Nontoxic, Natural and Earthwise.* She's nonbelligerent and nonjudgmental, and she didn't make me feel like a lowly worm just because I've been seduced by all those "New and Improved!" TV commercials. She recommends the following substitutions:

Scouring Powder:
Some harmful ingredients: dry chlorine bleach (prolonged exposure to this can damage lungs).

Try: Bon Ami Cleaning Powder or Bon Ami Polishing Cleanser, or sprinkle baking soda, borax, or dry table salt on the surface to be cleaned and scour and rinse.

Window and Glass Cleaner:
Some harmful ingredients: ammonia, artificial dye, aerosol propellants.

Try: 50 percent white vinegar and 50 percent water in a pump-spray and apply with newspaper or a soft cloth. But never wash windows when the sun is shining directly on them because the solution will dry too fast and streak. (I found vinegar and water worked well, as does a natural glass cleaner I bought from the health food store.)

Disinfectants:

Some harmful ingredients: cresol (chronic poisoning may occur from ingestion or absorption through the skin), phenol (fatal if swallowed in small amounts and thought to promote cancer), ethanol (ingestion of large amounts may cause nausea, vomiting, stupor, coma and death), formaldehyde.

Listen to what Debra Lynn Dadd had to say about disinfectants:

"If you believe the television commercials, we all need disinfectants to kill 'odor-causing germs.' Or we might have some on hand to kill germs when a family member is ill. There are other ways to disinfect, though, that are less toxic and actually work better. In fact, disinfectants can reduce the number of germs, but will not kill all the germs present. To make something totally germ-free, you have to sterilize it with boiling water."

Try: Borax. According to Ms. Dadd, "It's a very effective disinfectant. One hospital experimented with using a solution of a half cup borax to one gallon hot water for one year. At the end of that period, the monitoring bacteriologist reported that the borax solution satisfied all the hospital's germicidal requirements."

Furniture and Floor Polish:

Some harmful ingredients: nitrobenzene (particularly hazardous to pregnant women), phenol (fatal if ingested in even small amounts and thought to promote cancer).

Try: Mix together 1 teaspoonful olive oil, the juice of one lemon, and 1 teaspoon water (the odor will disappear after absorption and drying); or try Ecover Floor Soap or one of the Livos waxes (Livos Plantchemistry in Santa Fe, N.M., 800-621-2591).

To dust: Use cloths that capture dust because of the silica in them.

Mold and Mildew Cleaner:

Harmful Ingredients: Formaldehyde, phenol, pentachlorophenol (an additive that has been shown to decrease birth weights in the offspring of test animals), kerosene.

Try: Borax and water, or vinegar and water. Mix either combination in a spray bottle and spray it on. The mildew wipes right off. Borax also inhibits mold growth. Ms. Dadd also recommends using heat to take care of a major mold problem. Either use an electric hair dryer aimed at the mold for a few minutes, or bake the mold by using a portable electric heater in a closed room for a day. It will dry into a powder that you can brush right off.

Two other products that work well are AFM Safety Clean or AFM X158 Mildew Control from AFM Enterprises. I was not able to get these products in the health food stores I dropped in on; I ordered them from Allergy Resources catalog, or you could go right to the source at AFM Enterprises at 1140 Stacy Court, Dept. NNE, Riverside, CA 92507, 714-781-6860.

Laundry Detergent:

Harmful ingredients: naphthalene (can produce damage to the eyes, liver, kidneys, skin, red blood cells, and the central nervous system; can cause allergic contact dermatitis in adults and children), phenol.

Try: Borax with a little white vinegar, or Arm and Hammer Unscented Super Washing Soda, Ecover Laundry Powder, Granny's Power Plus Laundry Concentrate (cleans an average load with just a tablespoon and can be ordered from Granny's Old Fashioned Products in Arcadia, California, at 818-577-1825, or through the catalog of Allergy Resources, or the Janice Corporation; call 800-JANICES in Budd Lake, New Jersey).

It occurred to me, throughout the writing of this chapter, that one could become so suspicious of everything one breathes, drinks, eats, or even throws into the washing machine that one could stop enjoying life. The stress would be terrible. As my father used to counsel me, moderation is the key. Take care of the big environmental problems, and then embrace natural solutions one at a time. Rome wasn't built in a day; neither is a healthy home.

10. Ventilation Is the Name of the Game

....

I can just picture it. You search for a house for months, suffering severely from what I call real estate fatigue in the process. But your agent calls and you trudge off yet again to see a house that is just "perfect for you." You walk through the door, and—can it be?—it really *is* the house of your dreams, or at least it has almost everything you've asked for, and at the price point you can afford. It must be a pretty great house, because there are three other agents with their potential buyers pacing on the patio, waiting to get inside and probably start a bidding war.

Your real estate agent is giving you that now-or-never look, so you do one last walk-through. Suddenly, you turn on your heel and cry: "Stop everything! I can't buy this house yet. I have to check out the ventilation here first."

Right. Who ever gives a thought to ventilation? Insulation, maybe; ventilation—never. Yet, true health and comfort in a house can't happen without it, and horrible and expensive damage can happen to an improperly or insufficiently ventilated home.

Throughout the first year in our home, the subject of ventilation kept coming up, but because I didn't understand physics, I couldn't really grasp any of it. Two plumbers stood in my very hot boiler room, shaking their heads gravely and muttering something about the boiler not breathing enough oxygen (did that mean the boiler would die, or we would die?), and it is only now that I'm understanding the differences in combustion air and makeup air, the dangers of negative pressure in an improperly ventilated house, and the phenomena of backdrafting and reverse stacking in a furnace room.

And in the dog days of August, when the house becomes a hotbox by early afternoon, my carpenter just mused casually: "I wonder if your attic's properly vented? Your shingles will curl like fried bologna in the summer and take at least ten years off the life of your roof, and you'll get all this condensation from water vapor in the winter and rot the joists and trusses in the winter. By the way," he added, "did you have any ice damming last winter?"

No. (I was hanging on by my fingernails last winter, and that would have definitely put me over the top.) But my friends Elin and Bob suffered terrible ice dams on their roof, and it turns out better attic ventilation would have saved them the extremely costly repair as well as all the emotional angst they suffered.

At first, when the air turned arctic here and I was warm as toast in this obviously well-insulated house, I was absolutely thrilled we had ended up in a home so suited to my always cold hands and feet. But lately I've begun to wonder if the air is exchanging at a good enough ratio to rid the house of toxic buildup from carbon monoxide, formaldehyde, and all the other chemicals that get released in a house in a day.

Rot? Asphyxiation? Ice dams? Toxic buildup? I am tempted to scream like that teenager in the movie *Poltergeist: "Wha-a-t's happening here?"*

Nothing that couldn't be prevented with the right understanding about when and how to provide ventilation for my attic as well as for my family.

At first glance, the subject of ventilation may not seem all that sexy, but it has *everything* to do with a house that is durable, healthy, safe, energy-efficient, and comfortable. Besides, aren't you curious to know what some of those holes poking out of your house are called? (I must have been looking at louverlike openings in the sides of houses all my life, but it never occurred to me to ask what they were for or even to ascertain a name for them. Keep reading. You can find their name and function on page 332.)

There are two kinds of ventilation we're going to be discussing: attic ventilation and house ventilation. Along the way, we're going to catch up on Physics 101.

The Secrets of Attic Ventilation

Attic ventilation is vital for two reasons: It offers an escape route for all the water vapor that accumulates within a house, and it maintains the temperature of the underside of the roof sheathing so that it very nearly matches the temperature of the outdoors.

Let's start with the water vapor. Where does it all come from? From us, and all the bathing, cooking, and laundry we do in a day. An average family of four generates about 4 pounds of moisture a day simply perspiring and engaging in daily cleaning or cooking activities. Mopping the kitchen floor releases about 4 1/2 pints of water and washing the dinner dishes about 1/2 pint. In winter, vapor will rise to the attic through cracks, holes, and joints in an attempt to reach the dry outside air. But if the attic is not vented, allowing it to escape, it will hit the colder roof sheathing just under the shingles and condense. Now you have problems: Soggy insulation is practically useless, and if all the wood up there gets wet, it rots, and rotten wood could invite the neighborhood insects to move in to further destroy your home. Moisture condensation can leave you with peeling paint and the deterioration of ceiling and roof materials.

And then there are ice dams. If the roof sheathing remains cold thanks to proper ventilation, the snow will disappear during milder weather, gradually and evenly. All is well. If, however, the warm air from the house rises to the attic and escapes through the roof, then parts of the roof will become warm and the snow will begin to melt. And when the rivulets of melted snow hit the lower, colder sections of the roof, they will refreeze and begin to form the ice dams that will force a future batch of melting snow to pool and back up under the shingles.

Summer brings different headaches. If the attic is unventilated, the sun of a 90-degree day can raise the temperature of the roof sheathing to 170 degrees or greater. This heat can bake, buckle, and distort your shingles, causing them to die a premature death, and that pent-up heat radiating down through the ceilings of the living space will make you feel you've died and gone to hell. If there is not sufficient attic ventilation, the heat actually gets stored in the attic and begins to build up over a period of days.

Proper attic ventilation keeps the outside air moving between the insulation and the shingles, and the buffering effect of this air moving between the hot roof structure and the people in the rooms below is invaluable.

All of the above proves the importance of attic ventilation: It solves and prevents problems. But to really understand attic ventilation, we need to understand some of that physics stuff.

Physics 101

It is never just you and the house; it is you, the house, and Mother Nature. And she moves a lot of wind against a structure, causing all kinds of things to happen.

When a gust of wind blows into a house, it creates areas of pressure that are both positive and negative. At the point of impact, the force of the wind creates a positive pressure. It then fans out and jumps in either a vertical or horizontal direction, and within this "jump" expanse, a negative pressure originates.

If the physics of the wind force could be completely understood, the buffering effect of the moving air could be harnessed and channeled through the roof with the proper placement of intake and exhaust vents. Thus, intake vents could be placed in areas of positive pressure and exhaust vents placed in areas of negative pressure in order to guarantee a steady, cooling air flow in the attic.

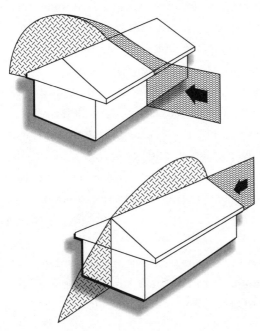

Outside wind direction

Negative air pressure

Positive air pressure

This sounds good until you remember that wind often changes direction—and a positive pressure area may become a negative one, and vice versa.

To complicate matters further, I have to tell you about two other natural forces at play in the movement of air that must be taken into account when designing a ventilation system: the **thermal effect** and the **inertia of moving air.** The thermal effect accounts for the fact that "warm air rises." Because the air in the attic is often warmer than the outside air and air wants to flow from a warmer to a cooler place, the warm air will rise and escape at the ridge—if there are vents placed there.

But the inertia of moving air is a far more important dynamic in maintaining good attic ventilation. This principle holds that air

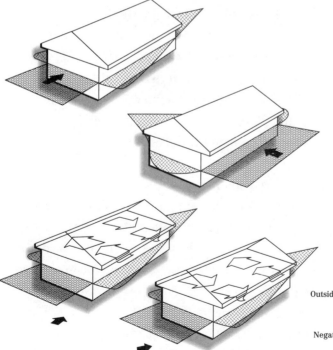

Outside wind direction

Negative air pressure

Positive air pressure

332   The Virgin Homeowner

in motion develops a momentum which tends to keep the air moving in the same direction. (The converse is also true. Air *not* in motion has a tendency to remain inert, and it requires more force to overcome the inertia and get the movement started than it does to maintain the movement once it has begun.)

So a superior ventilation system must take into account the impact of wind and a likely change in the direction of wind, and must work with the important characteristics of air: Warm air rises, and air moving in the same direction tends to continue to move in that direction.

So, understanding that there are laws of physics always at play in your house and particularly in and around the subject of ventilation, let's take a closer look at the roof vents themselves.

What Are Those Holes Poking Through My House?

The easiest vents to spot—if they're there—are the triangular or rectangular ones high up in the gable ends. These are called **gable louvers** or **end-wall louvers** and were the ventilation system used in houses built for years in this country. The problem of a gable-only system is that it's totally dependent upon wind direction, so often the gable vent is combined with **soffit venting** (the soffits are under the eaves of the house).

The soffits are a very good place for intake venting, because they are somewhat protected from rain and snow and the wind is parallel to the vent no matter which direction it's blowing. Therefore, with soffit vents on both sides of the structure, there is as much venting in a positive-pressure area as there is in a negative-pressure area, so it's always in balance. Nevertheless, even with gable and soffit venting, there is limited airflow across the underside of the roof deck—the roof sheathing—which is the part of the roof we need ventilated. The air tends to flow across the attic floor instead.

Venting

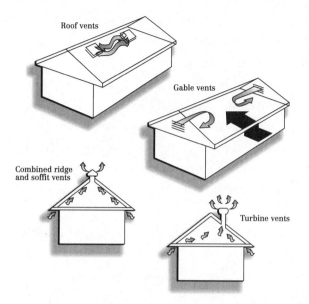

Roof vents

Gable vents

Combined ridge
and soffit vents

Turbine vents

Some home builders line the roof with roof vents—devices that cover holes cut in the roof near the peak—but the drawback to these is that the pattern of air circulation is negligible and limited to the space immediately surrounding the vent. Again, the majority of the roof sheathing goes unvented.

In the Midwest it is very common to see turbine vents, which are roof vents with a turbine wheel mounted on top. The turbine vent too offers limited air movement at all wind speeds, and it must be covered to prevent weather infiltration. Plus, such vents are highly unattractive and make your house look sort of like a diner.

In the 1970s, manufacturers discovered that a ventilation system of continuous soffit vents combined with a long vent all along the ridge (the high peak of the roof) accomplished exactly what the doctor ordered: Regardless of the wind direction, the air enters the roof at the soffit, moves up along the roof sheathing, and exhausts out the ridge.

Why should this be? Physics again. As the air strikes the house and jumps up over the ridge, the pressure above the ridge vent is lowered, and since air always moves from a higher pressure to a lower one, the air is literally pumped or sucked out of the attic. This is called the Bernoulli effect, after a Swiss mathematician who thought and wrote in the early 1700s.

Even if there is no wind, a ridge system utilizes the thermal effect to maintain air circulation across the underside of the roof sheathing. It rises and exhausts out of the ridge.

A ridge vent system brings ventilation air across the roof sheathing, where it can be extremely effective in minimizing the radiation of summer's heat to the floor of the attic and in maximizing the venting of winter's moisture through the ridge. Also, this cooling of the roof sheathing (combined with proper insulation and the sealing of air holes) goes a long way toward preventing ice dams.

To help clarify all of this, let me describe a video I watched while writing this chapter. It was produced to introduce people to the beauty of ridge vents, and it begins with the history of attic ventilation. In one section, a smoke machine was put in the attic and a number of different types of vents were put into place on the roof to see how effectively they cleared the smoke.

A few roof vents came first, and most of the smoke stayed in the attic, except in the areas directly underneath the vents. A turbine vent replaced the roof vents, and it was still impossible to see through the dense smoke inside the attic—and was it ugly!

Then the contractor replaced all this venting with a combination ridge vent and continuous soffit vents under the eaves. While I don't know if you actually could have held a tea party in the attic, there was a huge difference in the density of smoke. There seemed to be a very effective clearing.

You should understand that your warranty on the shingles of

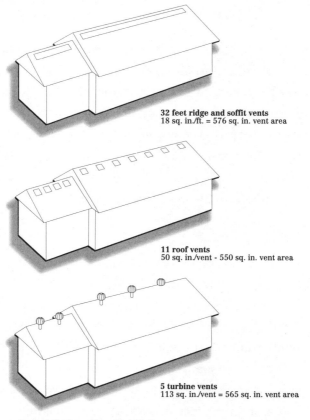

32 feet ridge and soffit vents
18 sq. in./ft. = 576 sq. in. vent area

11 roof vents
50 sq. in./vent - 550 sq. in. vent area

5 turbine vents
113 sq. in./vent = 565 sq. in. vent area

Source: Air Vent, Inc., a division of CertainTeed

your home depends upon proper ventilation going on underneath them. Shingle manufacturers generally require as much as 1 square foot of total net free ventilation area to 300 square feet of attic floor area. Air Vent Inc. of Peoria Heights, Illinois, a manufacturer of external baffle ridge vents,* provided a comparison sketch of houses and the amount of vents they would have to use to comply with the shingle warranty.

So, whether or not you warm to or understand physics, when

---

*The associate editors of *The Journal of Light Construction,* Sal Alfano and Clayton DeKorne, are of the opinion that external baffle ridge vents are preferable because they prevent fine wind blown snow from entering the vent and wetting the attic insulation. Also several ridge vent performance tests show that external baffles enhance the Bernoulli effect and better exhaust air from the attic.

it comes time to replace your roof, or if you're having any of the loathsome roof failure problems I've outlined above, have a ridge vent and continuous soffit vent system installed. It will accomplish maximum ventilation and ensure the health of a major section of your house. (In this case, you would close off your gable vents if they were present.) Do *not* attempt to solve problems with power vents. These are merely Band-Aids. Have good ridge and soffit vents installed and you'll have the best venting possible.

Venting a Flat Roof

I grew up in a flat-roofed modern house, and I started wondering how you ventilate them. After all, there is no peak or ridge. I did a little research and read some literature provided by the American Society of Home Inspectors. Apparently flat roofs are dicey when it comes to ventilation. Sometimes it's difficult to properly vent the cavity beneath this kind of roof.

Continuous soffit vents could be used if there are overhangs, or louvers placed in the fascia board may be adequate. But since there is little space between the lower ceiling and the underside of the roof structure, the insulation should be at least 1 1/2 inch thinner than the roof cavity. If not, condensation from the house air could be trapped in the insulation, rendering it useless and promoting rot and mildew.

It's especially important in flat roofs to see to it that all seams and leaks are sealed. This reduces the need for ventilation. Homeowners buying or contemplating building houses with flat roofs should consult with an engineer or architect to make sure that the house ceiling is extremely airtight so that warm, moist air can't find its way to the flat roof.

Once the attic ventilation is squared away, we need to look at the ventilation in the house proper.

Why Are We Suddenly Hearing So Much About Ventilation?

Houses used to be built without insulation, and they were built so loosely that the wind whistled right through them. It may have been cold and drafty inside, but there was always plenty of natural ventilation. The air found its way out of the house—**exfiltration**—and the air found its way in through cracks and openings around doors and windows and electrical sockets, etc.—**infiltration.** Moisture was removed, and roofs got so hot that snow melt was fast and profuse and there was much less ice damming. Also, there were many changes of air, and cooking odors and pollutants never concentrated and built up inside the house.

But, for a whole host of reasons, builders began to build (and consumers began to demand) tighter, more energy-efficient houses. Certainly a major impetus dates back to October 1973, when the Organization of Arab Petroleum Exporting Countries (OAPEC) announced a cutback in oil exports to North America in retaliation for America's backing of Israel during the Arab-Israeli war.

Gas was rationed, people stopped traveling, and for months the American public lined up anxiously every Sunday night at gas stations trying to get gasoline for the work week. It was a giant wake-up call for people who lived in a land of seemingly inexhaustible natural resources and the buying power to sustain their inventories.

But the OAPEC crisis was not the only shakeup. There was a sudden huge increase in the price of oil from Venezuela—400 percent in one year—with an accompanying 200 percent increase in the cost of extracting domestic oil. So from February 1973 to August 1974, the retail price of fuel oil shot up 60 percent.

A national energy policy began to form, and its clarion call was conservation. This meant promoting smaller, more fuel-efficient cars, lowering the highway's speed limit to 55, and giving tax credits to homeowners who added insulation to their homes. People began to insulate with a vengeance.

OAPEC provoked great changes in the way we build, but there were many incremental changes subsequent to that. In the early 1980s, a revolution in the design and manufacture of windows paved the way for very tight houses.

Up until then, double-glazed aluminum- or wooden-framed windows were responsible for some 35 percent of a home's total heat loss. In 1982, AFG of California introduced **low-E windows** (low-E means low-emissivity). These windows were coated with an invisible layer of metallic oxides that bounce the heat right back into a room instead of conducting it outside. A year later, window manufacturers built on this success story by figuring out a way to make low-E double-glazed windows even more energy-efficient. By filling the airspace in the windows with argon, a heavier-than-air gas, they slowed down the movement of heat to the outdoors even more.

I spoke to Mark LaLiberte, one of the owners of Shelter Supply, a company that has provided products for over 15,000 energy-efficient homes out of its headquarters in Minneapolis, Minnesota, about the changes in the building of homes and the advent of the better-insulated house. He told me that once windows stopped being such a great source of heat loss, low-energy builders turned their attention to the walls and envelope of the house.

"Since about 40 percent of the energy requirement is needed to replace heat sucked out by air leakage through the wall," he said, "it didn't take long for us to figure out that the best way to reduce air leakage was to line the inside of the house with a continuous layer of polyethylene. Then we began to frame a bit differently so that every corner of the house could be insulated. Next we protected the insulation and outer wall cavities with building wrap like Tyvek. This functions like Gortex—it lets the moisture out, but doesn't let the wind in. We tape and seal and caulk every hole.

"At the same time," he added, "door and window manufacturers began to install better gaskets around the doors and windows to reduce drafts and leaks, furnaces became more efficient, and in the late 1980s and early 1990s—for comfort, durability, and energy efficiency—our building became tighter and tighter."

Mark LaLiberte's wife, Cathy, remembers waking up in her parents' Victorian farmhouse and seeing her breath in the air on a winter morning. Once people experienced the luxurious comforts of a well-insulated, tight, low-E-glassed house, however, they would accept nothing less.

"But there was a compromise," said Mark. "We reduced the ventilation rate. Respiratory illnesses like asthma have increased significantly in children and adults, the indoor air quality is becoming worse and most likely unhealthy, and combustion appliances can backdraft into the living space because of negative pressures created in a tight house. To the parameters of energy efficiency, comfort, and durability must be added two more: safety and health."

Managed Ventilation for People

As Mark LaLiberte says, ventilation has become necessary for indoor air quality as houses have become tighter and more energy-efficient. These structures no longer have sufficient natural infiltration and exfiltration to assure enough air change for a healthful indoor atmosphere. (The idea that people need a steady supply of fresh air is not new. In 1865, Florence Nightingale noticed that patients recovered faster when a good supply of fresh air was provided.)

Usually the first indication that there's poor indoor air quality, most noticeable in winter, is high interior relative humidity. Too much humidity breeds mold, mildew, bacteria, fungus, dust mites, and the resulting respiration problems.

Also, as Linda Mason Hunter writes in *The Healthy Home:* "As many as 20–150 hazardous chemicals in concentrations 10–40 times those outdoors can be found in the typical American home. The EPA has called indoor air quality 'the most significant environmental issue we have to face now and into the next decade.' "

The two rooms that all houses have to ventilate are the bathroom and the kitchen. Think about the condition of your bathroom after someone takes a hot shower or bath. The humidity rivals that of a tropical rain forest. Not only does it feel uncomfortable to spend any time within this fog, but did you ever wonder where all that moisture goes in the cold months when a window is not cracked to usher it outside? It slyly finds its way through cracks and crevices in the walls, travels up through the ceiling fixtures into the attic ventilation, and gives a humid hug to all the wood framing and roof decking. On its odyssey, it causes great damage. The wood framing over the bathroom can deteriorate and the gypsum wallboard can be ruined. Other maintenance problems will develop: Wallpaper and paint will peel, grout will discolor, rust and mildew will abound, and the room will get harder to clean as the condensing moisture attracts dirt. Definitely not good.

An exhaust fan staves off all this devastation, because an efficient fan can expel the moisture ten times faster than if you let it wind its way through your home. (The fan must be ducted out of the home through the roof—not into the attic.) There are other bonuses to a good exhaust fan: You'll be able to apply makeup or shave after a shower, the room will smell better, and it will be a healthier place to be, because the fan will whisk away aerosol vapors from toiletries and cleaning supplies.

The Home Ventilating Institute (HVI) in Arlington Heights, Illinois, recommends that the fan have the capacity to change bathroom air eight times per hour.

To determine the cubic feet per minute (cfm) rating for a fan needed to ventilate your bathroom, multiply the length and width of the bathroom by 1.1 (assuming an 8-foot ceiling). For a 6-by-8-foot bathroom, the calculation would be as follows: $6 \times 8 \times 1.1 = 52.8$ cfm. Rounding off, the rating for the fan needed to properly ventilate this bathroom would be 53 cfm.

The first six months we lived in our house, I refused to use the exhaust fan because it was noisy and it bothered me too much. Of course, there was soon mildew sprouting and blooming on the ceiling.

The noise of a fan is rated by **sones,** and today's fans have much lower sone ratings. One sone has been described as the sound of one quiet refrigerator humming away in a quiet kitchen. Two sones is double that loudness, and so on. My fan must have had a 4-to-5-sone rating, because it was literally jarring.

I replaced it with a Preventilator I saw favorably reviewed in *Family Handyman* magazine. It was developed by Tamarack Technologies in West Wareham, Massachusetts, and it mounts on an outside wall. Because the fan is mounted outside there's much less noise, and it clears that bathroom of moisture in an almost miraculous way. It's 75 cfm at .25 static pressure. It normally takes an electrician about one hour to install.

Panasonic makes a bathroom fan that is .5 sone, and Pan America makes a .8 sone. (Shelter Supply sells both of these, and if you call 800-762-8399, you can request a copy of its catalog, read about them, and order one.)

Kitchen Fans

The kitchen is the other room in need of serious ventilation. (All that steam rising up from simmering pots, the dishwasher and sink faucet, all those cooking smells . . .) A kitchen range hood can expel heat, smoke, moisture, and odors from cooking, as long as it's ducted to the outside. The location and size of your stove determine the exhaust fan capacity. If the stove is installed against an outside wall, the Home Ventilating Institute (HVI) uses the formula of 40 cfm per foot of range width; if it is installed against an interior wall or an island, the HVI recommends 50 cfm per foot. Thus, a stove that is 3 feet wide needs a capacity of 120 or 150 cfm, depending on its location.

If you do the math, a professional range such as those made by Viking or Wolf might require only 250 cfm, but they're being sold to the consumer with 350–1,000 cfm exhaust fans. Such a huge-capacity fan forces so much air out of the house that a terrific negative pressure is created, and, if you remember the physics, if a cubic foot of air goes out, a cubic foot must come in. So much makeup air is needed that the air can be sucked right down the fireplace flue or other flues in the home, creating a very hazardous backdrafting situation.

Remember that bigger is not always better. Be careful when you size a fan to your beautiful new professional stove. Tell the salesperson that you don't want the turbo fan; you want the smallest fan that will still provide adequate ventilation for your stove. If it's too late, however, and the mother of all fans has already been installed in your beautiful new kitchen, try not to run it when the fireplace is burning, and open up at least two windows anytime you do turn it on.

The best way to ensure that backdrafting can't occur with

combustion appliances—especially in a tight home—is to make sure that the furnace is a newer sealed-combustion model which draws air from *outside* the house—not the furnace room. The water heater should be sealed-combustion also or power-vented. Power-vented, or induced-draft, appliances use a small fan to force combustion gases up and out of the house (see page 74 in Chapter 2, "The Inner Mysteries, Part I").

Mark LaLiberte feels that any house that has been tightened and every superinsulated house can only be safe if the combustion appliances are of the sealed-combustion or power-vented type.

This is what we did. We replaced the water heater with a newer model that was power-vented. It cost about $200 more. The small fan inside always expels the pollutants out in one direction; the stream of air can't reverse and endanger us. Now that I know about the creation of negative pressure and how it's forcing the house to search for makeup air, I crack windows when I run exhaust fans and pay attention to what's going on in the house when we're enjoying a fire in the fireplace. Also, I have my three carbon monoxide detectors to warn me of any potential dangers.

Whole-House Fans

My friend Denise built a home on a lake up in Charlotte, Vermont, and I asked her if she had had any kind of mechanical ventilation built into the house when it was constructed two years ago. She told me that she had some sort of whole-house fan up in the attic.

These fans cool a home during the summer months by helping it to "breathe." A fan is typically mounted in the ceiling, so that it pulls fresh air in through the windows and expels stale air out through the attic vents. These vents should be large, however—either gable vents or continuous soffit and ridge vents—so that the hot air has a chance to escape the house. The cooling breeze that is created can lower skin temperature by 2 to 8 degrees. A whole-house fan can save you money if you run it at night to flush the house with cooler evening air and reserve the air-conditioning for the hottest periods of the day.

Whole-house fans cost between $100 and $500 and are fairly easy to install.

How powerful a fan do you need? The HVI recommends that you multiply your home's square footage—excluding garage, basement, and attic—by three. So, a 2,000-square-foot house would need a fan rated at 6,000 cfm. If you live in a warmer or more humid climate, the total square footage should be multiplied by four.

This is not the kind of ventilation system you want if you have a tight, energy-efficient house, because the fan can create a negative-pressure situation that can cause the combustion appliances to backdraft. A tight house requires a balanced system that includes both exhaust and intake of air: a central ventilation system.

Central Ventilation Systems

Open windows is one way to satisfy the need for fresh air, but the problem with this technique is that we can't open them consistently. In the South, people button up the house for the cooling season; and in the North, people seal up the house for the heating season. Also, as we've become more and more concerned about home security, windows are firmly locked and we lose any source of ventilation, especially for eight hours at night, even if the climate outside is temperate.

So because natural ventilation is not a reliable way to provide fresh air to people living in a modern house in a society with enormous safety concerns, a mechanical ventilation system is becoming the reliable way to vent stale, moist air out of the house and supply fresh air to the living and sleeping areas—with no compromise in the arena of safety.

There are two major kinds of managed ventilation systems that can be installed in new, tightly insulated homes, or retrofitted into some existing homes when an owner wishes for better ventilation: **central exhaust** systems, and **heat-recovery ventilators (HRVs).**

An exhaust-only system is managed ventilation that uses fans to expel or exhaust the stale air, but does not use supply fans to bring air into the house. Instead, passive inlets are placed in bedrooms and living areas and the negative pressure caused by the air pushed out forces air back inside these one-way intake ports. American Aldes and Fantech—both in Sarasota, Florida—manufacture good-quality exhaust-only systems.

The inlet ports of an exhaust-only system must be placed properly, and the airflow pattern must be studied to ensure this makeup air circulates through the house. For instance, if there's an inlet port in the wall in a bedroom and you close the door and that door is long and close to the ground and there's a thick shag carpet butting up against it, the makeup air in that room is cut off from the house. In this case, louvers should be cut into the door to ensure the circulation of the air or the door should be cut down so there's approximately 1/2 inch of space underneath it for the air to travel through.

These systems are not right for a house in a cold climate or one with a radon problem: Cold air is coming in through those intake ports in the walls, and if radon is a problem, the negative pressure caused by the exhaust fans would create that vacuum effect in the basement and suck more radon into the house. If there is a potential for this or for the backdrafting of combustion appliances, a better option—especially if you live in a cold climate—would be the newest type of managed ventilation system, a **heat-recovery ventilator,** known as an **HRV.**

A heat-recovery ventilator is a centralized system designed to expel stale, moist air out of a house and pull fresh air in at the same rate, while transferring the heat or cool of the exhausting air to the fresh-air stream with no contamination. A homeowner gets fresh air that arrives preheated, even humidified or dehumidified. Many systems include filtration of this fresh air to further enhance comfort and consistent air quality.

It works like this. Inside an HRV, one fan blows stale air outside while another pulls outside air in. The two fans blow the air through a central heat-exchange core that wrests the heat from one airstream and transfers it to the other.

How does all this heat-transferring magic take place? Well, different manufacturers have come up with different technologies to accomplish this transfer. Several of the systems recover energy through a core (a flat plate) or a wheel. A flat-plate system uses polypropylene or aluminum sheets arranged to separate the airstreams yet transfer the energy. Both materials are efficient and are best suited for cold climates. In hot climates, a wheel system using a desiccant-coated material can actually attract humidity from the outside air and expel it to the exhausting, polluting air while ventilating continuously. This provides year-round ventilation that is reliable, efficient, and controllable.

What do HRVs cost? The unit models range from about $500 to $1,000, and then you have to figure ductwork, accessory material, and the labor of installation. In a house presently under construction, the installation of an HRV should run between $1200 and $2,500 installed. They can be installed in an existing house by using an existing forced-air furnace or by routing the ductwork through closets or chaseways behind walls.

How to Judge the Indoor Air Quality of Your Home

For those of us without HRV or ERV technology, a question remains: How do we know if we have an indoor air quality problem? David MacLellon of Tamarack Industries supplied a simple answer: He suggested you go outside for a walk for five or ten minutes and as you reenter your house—at the door—close your eyes and breathe in. What do you smell? If you smell yesterday's dinner or the furniture polish you slapped on two days ago, you don't have proper air exchange. This "nose knows" technology is surprisingly accurate as far as air exchange goes, but as Charles Schwartz, president of Environmental Assessments and Solutions in Hartsdale, New York, and one of the country's leading authorities on indoor environmental quality, told me, "there could be odorless or even sweet-smelling poisons and contaminants such as carbon monoxide, carbon dioxide, nitrogen oxide, formaldehyde, residual pesticides, volatile organic compounds, or microbial contamination—bacteria and fungi—polluting your living space." Persistent health problems may prompt you to have an indoor air-quality audit to try to nail down the culprit or culprits contributing to a problem inside your home.

I asked Charles about such audits and how to locate the people qualified to conduct them. He told me that the Yellow Pages are often a good place to start. "Look under 'Environmental and Ecological Services,' " he instructed. "But once you jot down the names and numbers, you have a lot of checking ahead of you. You want to ascertain the academic background of the people conducting the audit and make sure that the investigator's experience is relative to your particular concern. You also want a list of references. An expert with experience should be able to give you the names and phone numbers of schools, hospitals, and homeowners for whom he or she has worked. Finally, ask about the auditor's certifications and make sure they are also relevant to your suspected problem."

There is a virtual alphabet soup of these certifications, Charles Schwartz said. But some respected ones are CIH (Certified Industrial Hygienist), COHST (Certified Occupational Health Safety Technician), CSP (Certified Safety Professional), CEA (Certified Environmental Auditor), CEI (Certified Environmental Inspector), and CES (Certified Environmental Specialist).

Charles also told me to steer you toward an organization in Scottsdale, Arizona, called the Environmental Assessment Association (602-483-8100). This international organization has a membership of over 5,000 professional indoor air quality inspectors and specialists, and its office can give you the names and numbers of qualified people in your area of the country.

I should warn you that none of this is cheap. An environmental audit requires a detailed history, a lot of sleuth work, often quite a bit of testing with all different kinds of state-of-the-art instruments, and extensive lab work. Then, recommendations for lowering or eradicating levels of contamination—source removal, surface disinfectant, air filtration and air cleaning—as well as for beefing up the ventilation rate will be made. A complete home audit could range from $400 to $2,000 and even beyond. But if you are suffering from chemical sensitivities, have a family member suffering from asthma, or simply can't work at home without feeling logy by midafternoon, it is money well spent.

In the 1980s, we heard a lot about "sick building syndrome," and technologies and industries arose to diagnose and cure it. Today, a lot of this knowledge is being directed to the buildings in which we spend more than eight hours a day—our homes. While we certainly want to encourage tight construction for durability, efficiency, and comfort, we need to remember that ventilation is not a luxury, it's a vital necessity.

11. The Age of Innocence: Childproofing Inside and Out

Sometime last year, I was on the phone complaining to my friend Barbara Sand about how tired I was from running after Jordy, my then twenty-month-old toddler. She chuckled sympathetically and told me of an experiment she'd read about. Apparently, a man evaluated to be at an Olympic level of physical fitness set out to mimic the activities of a two-year-old, step for step, action for action. Within a short period of time, the toddler was just gaining steam, and the man in "peak" condition was prostrate on the couch.

No adult, not even Arnold Schwarzenegger, could keep up with the activity level of the under-three set. A child's insatiable curiosity, coupled with impulsive motility, often uncertain coordination, and a complete innocence about danger, makes him or her an invitation to disaster. The parts of the brain meant to "remember" things are pretty unconnected at this age. So the question becomes: If we can't be on top of them every minute, and they can't remember that those stairs could be dangerous, how do we keep them safe?

Our parents had the answer. They stuck us in playpens and we observed the world from a mesh-patterned remove. But parenting styles have changed and children crawl, toddle around, and race freely through our homes, observing the world up close and in a completely hands-on fashion. Only extensive childproofing and diligent supervision stand between them and the emergency room.

When my first son was five months old, I took every safety course I could find, including CPR, and childproofed our apartment with the fervor that only a first-time mother can muster. Naturally, my greatest nightmare was those ninth-floor windows. Safety bars were installed posthaste and checked more times than I care to think about.

It wasn't hard to remember how to childproof that small space for baby number two. But when Jordy was thirteen months old, we moved. Frankly, I was relieved when we bought a one-story house. No more neighbors' unprotected windows to worry about. We were entering a more benign environment.

Hardly. Now there were hazards inside *and* outside to worry about. Who knew that those beautiful azaleas and rhododendrons festooning the house were poisonous if ingested? Who understood the danger of untempered glass in the sidelights by the front door? (Who knew what sidelights *were*?)

I attempted to adapt my apartment knowledge of childproofing to this house: I covered every electrical socket, locked up all cleaning supplies and poisons, opened windows only from the top, covered cocktail tables with bumpers, and installed a gate (the wrong-style gate) at the top of the staircase. I cruised through large toy stores and made several expeditions to hardware stores for safety items, but I felt that the selection was not first-rate. My contractor couldn't install the latches I bought for the kitchen cabinets, and I ended up improvising with rubber bands or moving everything to high (and thus unreachable for me) shelves. (I finally get a decent amount of cabinets, and I can't even use them.) I always worried that my actions were ad hoc and that I might be missing something.

Somehow we survived, and here I am, gathering information from experts to pass on to you. In order to avoid the Leviticus-like lists of childproofing—all the "shalls" and "shall nots"—I wanted to walk you through a real house—this house—room by room, in the company of a professional child proofer.

"When They Start to Crawl It's Time to Call"

Frank Wright, president of Child Proofers, Inc., in Mamaroneck, New York, whose slogan you just read, has babyproofed close to a thousand homes in the metropolitan area. He was just finishing a job in the town next to us, and he agreed to come over and show me the childproofing ropes. Frank has been the subject of a spate of articles in the *New York Times, Smart Money, American Baby,* and *Child,* so I was a little nervous about the job we'd done here. On a very hot August afternoon, we began the interview and tour of this house.

I first asked Frank when a parent should rev up into the babyproofing mode, and he said: "You want to have all of this in place before the baby starts to crawl, so at about six months, you need to focus attention in this area. Do it once and thoroughly, taking all stages of development into consideration, and then you'll never have to guess what the child will do next and possibly miss out on a protection factor. Plus, you'll be used to handling the products and equipment and everything will seem second nature to you."

Because I am now about to mention a lot of very specific items, I'd like to steer you toward a wonderful catalog called *The Catalog for Safe Beginnings.* (In the industry this one is known as *the* kids safety catalog.) It has the largest selection of child safety products, it's organized room by room, and it comes complete with a lot of educational information about safety in the home and for children.

The Catalog for Safe Beginnings has "value added." It's produced in Billerica, Massachusetts, by Susan and Jeff Baril, who are both childproofers as well as parents of young children. These experts can talk you through ordering quandaries or any subsequent installation difficulties. Their prices were lower than those in one other catalog I looked at and competitive with those in another. It will not just show up at your house one day, however; it's available only by request. Call 800-598-8911.

I also don't want you to get confused trying to keep track of everything you're going to need to order. For the time being, just follow me and make mental notes about the potential injury areas. Near the end of this childproofing chapter is a work sheet that lists all the items and lets you go around the house and tally the necessary safety items, specific to your house and your child. As Frank Wright says: "There are the need-to-have and the nice-to-have categories." So, first total the absolutely essential safety items, and then determine how much—if any—budget is left.

Back to Frank and me, in the kitchen. Frank told me that he first asks parents what scares them most in the house, so he can address that right away. Often it's a staircase, a door that goes down to the basement, or a raised hearth. After that, and since there is a direct relationship between where you spend your time and where accidents take place, he starts in the kitchen. Since we were already standing just there, quaffing iced tea, he began to look around with a sharpened gaze.

"Counter level down is a child's universe," he told me as he launched into a discussion of passive latches. "Passive" means that the latches lock automatically, each time you close the drawer or cabinet—you don't have to remember to lock them. I told him how my contractor couldn't install the latches I'd bought, and when he looked at them, he figured out why. They weren't the right kind. Frank is a great believer in the latches manufactured by Mericon in Livonia, Michigan. Their products are sometimes marketed under the Fisher-Price logo. (He also likes the latches manufactured by Gerber Safety Products.)

Just about any latch will work on standard framed cabinets, but European-style cabinetry, where you can't see the frame, may require a little more investigation. Describe the kind of cabinetry you have to your salesperson. Each latch costs about $1.

Next Frank showed me something called a Tot-Lock. This item is for cabinets you don't *ever* want a child to get into, such as gun or liquor cabinets or those containing poisons or cleaning supplies. (This lock is well suited for European-style cabinets.) A Tot-Lock mounts inside the cabinet, and when the drawer or door is closed, it automatically locks. To release the lock, you need to place a special magnet key on the face of the cabinet. It also has a disengagement feature which allows it to be temporarily unlocked to allow normal use of the cabinet. (Tot-Locks are good items for grandparents' homes. They can employ the childproofing device only when grandchildren are scheduled to be around). If you install them yourself, they're about $5 each. Frank told me that this is the lock he would have installed under my sink where all the chemical cleansers and poisons sit.

Cabinets with double doors or with side-by-side pulls can be secured with a Side-by-Side cabinet lock that loops around the pulls or door handles. These are active locks and must be placed back on the cabinet each time. They cost about $2.50 each and require no installation.

While we were talking of lower cabinets, Frank spoke about that cabinet we all reserve for our children to play in while we're cooking in the kitchen. Typically we leave some pots and pans and kids and let them be a one-man/one-woman band. "That's fine," said Frank, "but make sure it's a cabinet and not a drawer that children can pull down on their heads or use as a step-up to the counter. Also, make it as far away from the cooking area as possible, and make it a plastic or Tupperware cabinet, not a pots and pans one. If they perceive a pot as a toy and see one on the stove, they could go after it and place themselves in grave danger."

Before we left the latch department, he pointed out a lower cabinet where I store some pot holders, a tea cozy, and my aluminum foil and plastic wraps. As we both stared at the serrated edge of the foil and plastic packaging, I realized how dangerous these could be to a crawling baby or child, and I knew immediately that either they should be locked in that cabinet or stored high out of reach.

Now to the stove. I told Frank I always turn pot handles to the back and try to cook on the back burner as much as possible. I never boil water for corn or pasta on any burner except the back ones. He discussed a product called Shield-a-Burn, which is a plastic shield that mounts on the top of the stove with metal clips and a special adhesive and helps prevent children from reaching hot burners, pot and pan handles, and dangerous utensils placed on the stove. I had had this in New York, and I can't say why I never put one in place in Connecticut. Jordy is three now and understands never to go near the stove, but if he were younger, I would definitely go for one. It costs about $30. Frank also said it's a good idea to remove the knobs of the burners, making it difficult for a youngster to turn on the gas (you'll still be able to maneuver the controls, however). And never store snack items above the stove or a little one having a sugar attack could attempt to reach the cabinet by climbing up and into dangerous territory.

The next big appliance we looked at was the dishwasher. Frank told me to keep it latched shut at all times when a child is around: an open door is an invitation for a flying fall. Also, he reminded me to store cutlery in the cutlery tray with the tines and blades facing down. I told him that the only time I ever had to call Poison Control was over the detergent in the soap tray. I had loaded the machine but not closed it up, and I turned around to see beads of it in Jordy's mouth. One thing I definitely didn't know when we moved here was that dishwasher detergent is highly caustic. (This was probably because I didn't have a dishwasher when Alex was a toddler, so I never picked up this bit of information.)

Anyway, because he had ingested only a tiny amount, Poison Control told me to wash it out of Jordy's mouth and have him drink milk. Frank told me to pour the detergent only at the last minute—just before I run the load.

As we began to shift our focus to the dining room and living room, Frank cautioned me about four more things: Make sure the garbage can locks and a baby or curious child can't get into it. Try not to use tablecloths when your child is in the pulling-himself-or-herself-up stage. If a child grabs onto the cloth, heavy items can be pulled down on his or her head. If you must use a tablecloth, tape the edges under the table with duct tape. Sharp corners on kitchen counters can be covered with Safety-Tips (Miricon, four for $1.50). Finally, make sure there are ground-fault circuit interrupters (GFIs) near the kitchen sink so water and electricity can't link up (see page 91) and there is no danger of electrocution.

Once we got onto the electrical system of a house, we spent the next fifteen minutes talking about the outlets and electrical wires. A crawling baby is generally within reach of places where electricity can cause shocks or burns and long wires pose a choking hazard. Outlet covers are a part of the great trio of childproofing (the other two being latches and gates).

Frank advised me to take a tally of all the outlets and divide them into categories: How many outlets do I use frequently? How many outlets do I use infrequently? And how many outlets are permanently in use?

For the frequently used outlets—say the ones I plug the vacuum into a couple of times a week—as well as those in easy view of a baby or toddler, he recommends a very good-looking Sliding Safety Plate. This replaces the existing outlet plate and comes in a white or ivory color. You insert a plug and slide it to the right. When you remove the plug, a locking mechanism snaps shut to cover the outlet. So you can never forget to replace a cap to the outlet, and there are no small parts that could break and end up in a baby's mouth. However, this type of outlet cover costs about $3, so you probably won't be using them on all eighty or so of your outlets. Opt for this type of outlet cover in areas where your baby spends a lot of time.

I had the cheap variety of plastic covers, but Frank has some concerns about these. "You tend to forget to replace them, they end up in a pocket or something, and they can stretch with constant use, and even break, and then they may pose a choking hazard, he says." He pointed me toward a product called Shock-Loks, manufactured by Mericon. Shock-Loks are attached to a strap which screws into an outlet plate. This feature serves as a reminder to reinsert the cap into the outlet after use, and helps guard against children chewing on misplaced caps. Ten of them cost about $6.

For outlets that have appliances plugged into them on a permanent basis, there is a cover that completely encloses the outlets and plugs and allows cords to thread through the bottom opening. These run about $3 each.

I was always pretty good about outlet covers, but I never was able to master the problem of cords and wires coiling all over the place. I finally improvised and used duct tape to gain some control over this sprawling mess of wire and keep them from tripping Jordy and his playdates, but they were still too much in evidence. Frank went out to the car and brought in a product called Cord-A-Way, which stores up to 8 feet of electrical cord by winding it up around an interior reel. He also showed me a neat item to replace the long spring-coiled cord on my wall telephone in the kitchen. He simply replaced it with the Cord Minder, a retractable yo-yo-like cord. Now Jordy can't pull the receiver down on his head from below or become entangled in the spring-coiled cord. The added benefit is that it's neater-looking and we're not always tripping over that wire ourselves. It costs $15.

Frank then introduced me to a Switch Blocker, a device that covers dangerous switches and locks them in an off position. This would be great for a garbage disposal switch or any other switch that a child should not fool around with. They cost about $1.50 each.

The objects in my living room and family room that concerned Frank were the tall, standing halogen lamps. "Anything taller than it is wide can be grasped by the newly cruising and toddling child for stability, and will fall over on the child." He advised me to put these lamps behind sofas and block them off.

The other "accident-waiting-to-happen" area is the raised hearth of the fireplace. Frank recommends a custom-made bumper that he orders from a company in Lilburn, Georgia, called Baby Bumpers. Its Hearth Guard has a wooden frame, and it's padded all the way around. It can fit odd angles and comes in half a dozen colors of Naugahyde. It's not a cheap item, however; it costs anywhere from $100 to $160, depending on the size and angles of your hearth. But, as Frank reminded me, "It's cheaper than a trip to the emergency room and it doesn't leave any permanent scars. Plus, you'll use it for five or six years at least." (Call Baby Bumpers at 1-770-717-0088, give your dimensions, and you'll get a price.)

If you have a very standard hearth, you could buy a ready-made adjustable hearth guard for as little as $65. Most catalogs, including *The Catalog for Safe Beginnings,* list them.

You need to put bumpers around cocktail tables and end tables also. I have a Toddler Shield that works like a dream. It's easy to stretch around the marble cocktail table and just as easy to take off when the adults sit down for hors d'oeuvres.

The High Toll of Untempered Glass

Now I admitted my gravest concern. I didn't know what untempered glass was until Jordy cracked a sidelight with his head. (These are the decorative glass panels of glass so commonly found next to entry doorways.) He wasn't hurt, but there was indeed a note of hysteria in my voice when I ordered replacements of tempered glass from the glass company.

I found out, almost the hard way, that when untempered glass breaks it separates into large, knifelike projectiles that your child can fall onto. This can be life-threatening. Tempered glass, however, is baked in an oven and cooled quickly, and its tensile strength increases fourfold. When it breaks, it shatters into tiny crystalline pieces.

In the two weeks it took to get the replacements, the man who grew up in this house came over to show his new girlfriend his "ancestral home," and we talked about that sidelight. He showed me scars where he'd had stitches after slamming into that untempered glass. He's lucky he's alive.

Older children and adults as well are endangered by old doors with low-placed untempered glass. Though it's illegal in Connecticut now, we had a back door and a basement door with untempered glass. I replaced both of them.

How will you know if there's untempered glass posing a danger in your home? Tempered glass usually has a small logo embedded in a corner. If you can't see this, take a glass cutter and try to make a mark in the corner of the glass you're investigating. If it's very difficult to scratch, it's probably tempered. But if the glass is in a door that appears to have been installed when the house was built in 1950, or you have a breakfront or see-through china cabinet that is an antique, you can bet the glass is not tempered and you should call a glass company and have it replaced. The glass of a stereo cabinet or a cocktail table should be tempered also. Look in the Yellow Pages under "Glass" to find a company to do this for you.

Frank told me that he would have covered that sidelight with a Plexiglas shield—on both sides—and the children would have been protected. He also covers French doors with Plexiglas panels. It is much cheaper than replacing all the panes with tempered glass.

Childproofing the Bathroom

The bathroom is a fascinating area to a baby: the swirling water of a flushing toilet, all those pretty (but unfortunately harmful) bottles of mouthwash, perfume, cologne, aftershave, nail polish, nail polish remover, shampoos and cosmetics, air fresheners, pot pourri . . . This is where most medicines are stored and where electricity and water can easily link up at the sink, and where scalding water can pour from the hot-water spouts. The bathroom needs careful childproofing.

I had already removed all cleansers and medications to a high shelf in a linen closet outside the bathroom, and my cosmetics are stored on high Lucite shelves in the bathroom. I had syrup of ipecac in the linen closet also, in the event a doctor instructed me to use it. I had dumped the pot pourri in the garbage as soon as I learned that it could be harmful to children (last week), so once Frank noted the ground-fault circuit interrupter (GFI) at the sink, we turned our attention to the toilet.

The best piece of equipment is called a Lid-Lock (another Mericon specialty). It not only protects your child from falling in, but protects your plumbing when he or she decides to play the eternal game of "How much toilet paper can be stuffed in this toilet?" or decides to experiment and see how long it will take Mommy's pretty jewels to "go bye-bye." A Lid-Lock on each toilet is a necessity. They cost about $10 each.

In Chapter 2 of this book, "The Inner Mysteries, Part I," I discuss the water heater and talk about changing the temperature setting of the hot water. If you have young children in the house, turn the water temperature down to 120 degrees, or to the lowest setting, so that scalds are avoided. When you give your baby or young child a bath, you want the temperature of the water to be about 98 degrees F. *The Catalogue for Safe Beginnings* features a Bath Pal Thermometer in the shape of a duck or a boat for $3.99, but, to me, this item falls into the "nice to have, don't need to have" category. Just feel the water and remember that "just warm is warm enough."

I would, however, purchase a bath spout cover that fits over the tub spout and prevents hard knocks on heads and fannies. One of these in the shape of a bear costs around $10.

Frank reminded me to remove from sight or reach all hair dryers, electric razors, electric toothbrushes, electric curlers, curling irons, etc., and to watch what I threw away in the wastebasket. He also cautioned me not to let cakes of soap get too small. They smell nice and a young child may think they might taste good. They represent a very real choking hazard.

And since every child locks himself or herself into the bathroom at least once, forcing us all to remove bathroom privacy locks as a last resort, you should know about the Gerber Door Knob covers which prevent a child from locking the door from inside. They cost about $4 for two covers.

Bedrooms

Frank did not like seeing the talcum powder on the changing table in Jordy's room, and suggested that I install a shelf above the changing table and put the canister and any other items like it up and out of reach.

He did, however, approve of the way I tied up the cords of the Levolor blinds, in the nursery and throughout the house. He said that a pinch clothespin would do the trick also. But I tend to worry about the long, dangling blind cords, and I have my eye on these Break-Thru Window Blind Cord Tassels that cause the cords to snap apart instantly when pressure is applied so that kids can't become entangled in them. They're $5 each and they're in the "nice-to-have" category, but I do spend an awful lot of time checking those blind cords, and these devices would free up my mind to obsess about something else.

Frank also gave me points for remembering to have my contractor nail the bookcase to the wall so it couldn't fall on top of Jordy (this happened to my neighbor's child, so it was a priority when we moved in). He did, however, want to see a smoke detector in the nursery. (There was one right outside in the hallway, but Frank told me that every bedroom should have one inside the room. See the discussion about this later in Chapter 12, "The Great Escape.")

But it was in the master bedroom that Frank pointed out a seemingly innocuous, totally unthought-of item that represents a real choking hazard for a crawling baby or young child: the doorstop with the little rubber tip on the end.

Of all the things I'd done wrong or omitted, this one really scared me, because I'd never heard anyone mention it before. You spend so much time checking under furniture for loose and dangerous coins, and you make such a big deal about so many other things, and all the while, sitting quietly behind the door, is a threat you didn't know existed.

Frank showed me the one-piece doorstop he recommends. It is simple and good-looking and costs $4.95. It is made by—who else?—Mericon; my house now sports several of them.

Windows

Frank and I sat down in the family room to have our long discussion about windows. I told him a story my friend Sydney had told me. Her sister was in the living room one day when she saw her four-year-old son shoot past the downstairs window. Only, he wasn't streaking by on terra-firma, he was dropping vertically, from above.

Apparently the little boy had been bouncing on his bed and shot right through the screen and down. Fortunately he fell into the bushes and was unharmed.

"Screens were made for bugs, not for boys," Frank commented dryly, and we were off and running on the subject of window safety.

The main safety item I had brought with me from the city was a Window Guard. These are the welded steel bars that you see all over New York City because it's required by law, and I thought they'd be a good bet in the one set of windows that have a bit of a drop to the ground beneath them. Typically, we never did get them up, and I simply began to open these windows only from the top.

"You'll get the same amount of ventilation," Frank said, "and you eliminate the risk of your child's falling through the screen.

"If you must open a double-hung window from the bottom," he continued, "install a nail or screw into the sash at the position where the bottom window ends when it is up three or four inches. This will prevent the window from being opened so much that a child can squeeze through it."

Frank went on to show me a new item called a Tot Stopper that he uses for just such windows and sliding glass doors. It's a round plastic suction cup with a square block on it and it's mounted so that kids can't open the window or slip out the door. It costs about $5.

But it was the casement or crank-out windows that were driving me crazy. We had one in the city, on the ninth floor, and although we devised a chain-linked solution, I always got the willies when I thought of that window and a climbing child. My neighbor Laurie was so exercised about the ones in her apartment that she had them soldered shut.

Now I move to the country, and there are all these casement windows. About six of them had drops below that would pose a danger for a very young child. Our solution was to never open them and to remove the cranks. But Frank told me that he would have installed a Plexiglas shield halfway up each window. That way we could have had the ventilation from the top of the window, and Jordy and any rambunctious playmates would have been safe. (Frank, where were you when I needed you?)

If you're thinking about putting serious metal between your child and a window, consider installing a stairway gate on the window frame. This will provide both sufficient protection from a fall and the ability to open a window quickly in an emergency. You always have to think of your egress in the event of a fire or emergency.

Safety Gates and Staircases

We next headed downstairs to the office and laundry room, but we paused at the top of the stairs to discuss safety gates. First Frank told me that there are two kinds of gates to buy: a pressure gate which is *not* for stairways but only to separate two rooms, and a hardware-mounted gate which is suitable for stairways. A stairway should have such a gate at the top of the stairs and one at the bottom.

We had installed a mounted gate, but Frank did not approve of the accordion-style gate we chose. "Do you see these diamonds where your child can get a toehold and climb the gate?" he asked. "Do you see where his fingers could get pinched?"

I asked him what he preferred, and he named the Gerry Wood Slat Gate and told me that *Consumer Reports* deems this one totally satisfactory. It typically costs about $25.

The Catalog for Safe Beginnings sells a Danish gate that is extremely good-looking (available in beachwood, $80, or white, plastic-coated metal, $60). These are admittedly expensive, but an adult can open the gate with one hand, so it's very convenient, especially if you're climbing the stairs with an infant. Plus, this gate will last through three rambunctious children at least. These are also 6 inches higher than other standard gates.

If those stairs you're climbing are spiral or DNA staircases as we refer to them around here, then the entire thing could be childproofed with mesh and Plexiglas, but you're looking at a bill of about $300. Any staircase that has balusters separated by more than 4 inches will need Plexiglas.

Many parents are frightened about going downstairs to a laundry room and having no hands free to latch the gate. They're concerned that a toddler or baby could follow and be injured. They should know about a Safety Door Closer that is spring-loaded and shuts up to a 150-pound door automatically. For $14.95, you get a lot of peace of mind.

Laundry Room, Exercise Room, Workshop, and Garage

Don't even think about letting your child spend time in these rooms. They should be locked from the outside or gated off. Detergents are ingested by children more than any other dangerous household product, and a stationary bicycle beckons little fingers with its spokes and gears. Weights can seriously damage a child, and the garage or workshop is close to impossible to childproof. Though you have to try.

As a precaution, and because children tend to follow you everywhere, keep all antifreeze, pesticides, paints, paint thinners, and any other chemicals and supplies locked up. Use the same cabinet and drawer locks you use in the house, and protect the electrical sockets. Make sure you unplug and store away any power tools, and keep saws, hammers, wire cutters, shears, etc. out of reach.

Store your ladders in a horizontal position so that your child doesn't attempt to climb them, and make sure all ropes are stored high or away. If you store a discarded or "holiday" refrigerator or freezer anywhere in the house, remove its door. An empty appliance can be a death trap for a curious child.

Check the automatic garage door and make sure it's the kind that reverses when it touches any object. Check it by closing it on a heavy cardboard box, and if it reverses, check it often to see that it's working properly. If it doesn't reverse, disconnect it and replace it immediately. Never let your child play with the opener, and make sure the manual switch is high up or protected with a Switch Blocker.

And finally, don't let your child play in a car parked in the driveway. Children have been known to ease the emergency brake and start the car rolling, they can lock themselves in, and there are still lighter knobs in cars that they might "accidentally" pull out.

Deck and Patio

Because most decks are raised above ground level, they must be childproofed just like the second floor of a home. Here again you're going to need installed gates—at the top of the stairs as well as at ground level. If the space between the deck balusters is greater than 4 inches, the space should be covered with cloth netting, coated wire screening, or clear Plexiglas.

You are also going to need to pay attention to the deck surface. Is the wood rough? Get it sanded or you'll be spending all summer with a needle and a match and a screaming child. Check that all nails are firmly pounded in place.

If you have a crawling baby, you might want to place a king-size sheet out on the deck so the baby's knees and hands are protected. If the deck is very slippery and you've got a road runner on your hands, you might consider some outdoor carpet.

Be extremely cautious with grills and grilling utensils and paraphernalia, and remember that charcoal embers stay hot a long time after the hot dogs have been scarfed down (see page 389).

Again, make sure there are ground-fault circuit interrupters in all outdoor electrical receptacles. And if you have sliding glass doors leading out to the deck, consider putting decals on them at the eye level of a child so that he or she won't run into them.

Pool

Each summer we entertain the fantasy of a pool in the backyard. But in my saner, less feverish moments, I remember that a pool takes a lot of effort to keep everyone safe, and an enormous effort to keep a young child from running over and pitching in. The following precautions must be taken to have a kid-safe pool.

Check your local building requirements first and find out the regulations for fencing. They are often very stringent. For instance, the gate typically must be 4 to 6 feet high, with slats or uprights spaced no wider than 3 or 4 inches. Fence the pool *inside* the yard, so that a child can't get to it from the house or any other side of the property. If you use chain-link fencing, be sure that it goes all the way to the ground so that no child or animal can squeeze under it. Make sure the links are small enough so that an enterprising youngster can't get a toehold and climb up the fence.

Never place furniture near the fence, because it might be used for climbing. Make sure nothing blocks the view of the pool from the house.

We were at a three-year-old's birthday party and the pool the kids swam in had something called a Protect-A-Child Pool Fence. This is a transparent mesh fence that indeed allows you to see the children as well as the beauty of your pool. Children can't climb the mesh, but if an unsteady toddler falls against the fence, it's very forgiving (metal is not). It is completely weatherproof and it doesn't rip, stretch, rot, or fade.

Holes are drilled into the pool deck surface and a permanent sleeve is inserted into each hole. The posts of each mesh panel slide into these sleeves. One of the pluses of the Protect-A-Child Pool Fence is that it can be disassembled and removed in about seven minutes. You simply pull out the mesh panels and cover the sleeves with flush, matching patio caps. So if you're having an adult luau, your patio and pool can still look fabulous.

This kind of fencing takes about a half a day to install and costs anywhere from $1,200 to $2,000. To locate one of the Protect-A-

Child dealers around the country, call the toll-free number at the company's headquarters in Florida, 800-992-2206, or look in the Yellow Pages under "Fencing" or "Swimming Pool Enclosures."

I would definitely invest in a pool alarm. And here again you have a number of choices. One type detects sudden motion in the water; another type shoots a light beam around the perimeter of the pool and sounds the alarm if the beam is broken. There are also fence-exit alarms. Check into all this carefully and decide which alarm is for you. When you make a decision, test the alarm frequently.

Vicki Lansky, the author of the excellent *Baby Proofing Basics,* also suggests the following:

- Keep a phone near the pool so you don't have to run inside to answer a call and in the event you need to seek emergency help.
- Post CPR techniques in the pool area and review them frequently.
- Make sure all outlets are protected by GFIs and test them frequently.
- Keep rescue equipment at poolside: a large pole with a shepherd's crook at one end, and at least one ring-shaped life preserver with a long rope. Install a safety line where water deepens to a point your child should not go beyond.
- Install textured concrete or other slip-proof material on the pool deck.
- Get an approved safety pool cover that will support at least 30 pounds of weight per square foot. Fasten the cover securely during the nonswimming months of the year, being sure there are no gaps that will allow a child to slip through. Remove the cover completely before anyone enters the water.

And finally:

- Don't rely on any of the various inflatable flotation devices available to keep your child safe. Most can be punctured or deflated and are not designed to keep a child's head above water. They "work" under ideal conditions, but can give both you and your child a false sense of security. Your vigilance is all you can trust.

Hot Tub and Spa

As relaxing as hot tubs and Jacuzzis are for adults, they pose several dangers for children. You have to look at a spa's cardinal features. The strong circulating action of a pump that helps ease the knots from your muscles can upend the balance of a little one. Never turn on the pump when a young child is present.

Some of the older spas have a floor drain with such strong suction that a child could be pulled underwater. Talk to your dealer about replacing such a drain.

Temperatures that might be comfortable or therapeutic for an adult could scald the skin of a child. Keep the water temperature no higher than 95 degrees F., and don't allow a child to soak for more than ten minutes. In fact, don't allow children under five in a spa or hot tub. Their lighter body weight and developing organs render them more vulnerable to stress from hot water.

A spa or hot tub needs the same protective fencing or sturdy locking cover as a pool.

Poisonous Plants

I remember being surprised to find out that holly and mistletoe and philodendron and pothos are poisonous, but it turns out that more indoor and outdoor plants are poisonous if ingested than are not. In fact, plants are the leading cause of poisoning in preschoolers. This list of poisonous plants in North America was compiled by Vicky Lansky in *Baby Proofing Basics* and reprinted with permission. Take an inventory in and around your house and neighborhood, give away any indoor plants apt to cause a problem, watch your children carefully, and teach them not to put plants, fruits, berries, and mushrooms in their mouths.

Poisonous and Nonpoisonous Plants

Indoor Poisonous Plants

Bird of Paradise pods

Caladium

Christmas Pepper

Diefenbachia (dumb cane)

English Ivy

Jerusalem cherry

Mistletoe

Philodendron

Pothos

Indoor Nonpoisonous Plants

African violet

Asparagus fern

Begonia

Boston fern

Christmas cactus

Dracaena

Easter Lily

Flame violet

Fuchsia

Gloxinia

Jade plant

Kalanchoe

Palm (all types)

Peperomia

Poinsettia (but can cause irritation)

Purple passion vine

Sansevieria (snake plant)

Schefflera

Spider Plant

Tahitian bridal veil

Ti plant

Outdoor Poisonous Plants

Azalea

Bloodroot

Caladium

Castor bean

Daffodil and jonquil

Delphinium

English Ivy

Fruit pits from any tree fruits

Foxglove

Holly berries

Hyacinth

Hydrangea

Iris

Jack-in-the-pulpit

Lantana

Larkspur

Laurel

Lily of the valley

Morning glory

Mushrooms (most)

Narcissus (bulbs)

Nicotiana

Oleander

Pokeweed

Poison Ivy

Privet

Rhododendron

Rhubarb (leaves)

Sweet pea

Tobacco

Tulip

Wisteria

Yew

Outdoor Nonpoisonous Plants

Bachelor button

Coleus

Dandelion

Impatiens

Marigold

Petunia

Rose

Salvia

Viburnum

Finding Mr. Wright: Hiring a Child Proofer

Frank Wright and I finished up the tour of our house, and I finally turned and asked the question that had been on my mind throughout the entire discussion: How much would it cost for a professional childproofer to do a house? "Without all the bells and whistles," he answered, "this house would cost between $450 and $500." (Remember, my house is rather sim-ple; there are no elaborate staircases, and I have a patio rather than a deck, and no raised hearth, no Jacuzzi, and no pool.)

Even though "What price, the safety of a child?" is my motto, this is a weighty figure for anyone, but especially for a new home-owner already hemorrhaging money from the new mortgage and points, the insurance transactions, the move, the setup costs, and all the new bills that come pouring in.

I asked Frank to break down the necessary safety items that I would have to purchase without the aid of a professional child-proofer, and that tally came to about $300. His two visits, ordering, and labor and installation came to about $200.

Frank put it this way: "It might take you an hour to orient yourself to a catalog and quite a bit longer to shop through stores making purchases. Once you order everything, you'll probably spend two days reading directions and doing the installation. For $200 you bought yourself the weekend and then some."

This makes sense to me, especially as I have no mechanical proclivity. (We never even installed that one set of window bars.) But even more important would be the peace of mind that comes from knowing that everything in my home was examined by a pro-fessional who educated me and eliminated hazards. I wouldn't be operating with minimal knowledge, guessing where the problem areas are and how best to remove them.

So, where do you find a professional childproofer? Your pedi-atrician might be able to recommend someone, or you could look in the Yellow Pages under "Safety Consultants," but probably your best bet is to flip through one of the parenting or "family and kids" magazines that you'll often find at Y's or pediatrician offices or in libraries. If there's a childproofer in your area, he or she will no doubt advertise in such places.

Shopping for Child Proofing Products

As promised, I've compiled a work sheet of the safety items you might wish to purchase when childproofing your home. First tally the "big three" of childproofing essentials: gates, outlet covers, and passive latches. Then follow the room-to-room path that Frank and I took and expand your list. Remember that these prices are approximate. They were noted in 1996 and included just to give you an idea for the total budget.

Gates

..........Mounted slat gates (for stairways; one at the top, one below; $25–$60 each)

..........Pressure gates (for thresholds only and to separate rooms; $20–$35)

Outlet Covers

..........Sliding Safety Plates (for frequently used outlets; about $3 each)

..........Shock Loks (Mericon product that screws into outlet; ten for $6)

..........Twistplug Outlet Plate (for permanently in-use outlets; two for $7)

Passive Latches

..........Tot Loks (magnetic locking system for high security; two for $13)

..........Passive drawer and cabinet locks (one-piece or two-piece; $1 each)

..........Side-by-Side Cabinet Lock (for cabinets with double doors or with side-by-side pulls; $2.50 each)

The Kitchen

..........Shield-A-Burn (for the stove; a 36-inch shield is about $30)

..........Switch Blocker (locks garbage disposal or other dangerous switches in the off position; $1.50 each)

..........Cord-A-Way (stores up to 8 feet of electrical cord; three for $7)

..........Cord Minder (replaces spring-coiled cord on wall phone; $15)

..........Safety-Tips (for sharp 90-degree angles on countertops; four for $1.50)

The Living Room and Family Room

..........Hearth Guards for fireplaces (about $100–$160 each)

..........Toddler Shields (gathered bumpers for cocktail and end tables; $30–$60)

The Bathrooms

..........Lid Locks (secures toilet lids; about $10 each)

..........Bath Spout Cover ($10 each)

..........Bath Thermometer ($4)

..........Gerber Door Knobs (keeps toddler from locking himself or herself in; two for $4)

..........Bottles of syrup of ipecac

..........Activated charcoal

..........Epsom salts

Windows/Doors

..........Child-Safe Window Guards (about $15 each)

..........Tot Stopper (round suction cup that prevents windows from opening too wide; $5 each)

..........Safety Tassels for Blinds ($1.25 each)

..........Safety Door Closers (automatically shuts doors; $15)

..........One-Piece Door Stopper (No more rubber tips that are a choking hazard; $1.50 each)

Special Orders: Plexiglas panels for casement windows, French doors, stairways, or sidelights:

....

....

....

....

Mesh for decks or stairways

....

....

Each adult in your household and any caregiver who spends time with your children should take a child-safety/CPR course, and no parent should be without a copy of the book *A Sigh of Relief* by Martin Green (Bantam Books; $16.95). This is a totally unique first-aid handbook for childhood emergencies that gives every aid to a parent or caretaker. It features a back cover index that allows you to locate the emergency you're dealing with in less than a second, and step-by-step-illustrations with fast, simple instructions. This book boosts my confidence that even in a panicked situation, I would be able to remember the emergency training I've had and handle the problem.

12. The Great Escape: Protecting Yourself, Your Family, and Your Property from Fire

Very few things in life are as terrifying as the idea of you or your family being trapped in a house when a fire has broken out. Yet today, armed with knowledge, smoke detectors, fire ladders, and safety plans, you and your family have the greatest possible chance of surviving just such an emergency.

When we first moved, we dutifully went out and bought the requisite smoke alarms (one for the downstairs room, one at the top of the stairs, and one in the hallway of the bedroom wing) and three fire extinguishers. But a few months ago, I saw a segment on *Prime Time Live* in which a smoldering fire was started in a wastebasket in a condemned house. It was eye-opening.

There was a smoke detector, but it didn't go off until the fire had spread quite far, and the fire was like nothing you see in the movies. You literally *couldn't* see—it was profoundly dark. Black. Soot completely filled the air and covered everything.

The segment also revealed that there could quickly be a 500-

degree difference in the temperature at belly level on the floor and the temperature at eye level as you stood up. The body shuts down at 150 degrees F. The picture I had of our early warning thanks to the protection of our few smoke detectors and our walking our children quickly to safety, backlit by the fire, got blown away long before the commercial break.

So I was particularly interested in having a conversation with a fire specialist at the Westport Fire Department and getting very clear about the realities of a fire in the home. I was lucky to speak with Deputy Marshal Fred S. Baker. He became a real hero in our town recently after he entered a house completely engulfed in flames and rescued a baby trapped upstairs in her crib.

Fred and I sat down late one afternoon and I got the chilling details, but also the hopeful information that you can safeguard yourself and your family and friends from the tragedy of fire.

He had caught that segment on *Prime Time Live* also, and the first thing I did was bring up the subject of that smoke detector that didn't sound for such a long time. "How come," I asked, "I can't take a shower or cook a meal without the smoke detector going off, and this one took so long?"

"This house was not adequately protected by the correct number of smoke detectors," he answered. "The one it had was too far from the fire, and the fire had to really get going to produce enough smoke for it to finally reach that detector.

"At the risk of sounding like a broken record," he continued, *"there's just no such thing as too many smoke detectors in a home.* The more you have, the more you increase your chances of surviving a fire. About 90 percent of all residential fire deaths and 80 percent of all residential fire injuries occur in homes without working smoke detectors.

"There should be one *inside* each bedroom, and one in the

hallway of each sleeping area. If the hallway is longer than 40 feet, then two detectors should be installed. Two detectors should be protecting your stairs, the primary path of egress, also. Place one at the top of the staircase and one at the bottom.

"Then you should have a smoke detector on each level of the home. In the basement, place a detector on the ceiling, not at the top of the stairway leading down to it. This is because smoke is initially not that hot and it will stratify in the air and take a while to rise. Eventually it will rise up, but not until there's quite a fire going underneath it."

He added: "Current code for new construction here requires all of these smoke detectors, and if they run on house current, they must have battery backup. They are also interconnected, which means that if one goes off in the basement, they all begin to sound."

I was surprised that each bedroom needed a detector, but Fred explained: "Fires do start in bedrooms—people smoke or a child throws a shirt on a lamp. If the door is closed, it will prevent the smoke from reaching the hallway detector for quite a while. Too late for the person sleeping inside that room."

I have a pretty good "nose," and I always thought I would wake up and smell the acrid smoke, but I was disabused of that notion pretty quickly. You don't smell while you're sleeping, and the carbon monoxide in the smoke acts as an anesthetic and puts you into an even deeper sleep. Only the piercing sound of a smoke detector will awaken you and buy you the extra time you need to escape with your life.

Fred also told me that there are now special detectors for the hearing-impaired that use a 177-candela strobe light paired with an 85-decibel alarm to wake and warn a person, so if you have an elderly parent staying with you or a guest whose hearing is diminished, place one of these detectors in that bedroom. They're man-ufactured by First Alert.

Most people are under the impression that they have about ten minutes to dress, grab their jewelry, and gather cherished objects. This is a deadly misapprehension. *You have no time.* Fred Baker lent me a video called *Fire Power,* and the First Alert educational office sent me an unforgettable video based on a series of reports by Dr. Frank Field called *Plan to Get Out Alive.* (The video costs $9.95 and is available through Media Tech, 110 W. Hubbard St., Chicago, IL 60610; 312-828-1146. An accompanying book, titled *Get Out Alive,* is published by Random House.) Both videos make it very clear that you may have about two minutes to escape a fire. That's 120 seconds. A fire burning in a house for one minute grows to three times its original size. In four minutes it grows to eleven times, and in six minutes, it reaches fifty times. Therefore, you cannot go look for the fire, get dressed, or gather valuables. Use the precious little time you do have to alert everyone in the house and to get out.

Give up the notion that you will ever stand up in a fire. Don't even sit up in bed. Instead, roll to the ground. The smoke and fumes will numb your brain and make it extremely difficult to move your arms and legs. A survivor in the *Plan to Get Out Alive* video recalled getting out of bed and walking to the door. He could see the door, he knew he wanted to get to the door, but he couldn't move. He began to feel paralyzed, grew dizzy, and collapsed. He was saved only because his father was crawling on the floor and was able to pull him out of the house.

Dr. Frank Field asks a pertinent question: "If it takes two minutes for smoke to trigger the detector, you have about one minute. Could you and your family escape your house in one minute? Disoriented? In the dark?" You have to have well-laid plans that are second nature to you if you're going to pull this one off.

I asked Fred Baker to describe the kind of drills we should all be running with our children and baby-sitters or secondary care-givers. That night, following his instructions, Demitri and I ran the drill with our nine-year-old, Alex, and our three-year-old, Jordy. (Jordy kept shaking his head, whining that he didn't want to be dropped into the bushes, but Alex really got into it.)

First Demitri pushed the button of the smoke detector, and we explained that this sound means there's a fire somewhere in the house, and they have one thing to do: Get out of the house as quickly and calmly as possible. I had a floor plan of the house, and we discussed two exits from each room. There were multiple choices from the living room, kitchen, and family room, but the bedrooms were the area that needed the most discussion and practice.

Alex was instructed to roll out of bed and get on his belly and crawl like GI Joe to the door. We told him to keep his head about 12 to 24 inches from the floor, because the best air would be there in the event smoke was in the area he was crawling through. When he reached the door, he was to feel it with the *back* of his hand, not the palm. (We didn't want him to burn his palm if the door was hot. He would need a good grasp to open doorknobs or windows or ne-gotiate a fire ladder.) If the door was hot, he wasn't to open it; if it was cool, however, he was to open it just a crack and put his hand out and see how warm the air was. If all seemed relatively clear, he was to belly-crawl to the front door and stand only to exit. We ex-plained about the enormous difference in temperatures from the ground to midlevel of the room, and told him that the air at belly level would be cooler and clearer.

If, however, when he opened the door to his bedroom, the smoke seemed dense, he was to slam the door fast and go out his second exit—the window of his bedroom. (A closed bedroom door can be lifesaving in the event of fire.)

We also told him that he had about one minute to get out of a burning house and he wasn't to go back and get the dog or any treasured item. If Jordy was sleeping in his room that night, Alex was to pull him onto the floor with him and boost him out of the window before he, Alex, climbed out. Crawl, test, crawl, and get out was the order of things.

We designated a spot across the driveway where we were all to meet and do a head count before going to our neighbors' to call 911. Demitri underscored the point that we might not all go out together or through the same exit and that Alex wasn't to wait for us.

Because the soot of a fire makes for zero visibility, we ran the drill again in the dark. And we turned Alex around and around so he was disoriented in the room. We wanted him to learn to "feel" and memorize guide points for himself so he could orient himself and move toward the chosen exit. (Alex chose to exit the bathroom window this time, and he would like you all to know that he bumped his head on the toilet bowl as he rose from his crawling position.)

Because we live in a ranch house, exiting from the bedrooms is not too difficult, although Fred advised me to check that screens and storm windows were not difficult to remove. Because our old windows have a tendency to stick, however, we're earmarking money to replace them.

Fred told me that I didn't actually have to drop Jordy out the window and into the bushes during the drill, but people who live in two- and three-story houses have to purchase escape ladders for each bedroom and must practice going down them. They take a bit of getting used to.

When you practice, the adult should go down first and help steady the child on the descent. If you have an infant, you have a more difficult task ahead of you. It's impossible to hold an infant and negotiate an escape ladder. Some people suggest that you always keep a Snugli near the bed so that you can wrestle the baby into it and escape. But since I used to allow forty-five minutes to remember how to get the Snugli on me before a doctor's appointment, this does not seem like a good option. I asked Fred what to do, and he said: "Keep a long piece of rope under the bed and grab a pillowcase off the bed. Put the baby in the pillowcase, tie it up with the rope, and lower the infant to the ground. If two of you are at home during this escape, one parent can go down first and be ready to receive this squirming bundle on the ground and quickly open the sack. If only one parent or caregiver is home, lower the baby and climb down and attend to the baby."

Fred assured me that the baby would not suffocate in the pillowcase. Still, this scenario gives me the shivers. Practice this drill with a doll the size of your infant—don't run it with an actual child.

You can buy fold-up escape ladders at hardware stores or Home Depots, or through safety catalogs (*The Catalog for Safe Beginnings* mentioned on page 353 has two of them, as does *The Safety Zone*). First Alert just came out with a fire escape ladder that has several nice features. It's lightweight, is made of heavy-duty plastic that folds up, and has stand-offs, which allow for a better footing when descending. (The stand-offs are short, horizontal projections from every rung that hold the ladder about 3 inches away from the side of the house, giving you more room to place your feet and adding to the stability of the ladder.) It retails for about $85. (Call 800-323-9005 to find out who sells such a ladder near you.)

Never store an escape ladder in a closet where it's sure to be buried by clutter. Instead, store it right by the window, or under the bed. Run the drill periodically and check that your ladders haven't been hauled off to the new tree house down the street.

Fred and I agreed that it might not be a bad idea to install infrared floodlights that will automatically light your way out the window (see Chapter 8, "The Univited Guest, Part II").

The last exit that Fred and I discussed is the one from the laundry room of my home. It's a double metal door with a double deadbolt lock—the kind you have to open with a key from the inside. This kind of lock is great for security from burglary, but a serious hazard in the event of fire. Fred asked me where the key was. "I have two up on a nail, near the door," I told him. As the words came out of my mouth, I realized that a child might not be able to reach the key, but that wasn't where Fred was heading.

"You don't want to stand up or have a child get up on a chair if there's a fire in that room. The key should hang at baseboard level." (I have yet to work this problem out, because a small key is a choking hazard for a young child, and the chances that the key will not be removed and lost by a three-year-old are dim.)

I told Fred that we always seem to be juggling the need for security with the need for fire safety with the need for childproofing. He nodded sympathetically, and we briefly touched on the subject of bars to protect a child from falling out a second-story window. He advised homeowners to look for gates or bars that open easily from within and to always keep one window free of a gate or bars of any kind.

The Placement of Smoke Detectors

I was convinced of the lifesaving importance of smoke detectors, and I realized how underprotected we were with our three detectors, so I immediately ran out and bought eight more. I even decided to try my hand at the electric drill and install a few myself. This apparently was such an event that Demitri felt the need to gather the children to watch and to videotape the sight for posterity.

Peanut gallery aside, I started obsessing about the placement of each detector in each room. Here's what the instructions tell you.

The optimal spot for a detector is in the middle of the ceiling. If this bothers you aesthetically or is not an option, place it on the periphery, but never closer than 4 inches from where the wall meets the ceiling (8 inches would be better). Never install one at the exact point where the ceiling and wall meet. This place has proved to be a "dead air" area in a room, just out of reach of the roll and puff of smoke and fumes.

If you wish to wall-mount a detector, place it between 6 and 12 inches from the ceiling. Never place a smoke detector in front of an air vent, because the continuous sweep of "clean" air may pass through the detector and prevent smoke from reaching it.

There are two kinds of smoke detectors: ionization and photoelectric. Most of the smoke detectors you see and can buy are of the ionization type. Patrick Coughlin, the director of the International Association of Fire Chiefs, explains the differences: "The ionization type monitors ions, or electrically charged particles. Smoke particles entering the sensing chamber change the electrical balance of the air. The detector's horn will sound when the change in electrical balance reaches a preset level.

"The other type of detector is called photoelectric because its sensing chamber uses a beam of light and a light sensor. Smoke particles entering the chamber change the amount of light that reaches the light sensor. The detector sounds when the smoke density reaches a preset level, also."

Photoelectric detectors are more sensitive to large particles of combustion—those emitted by a smoldering fire—while ionization detectors are more sensitive to tiny particles of combustion—those emitted by a flaming fire. "Thus," says Patrick Coughlin, "the response time of the two detectors will vary, depending on the mix of small and large particles in the fire. But test results show that the differences in response time are small enough that both types provide enough time to escape."

When I asked him if I should supplement my now abundant supply of ionization detectors with a few of the photoelectric variety, he answered, "The number of detectors is more important than the type. It's not a bad idea to install a few photoelectric detectors or replace a few of your ionization detectors with a model that has both types of sensors in the same unit, but of course these models are more expensive than those with a single sensor." He made the point again: "If the choice is between having only one of each type or having more of the same type, more detectors is the better choice."

Several of my friends mentioned that they had heat detectors instead of smoke detectors so they wouldn't have to deal with nuisance alarms, especially in the kitchen. These detectors are set off not by smoke, but by heat; a piece of metal is specially formulated to melt or bend in the presence of increased temperature. Alarm companies install them and hook them into a central alarm system.

These heat detectors are not a substitute for smoke detectors. They work only when they are close enough to a fire to sense the heat, and will not warn you of the extreme dangers of the poisonous gases and fumes of a smoldering fire. They are actually supplements to smoke detectors and are a good choice for areas with harsh environments which may disable a smoke detector or cause false alarms (for instance, in a dusty or too hot attic, or in a garage or workshop where it gets both very hot and very cold).

Get into the habit of changing the batteries of the smoke detectors at daylight saving times—once in the spring and once in the fall. "Change your clocks, change your batteries" should be your new motto. (If you live in Arizona, Hawaii, or the eastern part of In-

diana, where daylight saving time is not observed, pick a special day
or anniversary to help you remember to change the batteries—perhaps April and October tax schedules?) Or, if this task sounds bur-
densome to you, invest in First Alert's new Six-Year Lithium Battery
Smoke Detector, which eliminates the need for frequent changing.
These retail for about $35.

Because dust can impair detector sensitivity, you should vacuum each one at least once a year. Haul your vacuum into each
room and simply hold the vacuum cleaner nozzle to the smoke-entry
opening on the detector. Never paint a detector, as paint can damage the unit.

If you have any questions about detectors, or any aspect of residential fire safety, call Operation Life Safety in Fairfax, Virginia.
The number is 703-273-9815, ext. 319.

How Can We Prevent Fires?

I'm so glad we have the smoke detectors in place and that we
know the drills, but I hope never to hear the sound of the alarms or
have to implement the emergency escape plans. So naturally I asked
Fred Baker how fires happen and what we can do to prevent them.

"A lot of fires are the result of smoking—someone drops ash
on a sofa or bedding, or throws an unextinguished cigarette or
match in a wastebasket," he began. "We've seen fires break out
after a person has seemingly extinguished the embers that dropped
into the overstuffed sofa or bedding, and hours later, one tiny ember
can ignite." He reminded me to check under sofas and chairs after
a party and to dispose of the contents of ashtrays in a metal can.
(Demitri's old pipe tobacco cans work really well. They have a nice
tight-fitting metal top. Irish Oatmeal cans are a good bet too.)

Unbelievably, Fred told me of a couple who enjoyed a fire in
their fireplace on Friday evening and waited until Sunday to shovel

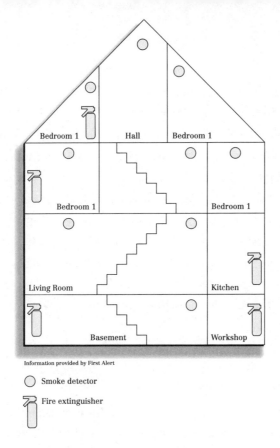

Bedroom 1 Hall Bedroom 1

Bedroom 1 Bedroom 1

Living Room Kitchen

Basement Workshop

Information provided by First Alert

○ Smoke detector

🔥 Fire extinguisher

the ashes into a bag, which they disposed of in the trash can in the garage. Sunday evening, their garage burned down. One tiny glowing ember, protected by the bed of ash, was all it took to ignite the combustibles around it.

Fred advises that you leave the ashes after a fire for at least a week. If you must clean them out, shovel them into a metal container and store them away from any structure or combustibles for seven days or longer.

Cooking oils are another fire hazard if not handled correctly. Heat deep wells of oil *slowly*, with *patience* and a *hawk eye*. Too often, people turn the gas on high to get those french fries going and then a phone call or other interruption takes them away and the oil eventually heats to its flash point. Fred's advice is to heat oil slowly on a low to moderate flame and to watch things carefully. He always sets a timer to call his attention back to the stove in the event of an interruption. If a fire does break out in a pot, just stick a cookie tin on top or take the lid and drop it over the pot by sneaking up on it from below—as though you were climbing a mountain and then landing on top.

I'm keeping a cookie tin in my oven so it's always there or on the counter next to the stove if I happen to be using both the oven and the burners (on a *good* day I can't find the lids to the pots without a struggle). Also, I've put a big, opened box of baking soda covered with plastic next to the stove, because it will extinguish a grease fire if you keep pouring it on. Expect a flare-up, but keep pouring.

Never throw water on a grease fire, and *never* use flour. Flour could cause it to explode. (I'll discuss the possible use of a fire extinguisher on page 393.)

Any organic-based oil must be handled extremely carefully. Linseed oil and other oils for furniture, mineral oil, and neat's-foot oil (for softening baseball gloves or other leather) are examples of organic oils. When these oils decompose on a rag, they can heat up and burst into flame. Rags used to spread these oils are extremely dangerous.

I went to the hardware store to take a look at some of these oils, and the back panel of a can of linseed oil read:

"Oil-soaked rags or other oily waste are subject to spontaneous combustion (may ignite without an ignition source such as a spark or flame). The time frame and conditions under which spontaneous combustion will occur is unpredictable. If rags or other application materials are to be set aside, even for short periods of time, they should be placed in airtight or water-filled metal containers until final disposal."

What comes next is almost too eerie to talk about. But two days after I typed the above paragraph, I got a call from my sister in California. Remember my brother and sister-in-law's home out there? The one featured in Chapter 9, "The Healthy House"? They spent years and a fortune building this truly spectacular house, and it was a physical and spiritual haven. But a fire broke out, apparently caused by spontaneous combustion. The house burned to the ground, and Rob and Dianna lost everything. (Fortunately, they were in Rome when it happened, but they are absolutely heartbroken.)

Naturally, the mysteries and awfulness of spontaneous combustion have been a big topic around here lately, but I was floored to learn that wet newspapers can spontaneously combust, also. As the ink dries, the paper can ignite. I guess it makes sense—the oils in the ink—but I had never heard about this.

I called Rob and Dianna in Rome to express my condolences about the house, and we talked about their installing a sprinkler system when they rebuild. They hadn't done it the first time because they were afraid it would discharge accidentally and cause damage.

It turns out that there is little likelihood of this happening, and sprinkler systems really work. The video, *FirePower,* that Fred Baker lent me showed a room in flames within minutes of a smoldering cigarette igniting. The fire blew all the windows out and melted everything in the room. Then the director reshot the same scene in a room with all the same furnishings and set the fire again. As soon as the temperature reached 165–175 degrees F., the sprinkler released a spray of water and completely doused the fire.

Sprinkler systems are expensive, however; they cost between $1 and $2 a square foot. But you should know that insurance companies lower your rates 5–15 percent if you have them. Rob and Dianna are installing them when they rebuild.

Fred and I got back to our topic: preventing fires in the first place. He told me that many fires start because woodstoves are installed incorrectly and not cleaned each year. He urged me to tell you to have all your heating equipment checked by a professional and to have your chimneys cleaned annually. Also, fires can break out in clothes dryers if the lint filter or hose gets clogged. These should be cleaned regularly to avoid lint buildup, and I've made reminder notes on the "On-Track" Calendar in the appendices of this book. Clean the lint from under your dryer, also. In the event that a fire does break out and you are on the scene, keep the dryer door shut, and if you can safely unplug the dryer, try to do so. If not, shut off the power at the main panel, or in the case of a gas dryer, shut off the main gas valve, and let the fire burn out.

And, finally, we talked about electrical fires. Fred explained that many of these are caused by the loading up of extension cords. "People don't seem to realize that an extension cord should only be a very temporary solution, not a way of permanent wiring," he said. "The 15-amp circuit breaker protecting an outlet is only protecting the wiring in the walls to that outlet, it is not protecting what's going on from the outlet through an extension cord. So, if you buy a 7- or 8-amp light extension cord and load it up over the 8 amps, the circuit breaker cannot monitor the situation—the circuit breaker does not trip, the fuse does not blow—and the wires can heat up and cause a fire."

If an electrical fire does break out, however, *don't throw water on it.* If you can somehow safely pull the plug, do so. If you can't, and the main electrical service panel is in the garage, switch off all the power. (If it's downstairs, don't attempt to get to it. Don't risk being trapped in the house. Spend the time getting everyone out and call 911.) If you are trained to use a fire extinguisher and the fire is small, make a thirty-second attempt to spray it with a C-, BC-, or ABC-rated fire extinguisher (see discussion below).

Fred finished by stating: "If a 1990s family wants to live in a 1940s house, they should have an electrician put new receptacles in place and completely eliminate the need for extension cords." (See page 90 in Chapter 2 for a discussion of electrical upgrades.)

Fire Extinguishers and Other Ambiguities

The late-afternoon sun was vanishing when we launched into the topic of fire extinguishers. I was all primed to learn what the A-B-C meant and how to properly fight a fire, but an uncomfortable look crossed Fred's face. "I have hesitations about people using fire extinguishers," he said. "Some people get this macho idea that they can handle fire, and this is a false and dangerous impression to hold. A home extinguisher won't handle more than a little pot on a stove, anyway, especially in untrained hands, and you might only make the situation worse."

He continued: "There's skill involved in using an extinguisher, and if you want to be able to use one, make an appointment with your local fire department. They can light a fire in a pan and teach you the technique. Still, I would prefer you call 911 and let professionals fight the fire for you."

I said: "But what if it's just a small fire? By the time you got here, it could be much bigger."

"Our response rate is about three minutes. Your job is not to be Fireman Fred. Your job is to alert everyone in the house that there's a fire, get everyone out of the house, and call 911."

He then said very emphatically: "Never, never be afraid to call the fire department, even if it's just a tiny problem. No one will laugh at you—they'll think you're smart and know what you're doing.

You'll get over the embarrassment of the fire truck careening to your front door. But scars from burns never fade."

If you are trained to use a fire extinguisher, and you're in the room when the fire flares up, you have thirty seconds to fight it. There are three kinds of extinguishers: Class A, Class BC, and Class ABC.

Class A extinguishers work on fires associated with wood, paper, clothing, furniture, and plastics; Class B are for flammable liquids such as kitchen grease, kerosene, gasoline, and paints and oils; and Class C extinguish small electrical fires. An all-purpose ABC extinguisher is what most homeowners place around the house.

Most people, myself included, think they have the time to read the directions on the extinguisher just before saving the household from fire, but as I said before, you have all of thirty seconds to put out a small fire before it grows out of control. Evelyn Wood couldn't speed-read fast enough.

Operating a Fire Extinguisher

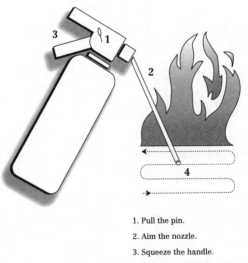

1. Pull the pin.

2. Aim the nozzle.

3. Squeeze the handle.

4. Sweep the nozzle from side to side at the base of the fire.

The New York Office of Fire Prevention and Control uses the acronym PASS to remind you of the basics of fire extinguisher operation. Pull, Aim, Squeeze, Sweep. You pull the pin, aim the nozzle, squeeze the handle, and sweep the nozzle from side to side at the base or bottom of the fire. All of this is done about 6 feet away from the fire. (I blocked it out in my kitchen so I'll understand what 6 feet means in this particular space.)

If you have taken the trouble to learn how to use an extinguisher, you need to learn about the proper maintenance. Read the instructions on the canister. Every few months an extinguisher needs to be shaken up so the fine powder inside doesn't compact and clog. Fire extinguishers have a life expectancy of about five years, and you must check the dial periodically to ensure that they're fully charged.

It was night now, and Fred Baker was going home to his family. I was going out to hunt up my arsenal of smoke detectors and prepare for our first drill. Fred closed our conversation with this final statement: "Teach your children that matches are tools, not toys, and that we must always handle them with knowledge and respect. Let them help you build the fire in the fireplace and instill in them a sense of responsibility and good judgment. Teach them to 'stop, drop, and roll' if their clothes ever catch fire. Show preschoolers an exit sign and explain what that means. Educate everyone who spends time in your home and with your children about fire safety and what to do in the event of an emergency."

13. Finally Home

I remember my friend Carlos saying to me right before we moved: "It takes a while, but you're a very outgoing person and you'll have lots of friends here in a year." My brother echoed this sentiment sometime later, but shortened my adjustment time to a few months. "As soon as you get settled in a routine," Rob told me, "you'll forget all about your life in New York. In fact, you'll see how crazy it was that you ever lived there in the first place."

As with all things in life, the move was a mixed bag. I was ready for a change, I was excited about our new life and all the potential it held, and I was afraid. But I agreed with Carlos and Rob. After a few tough months, I would swing into a routine and adjust to what was sure to be a healthier new life for all of us. The holiday letter I sent out four and a half months after our great move opened like this:

"If you heard a lot of sobbing and wailing on July 31 of 1993, it was only the sound of Janice Papolos leaving New York City for the last time, after twenty years."

After a lot of pathetically funny stories about the travails of house-hunting, I described this house and then got right back to how blue I was feeling: "I keep missing my life in New York and when my friends come up and visit or even if I watch the opening scenes of *NYPD Blue,* I say: 'Demitri, I'm getting all *verklempt.*'* I keep having these 'moments' where I am so mournful, or at the very least, wistful about the change in lifestyle."

The letter amused my friends, but was written too early to convey the enormous adjustment I was experiencing. More was being stirred up than I'd suspected.

I held on by my fingernails through the worst winter in two decades, and began to feel things I didn't remember feeling before: a distinct lack of stamina, as though anything could put me over the edge. I was with my family, but I still felt this huge sense of loss.

I suffered through and began to hate the house as everything that could go wrong did, stretching our already weakened finances. I felt torn in so many directions as I tried to help everyone in my family adjust and get settled, and as I attempted to create a new life for us all.

In the winter of my discontent, I wasn't alone in my misery. Calls to my friends Denise Shekerjian in Vermont and MaryEllen Landon in her new home in El Paso, Texas, and lunches with Kathy Terkelsen, newly settled in Ridgefield, Connecticut, netted me plenty of company. Kathy said: "I don't think I can stay here. We have family in Cape Cod—perhaps we should think about settling up there. Every time I look at the videos of my old house, I cry and cry."

I think we had all underestimated the psychological impact of a move. I was beginning to understand why psychologists place moving just after death and divorce on the scale of stress.

*See *Saturday Night Live*'s "Coffee Talk."

But why should this be so? Ostensibly, we'd made a wonderful move, and we should all be flourishing. What was really going on here?

That first winter, as I watched my then eighteen-month-old toddler negotiating separation from me and venturing out into the world, I also saw him always returning to refuel. He was full into "stranger anxiety" and would hide behind my skirts when introduced to new people. I watched him and, noting the strange feelings I was having, thought: "I've left my 'skirt,' big-time. All my routines, my friends, my signposts are missing, and I'm wandering around up here with no refueling station."

Now, you're not listening to the wife of a psychiatrist for nothing. The only thing I could think was that these early issues of separation were being stirred up in this new and not yet comfortable situation. Outgoing or not, I was suffering a major case of stranger anxiety. We knew only two people here, and the enormous task of introducing ourselves to a community lay ahead of us. It had been twenty years since Demitri and I had left Boston for New York and been in this position, and we had gotten very used to the comfort of friends, looking at us through eyes of love and shared memories.

Recently, and about a year and a half after some of our most distraught conversations, Kathy invited us up to Ridgefield again. Sometime during dinner, I overheard her say to her table companion. "Oh, I feel very connected here. This is such a wonderful community."

Denise, beginning her third year up in Vermont, was sounding suspiciously brighter too. She told me all about the library building committee she's spearheading and about the new book she has started. And—this is still hard for me to believe—I actually felt a thrill the other day watching a vee of Canada geese flying on their migration pathway, honking loudly over this property. Me, the person who likes the sound of traffic and sirens.

Now what was going on? Had pods been placed under our beds à la *Invasion of the Body Snatchers*? Did we just wake up happier citizens one day?

I was starting to appreciate that, as disruptive and uncomfortable as the move had been (and I don't think seventeen snowstorms and a narrow escape from death by electrocution helped speed my adjustment), there's new growth and a new integration that comes with such a major change.

How long does it take until this great transformation happens and you feel connected to a community? Well, I've enriched the coffers of MCI doing an informal poll all over the country. And I discovered that the span most people quoted was two to three years. Maybe Carlos and Rob are more adjusted than the rest of us, or maybe they were trying to ease my anxiety, but it takes two to three years to stop looking back to the previous fount of all your memories and drive in the driveway *here* and feel home.

And it doesn't seem to have anything to do with how superior your new place is to your old. I look around this house and know there's no comparison to our cramped city apartment, but every corner of that apartment held a memory—or three, or four. That was where I'd brought Alex and Jordy home from New York Hospital, that was the scene of so many dinners with friends, birthday parties, anniversary celebrations. It was in that chair, by that window, that I got the idea to write my first book.

The new house held no memories. It felt cold. Only time would provide that layer of memory molecules that circulate about a house, transforming it into a home. The resonance and richness had yet to be added. There was no "there" here.

So what do you do in the meantime? How do you turn a house

into a home and a town into *your* community? It's a process that seems to proceed in stages, and you can help yourself if you're aware of them, I think.

First, get comfortable with the house. You get to know the house; it gets to know you. I love how David Owen describes the beginning of the relationship between home and homeowner in *The Walls Around Us:*

". . . I now believe that when a new family moves into a house, the house suffers something like a nervous breakdown. A few days after the deal is closed, water begins to drip from the chandelier in the dining room, a heating pipe bursts, and even the oven stops working. The house is accustomed to being handled in certain ways. Then, suddenly, strangers barge in. They take longer showers, flush the toilets more forcefully, turn on the trash compactor with the right hand instead of the left, and open windows at night. Familiar domestic routines are destroyed. While the house struggles to adjust, many expensive items—including, perhaps, the furnace—unexpectedly self-destruct. Then gradually, new rhythms are established, the house resigns itself to the change of ownership, and a normal pace of deterioration is restored.

"There is another possible explanation. It may be that it simply takes several months for a new homeowner to become numb to the cost of maintaining what is essentially a huge box filled with complicated things that want to break—a box that sits outside, day and night, in the rain and snow, surrounded by creatures that would like to eat it."

How I wish I'd read those paragraphs early in the game when I viewed the house as pitting itself against me and the balance in both checking and savings accounts.

If you've read this book, you already know quite a bit about your house and the systems in it, but soon you'll need to turn to-

ward the greater community and become a part of it. As Thomas
Moore describes it in his book *The Care of the Soul:*

". . . the goal is a richly elaborated life, connected to society
and nature, woven into the culture of family, nation, and globe. The
idea is not to be superficially adjusted, but to be profoundly connected in the heart to ancestors and to living brothers and sisters
in all the many communities that claim our hearts."

I've been trying to think about how these connections are
made, and I've called and corresponded with several friends who
have made a move in the past two or three years and asked them
to share advice on how to ease the transition. Moving your boxes
and bodies is the easiest part. But your mind and heart often linger
behind awhile back there, in the place they've long called home.
How do you unpack your "psychological bags," as author Victoria
Secunda puts it?

I spoke with her for a long time recently about how she negotiated a big move after living in her old community for twenty years.
She told me that moving brought her a mixture of excitement and
dread: "Dread because I was leaving the familiar; excitement because I was leaving the familiar."

Victoria told me that she really had to stick her head out. "It's
like dating," she said. "You must flirt and be inviting and make an
effort.

"Introduce yourself to your neighbors as soon as you move in,"
she advised. "Let them know a friendly presence has moved in."

Other people have "stranger anxiety" too, and we all must
make an effort to allay it. Victoria spent a lot of time, outside gardening, waving to people who drove by. It gave people a chance to
stop and introduce themselves and talk gardening at the very least.

She also threw a party, mixing old friends with new neighbors,
about six months after she and her husband, Shel, moved in. "You

can't wait for people to find you, befriend you, and make time in their schedule for you," she explained.

Victoria talked seriously about the downside of moving: "Something is also lost when you move," she told me. "There's always a loss. At the very least, a loss of the familiar. But without it you wouldn't develop new strengths."

Victoria continued: "I was feeling uprooted and fairly wilted, because all my landmarks were gone. Now everything was up to me. I was going to have to put down my own taproot. Gardening seemed like an appropriate metaphor. I said: 'I'm going to make this land bloom.' And in the process, I bloomed. My plants grew, my network grew; *I* grew."

She has a theory of sweat equity: The more you put into your house and land, the more you see yourself reflected in it and the more it becomes a part of you, and you a part of it.

Before we rang off, Victoria advised me to pass on a few other tips she found helped her get settled: "Join the library. It's often a hub of the community. Take the local paper so you know what's happening around town and can decide where you'd like to participate. Introduce yourself to the chief of police—it will make you feel more secure. Introduce yourself to the branch officer of your bank. Try to get a project going for yourself. Set some goals. Take a college course. Improve your tennis game. If you and your partner belong to any national organization, check to see if there's a local chapter and show up for meetings. Get out and about. Remember, there are little epiphanies, little grace notes, that can happen out there and that add luster to your life."

She concluded by saying: "You know, gardening metaphors keep occurring to me. Recently I was talking with a landscaper and bemoaning a treasured peony bush I had transplanted. It looked like it wasn't going to make it. He turned to me and assured me of its viability. 'The first year it sleeps,' he said. 'The second it creeps, and the third it leaps.' Mother Nature seems to be providing some wonderful cues about the stages of our kind of transplants, too, I think."

Novelist Denise Shekerjian, up in Vermont, wrote me a long letter about her gradual adjustment to small-town life. "My worry about leaving life in a metropolitan area was that I would be cut off from the energies I thought necessary to fuel creativity," she said. "No museums, no concerts, no theaters, no bookstores of note, no funky neighborhoods, no delis or Greek diners . . . death. Of course, I was an utter fool, as this didn't turn out to be the case at all. In fact, I now know that leaving was the best thing that ever happened to my writing. The quiet of my days allowed me to calm down and really concentrate—and I needed to do both to produce, as I now realize."

She also put down on paper something that I was doing obsessively in the year after our move: concentrating only on the flaws of the house. "I wasn't sure I liked our new house," she wrote. "Okay, so we built it, but that doesn't mean it meets our dreams. For a while, all I'd see was the mistakes: the too-small closets, the wrong choice of tile, the too-cheap fixtures, an inferior carpeting choice, an unfortunate color choice . . . and yet we had paid a fortune for it (another reason not to like it), or so it seemed. Shouldn't I have liked it more? Now I'm past all that and the house is fine— more than fine, really, and in the end, there are more important things in life."

She went on to say that it took a while to meet people with whom she felt simpatico. "People were pleasant, but there wasn't any connection. Again, in time, that changed," she wrote assuringly.

Denise said that getting involved in a town project worked for her. Her volunteer activities center around building a library. "I'm meeting a new crop of people outside of my usual life. I'm learning new skills, like fund-raising. And I'm useful to the town, which brings a curious sense of achievement and satisfaction. In the next year or two there will be a library in the new town center and it will, in part, be thanks to me. That's nice."

She closed her letter with several other thoughts: "Keep an open mind. Who's to say that what you left will be better than what's to come? There's a lot of charm to country life. I've learned that I love gardening, open space. I've come to appreciate the quieter, more contemplative rhythms. The interpersonal dynamics of a small town are endlessly fascinating to me and will probably work themselves into a book down the line. Give it time. Making a house a home is a process, and it happens one day after the next. It's not quick and deliberate. It just happens as you forget about the need of it. When you can, leave for a long trip. When you return you realize that this new place is in fact *home*."

Her very last suggestion: "Get a dog or a cat."

And what of Kathy Terkelsen up in Ridgefield? Well, she admitted having a "real case of vapors on the couch and acting like Camille for a while," but she told me that she finally realized that "nobody was going to knock on the door and drag me out to meet people.

"I went back to myself and began to pick up a thread of my previous life where I was the village historian. I started going to the library and reading a lot of things about the history of Ridgefield," she said. "Then I called the Keeler Tavern Museum and found out they needed docents. I became a guide there, and learned through a colleague that a position was opening in museum archives. Before I knew it, I had a new job—and in many ways, I feel like I've found myself again.

"I now sit on the board of the Keeler Tavern Museum, and I live a hectic but very interesting life. Finding this museum was a lifesaver for me—it was an incredible meshing of their needs and my needs."

Kathy added: "I'm not unaware of what a huge effort it is to connect yourself. You can easily get into a rut. You'll manage, but you won't thrive. You really have to push yourself to get involved."

Victoria and Denise and Kathy and I were East Coast people moving within the East Coast corridor, and not an impossible distance away from old friends and old haunts, either. But how do people move to a different region of the country, where they really have even fewer connections and may find themselves judging and being judged as an outsider?

Cheryl Gallan moved from New England to North Carolina, and initially had a very hard time of it. But she took the concept "Bloom Where You Are Planted" to heart and got involved with the local arts council. She began to purchase art and crafts indigenous to the area and found it added a whole new dimension to who she was as a person. "My palate was expanded, so to speak. I accepted new ideas and defined myself in high relief against another culture."

Because this was indeed a different culture, she didn't have a cocktail party, but wrote out invitations for coffee . . . and delivered them personally to immediate neighbors. This practically guaranteed that everyone would feel more comfortable and connected. No matter how different people seem, Cheryl tried to keep saying # 552 of *Life's Little Instruction Book,* Vol. II, in mind: "Remember that everyone you meet is afraid of something, loves something, and has lost something."

Cheryl, Denise, and Victoria made a point of mentioning professional counseling if you fall into a funk that lasts too long. "Your problems are portable," Victoria said. "If you're looking to the community to define you and make you happier than you've ever been, you may be disappointed. On the other hand, if you're challenged by the idea of putting your personal stamp on your new environment—both changing it and being changed by it—that's where the epiphanies are. Don't be afraid to seek out a professional who can help you through the transition period and sort out some of the feelings that may be stirred up."

Harriet White and I spent hours on the phone. Three years ago she and her family left Boston for Tucson. She also confirmed that it had taken about two years for them all to look at the desert as home, but she had nothing but wonderful things to say about their new, easygoing lifestyle. The splendor, the majesty, and the tranquillity of the environment had a tonic effect on all of them.

"My philosophy was 'When in Rome . . . ,' so I bought a pair of cowboy boots and signed up for a country-and-western line-dancing class, even though my children were laughing at me. We began eating Mexican food five out of seven nights a week, and we began to share in the culture. My daughter and I began riding, and I got certified in a therapeutic riding program, which was a wonderful inroad to other people. I took risks and so many dimensions opened up for me.

"I no longer pigeonhole myself," she reflected. "I went from a historic preservationist on Beacon Hill in Boston to a cowgirl wannabe. These changes, or newly discovered facets, would never have come about or seen the light of day without the healthy jolt of the move and the change in environment."

The men I interviewed seemed to have a more difficult time connecting in their new situations. Several I spoke with told me that they experienced their new communities from the secondary remove of their wives' and children's lives.

Dewey Loselle, who grew up in a military family and who had moved eighteen times throughout his school years, wanted nothing more than to put roots firmly down in a community. Yet he was away at work most of the day, and he began to feel disenfranchised from the community here.

When he and his wife, Susan, shopped around Westport, he became aware that everyone seemed to know her and stopped to chat, and that he was constantly being introduced. Again the new boy in town.

"For the first year, it was easy to get absorbed in the house and spend all weekend long fixing things and attending to things," he recalled. "But after this, I began to sense that I wasn't connected, and I tried to figure what to do about it."

Susan eventually became president of New Neighbors of Westport, which is a wonderful organization joined by new arrivals with all kinds of monthly activities designed to take some of the strangeness from the move. Dewey started a men's dinner group and has been active in the monthly dinner club. "The first time we went to New Neighbors, we didn't have a great time. We felt that everyone else knew each other. Only by forcing ourselves to go back again and again did we start to relax and did people start opening up to us. As we became familiar faces, we made the point that we were here to stay so that people *could* turn to us.

"You just can't go to something once and write it off. Nothing ever comes of that. Try it four or five times before you decide it isn't your cup of tea," he advised.

"I also found that it's a good thing to become a part of a project, be on a committee with other people. You get to see how other people think and what their talents are. You get to sense who you'd like to know better and with whom you'd like to spend more time. For instance, I answered a 'calling all hands' notice to help build the children's playground at the elementary school. It was an amiable group and there was a terrific payoff at the end: a playground that our children could enjoy. Admittedly I wasn't one of the guys who showed up with work belts strapped on and ropes coiled on their shoulders—I got to schlep gravel bags and fetch coffee—but it was easy to talk and joke with people as we worked. There wasn't the stiffness of a social situation."

Gary Roth also felt divorced from his community because of work and travel, but after about three years, he made the decision to devote himself to two outside projects. He wanted to get involved with his boys' soccer teams, and he agreed to be on the board of a charitable organization. "I feel like a cog in the wheel now, not just someone listening to Czaschka and the boys talk about their lives out and about in the community," he confided.

Photographer Shel Secunda went through a few low periods in the first months of their move. "It was such an upheaval, starting a new life, getting a new business going," he recalled. "But we were fortunate in having a very warm friendly real estate agent who invited us over and introduced us to people. Then, two new neighbors moved in right after us, and we all managed to break the ice and begin the path that leads to real friendship. I also tried to mesh my talents with the needs of the community. When I was asked, I contributed my work to charities and hospitals. It was nice to think that one of my portrait sittings was going to benefit the Danbury Hospital."

Shel summed up his thoughts by telling me: "You can't believe people are just going to come a-calling. When we met people, we invited them over. When people invited us, we invited them back in a timely fashion. You've got to keep the ball rolling and nurture the fledgling relationship."

I am in awe of the transition that these people have made and the grit they've mustered in a time of stress. In each case, no matter what the difficulties of the transition, they have become richer, more complete people and have given a lot back into their communities.

You know, the Aborigines of Australia don't celebrate birthdays. They don't understand throwing a party simply because another year has passed. They do, however, celebrate a tribe member acquiring a new skill or expressing more of their "beingness." They even change their names within the community to reflect that growth. I feel that the fine people who shared their thoughts and reflections in the pages above deserve a feast honoring their mastering this major change with such grace and humanity.

Who knows? There may be a part of me that is not quite so helpless and "all thumbs" as I've always believed. It still comes as a pleasant shock to me that I can discuss backdrafting with an HVAC engineer or get into a spirited discussion about ice dams and ridge ventilation options. Someday I may even throw a party and announce that I am henceforth to be known as "She Who Walks with Wrench." (This sentence will set off gales of laughter in my husband and sons, but I'm going to be open to the possibility, just the same.)

It's time, now, to bring this book to a close. Writing *The Virgin Homeowner* was a wonderful project for me during this difficult transition period and moved me well along the path of Stage I: getting to know my house and letting the house get to know me. Thank you for accompanying me on the first leg of this journey of adjustment.

On a glorious September day, many years ago, the judge who married Demitri and me closed the wedding ceremony with a wish for our life together. He said: "May you care more for the dimensions of a home than the details of a house."

While all this time later I still thrill to this sentiment, I think now that the dimensions come only *after* we attend to the details. Only then can our dwelling places become, in the words of French philosopher Gaston Bachelard, "an instrument with which to confront the cosmos."

Relish the details, and may your dimensions increase a thousandfold.

Best wishes,
Janice Papolos
(Finally home in Westport, Connecticut)

The "On-Track" Calendar

September

Have septic tank inspected and pumped.

October

Check smoke detectors and change batteries.
Run fire-safety drills and check extinguishers.
Bleed radiators (if your house has hot-water heat).

November

Clean gutters and splash blocks.
Flag fuel line.
Turn off outside water supply.

December

Clean lint from clothes dryer hose.

January

February

Drain water heater.

March

April

Check smoke detectors and change batteries.
Run fire-safety drills and check extinguishers.
Put screens in windows and doors.
Tour exterior of house and check roof/siding.

May

Have chimneys cleaned.
Have furnace or boiler serviced.
Wash and brighten deck.
Clean gutters and splash blocks.

June

Have air conditioners serviced.
Have heat pump serviced.
Go on a termite hunt.

July

Clean lint from clothes dryer hose.

August

(Note: Adjust some of these maintenance chores to suit the climate changes in your region.)

House Doctors Directory

Plumber:

Telephone:

Address:

Emergency Beeper:

Electrician:

Telephone:

Address:

Emergency Beeper:

Septic Engineer:

Telephone:

Address:

Chimney Sweep:

Telephone:

Address:

Oil Company/Gas Company:

Telephone:

Address:

Contractor/Roofer:

Telephone:

Address:

Emergency Beeper:

HVAC Engineer:

Telephone:

Address:

Pest Inspection Company:

Telephone:

Address:

Others: (Landscaper, Tree Surgeon, Snow Removal Service, etc.)

Home Insurance Company:

Telephone:

Policy No.:

Paint Palette Directory

Painter:

Telephone:

Living Room: brand of paint:

Ceiling color: No.

Molding color: No.

Wall color: No.

Where purchased?

When painted?

Dining Room: brand of paint:

Ceiling color: No.

Molding color: No.

Wall color: No.

Where purchased?

When painted?

Master Bedroom: brand of paint:

Ceiling color: No.

Molding color: No.

Wall color: No.

Where purchased?

When painted?

Bedroom 1: brand of paint:

Ceiling color: No.

Molding color: No.

Wall color: No.

Where purchased?

When painted?

Bedroom 2: brand of paint:

Ceiling color: No.

Molding color: No.

Wall color: No.

Where purchased?

When painted?

Kitchen: brand of paint:

Ceiling color: No.

Molding color: No.

Wall color: No.

Where purchased?

When painted?

Bathroom 1: brand of paint:

Ceiling color: No.

Molding color: No.

Wall color: No.

Where purchased?

When painted?

Bathroom 2: brand of paint:

Ceiling color: No.

Molding color: No.

Wall color: No.

Where purchased?

When painted?

Powder Room: brand of paint:

Ceiling color: No.

Molding color: No.

Wall color: No.

Where purchased?

When painted?

Bibliography

For general information about the systems of a house as well as home maintenance, I relied upon and highly recommend:

Abram, Norm. *Norm Abram's New House.* Boston: Little, Brown, 1995.

Better Homes and Gardens. Complete Guide to Home Repair, Maintenance and Improvement. Des Moines: Meredith Corporation, 1980.

Blackburn, Graham. *Year-Round House Care.* Yonkers, N.Y.: Consumer Reports Books, 1991.

Johnson, Duane. *The Family Handyman's How a House Works.* Pleasantville, N.Y.: Reader's Digest, 1994.

Kidder, Tracy. *House.* New York: Avon, 1985.

Locke, Jim. *The Well-Built House.* New York: Houghton Mifflin, 1992.

Madorma, James. *The Complete Guide to Understanding and Caring for Your Home.* Whitehall, Va.: Betterway Publications, 1991.

Owen, David. *The Walls Around Us.* New York: Vintage, 1991.

Time-Life Books. *How Things Work in Your Home.* New York: Henry Holt, 1985.

Vandervort, Don. *Home Magazine's How Your House Works.* New York: Ballantine Books, 1995.

Warde, John. *The New York Times Season-by-Season Guide to Home Maintenance.* New York: Times Books, 1992.

In addition to the above books and the many interviews I conducted, I turned to the following for specific chapters:

Chapter 1: Home Inspection

Becker, Norman. *The Complete Book of Home Inspection.* Blue Ridge
    Summit, Pa.: TAB Books, 1993.

Boroson, Warren, and Kean Austin. *The Home Buyer's Inspection Guide.*
    New York: John Wiley & Sons, 1993.

Fredriksson, Don. *The Complete House Inspection Book.* New York: Faw-
    cett Columbine, 1988.

Huang, Nellie S. "The Great House Detective." *Smart Money,* August 1994.

Madorma, James. *The Home Buyer's Inspection Guide.* Whitehall, Va.:
    Betterway Publications, 1990.

Murphy, Michelle M. "Home Ecch." *Connecticut,* May 1995.

Salant, Katherine. "Hiring a New Home Inspector Can Produce Peace of
    Mind." *Washington Post,* September 23, 1995.

Ventolo, William L., Jr. *The Complete Home Inspection Kit.* Chicago:
    Dearborn Financial Publishing, 1990.

Ventolo, William L. *Your Home Inspection Guide.* Chicago: Dearborn Fi-
    nancial Publishing, 1995.

Vila, Bob, with Carl Oglesby. *Bob Vila's Guide to Buying Your Dream
    House.* Boston: Little, Brown, 1990.

Chapter 2: Plumbing and Electricity

Arosteguy, Julia. "An Electrical Makeover." *Home,* November 1995.

Barlow, Ronald S. *The Vanishing American Outhouse.* El Cajon, Calif.:
    Windmill Publishing, 1992.

Bartholome, Jean. "Clogged Pipes: How to Get Them Flowing Again."
    Family Handyman, September 1995.

Burch, Monte. *Basic House Wiring.* New York: Sterling Publishing, 1987.

Colman, Penny. *Toilets, Bathtubs, Sinks and Sewers.* New York:
    Atheneum, 1994.

Frederiksson, Don. *Plumbing for Dummies.* Indianapolis: Bobbs-Merrill,
    1983.

Johnson, Duane. "How a House Works: Why Water Heaters Wear Out." *Family Handyman,* July/August 1994.

Johnson, Duane. "Electrical Overloads." *Family Handyman,* March 1995.

Levine, Leslie. "Your Home's Electrical System." *Woman's Day Home Improvement,* Vol. 4, No. 1 (1994).

Sunset Books. *Sunset Basic Plumbing.* Menlo Park, Calif.: Sunset Publishing, 1992.

Time-Life Books. *Basic Wiring.* Richmond, Va.: Time-Life Books, 1994.

Chapter 3: Heating and Cooling

Holohan, Dan. *The Lost Art of Steam Heating.* Bethpage, N.Y.: Dan Holohan Associates, 1992.

Hunter, Linda Mason. "The Gas Equation." *Home,* December '95/January '96.

Lehrman, Celia Kuperszmid. "Turning Up the Heat." *Woman's Day Home Improvement,* Vol. 5, No 4 (1995).

Levine, Leslie. "Your Home Heating System." *Woman's Day Home Improvement,* December 1994.

Petroleum Marketing Education Foundation. *Oil Heat Technician's Manual.* Alexandria, Va.: Petroleum Marketing Education Foundation, 1985.

Time-Life Books. *Home Heating and Cooling.* Richmond, Va.: Time-Life Books, 1994.

Trethewey, Richard, with Don Best. *This Old House Heating, Ventilation, and Air Conditioning.* Boston: Little, Brown, 1994.

Vandervort, Don. "Central Air Conditioning." *Home,* May 1995.

Woman's Day Home Improvement. "Ground Source Heat Pumps," Vol. 4, No 1. (1994).

Chapter 4: Septic System

Alth, Max, and Charlotte Alth. *Wells and Septic Systems.* 2nd ed. Blue Ridge Summit, Pa.: TAB Books, 1992. Revised by S. Blackwell Duncan.

American Ground Water Trust. "Everything You Ever Wanted to Know
    About Septic Tanks, but Didn't Know Whom to Ask." 1990.
Wilcox, Kevin. "Little Common Ground in Septic Tank Additive Debate."
    Small Flows, July 1992.

Chapter 5: Chimneys

"Building a Fire." *Living,* February/March 1994.
Johnson, Duane. "Is Your Chimney in Good Shape?" *Family Handyman,*
    April 1994.
Romano, Jay. "Hiss! Crackle! Sputter!" *New York Times,* October 22,
    1995.

Chapter 6: Water Leaks

Kolle, Jefferson. "Choosing Roofing." *The Best of Fine Homebuilding.*
    Newtown, Conn.: Taunton Press, 1996.
Lewin, Jan. "Getting to the Bottom of Leaky Basements." *Home,* July/August 1994.
Wentz, Mac. "Defeating Ice Dams." *Family Handyman,* September 1994.

Chapter 7: Insects and Other Pests

Bayatt, A.S. *Possession.* New York: Random House, 1990.
Becker, Vivienne. *Art Nouveau Jewelry.* New York: E. P. Dutton, 1985.
Klass, Carolyn, and Diane M. Karasevicz. "A Guide to Pest Management
    Around the Home." Cornell Cooperative Extension Publication,
    1993.
Limburg, Peter R. *Termites.* New York: Hawthorn Books, 1974.
Miller, Griffin. "New Ways or Old, Pest Control's Tough." *New York Times,*
    January 13, 1994.
Mills, Joanne. "Diatomaceous Earth Kills Insects Without Harming Environment." *Montreal Gazette,* June 25, 1989.

Olkowski, William, Sheila Darr, and Helga Olkowski. *Common-Sense Pest Control.* Newtown, Conn.: Taunton Press, 1991.

Raftery, Miriam. "Pest Control Without Poison." *Home,* June 1994.

Souza, D. M. *Insects Around the House.* Minneapolis: Carolrhoda Books, 1991.

Zim, Herbert S., and Clarence Cottam. *Insects.* Racine, Wis.: Western Publishing, 1987.

Chapter 8: Physical and Electronic Security

Barry, Dave. *Dave Barry's Homes and Other Black Holes.* New York: Fawcett Columbine, 1988.

Collins, Clare. "New Strategies in the Pursuit of Safety." *New York Times,* August 18, 1994.

Consumer Reports. "Door Locks: Which Are Most Secure?" May 1994.

Daily, Laura. "Creating Safer Homes and Neighborhoods." *Geico Direct,* Fall 1994.

Heberle, David, and Richard Scutella. *The Complete Guide to Making Your Home Safe.* Cincinnati, Ohio: Betterway Books, 1995.

Johnson, Duane. "Motion Detectors." *Family Handyman,* November/December 1994.

Maxwell, Helen, with Mike Maxwell. *Home Safe Home.* Far Hills, N. J.: New Horizon Press, 1992.

National Burglar and Fire Alarm Associates. "Safe and Sound: Your Guide to Home Security." Bethesda, Md., 1994.

Phillips, Bill. *Home Mechanix Guide to Security.* New York: John Wiley & Sons, 1994.

Wacker, David Alan. *The Complete Guide to Home Security.* Whitehall, Va.: Betterway Publications, Inc. 1990.

Wood, Robert W. *All Thumbs Guide to Home Security.* Blue Ridge Summit, Pa.: TAB Books, 1993.

Chapter 9: The Healthy House

Bai, Matt. "Don't Drink the Water." *New York,* January 16, 1995.

Berger, Warren. "Getting the Lead Out." *New York,* April 5, 1993.

Berthold-Bond, Annie. *Clean and Green.* Woodstock, N. Y.: Ceres Press, 1994.

Bower, John. *The Healthy House.* New York: Carol Publishing Group, 1993.

Brody, Jane E. "Why You Need a Carbon Monoxide Detector." *New York Times,* December 13, 1995.

Charles, Eleanor. "Waterborne Radon Joins Airborne Type as Problem." *New York Times,* February 19, 1995.

Consumer Reports. "The Pollutants That Matter Most: Lead, Radon and Nitrates." January 1990.

Consumer Reports. "Radon: The Problem No One Wants to Face." October 1989.

Dadd, Debra Lynn. *Nontoxic, Natural and Earthwise.* New York: G. P. Putnam's Sons, 1990.

Dadd, Debra Lynn. *The Nontoxic Home and Office.* New York: G.P. Putnam's Sons, 1992.

Greenfield, Ellen J. *House Dangerous.* Revised. New York: Interlink Books, 1991.

Hamlin, Suzanne. "Baking Soda to the Rescue!" *New York Times,* July 18, 1995.

Henderson, Nancy. "The Day I Decided to Get the Lead Out." *Kiplinger's Personal Finance Magazine,* July 1992.

Hsu, Karen. "Deadly Parasite in Water Spurs Scientists to Improve Detection." *New York Times,* August 16, 1995.

Hunter, Linda Mason. *The Healthy Home.* New York: Pocket Books, 1990

Leclair, Kim, and David Rousseau. *Environmental by Design.* Point Roberts, Wash.: Hartley & Marks, 1992.

Louie, Elaine. "A Couple Builds a Home So Healthful It Passes the Sniff Test." *New York Times,* December 3, 1992.

Murphy, Michelle M. "Home Ecch." *Connecticut,* May 1995.

Pearson, David. *The Natural House Book.* New York: Simon & Schuster, 1989.

Radon Program of the State of Connecticut. "Radon and You: Testing and Reducing Radon Levels in Connecticut Homes."

Ritchie, Ingrid, and Stephen J. Martin. *The Healthy Home Kit.* Chicago: Dearborn Financial Publishing, 1995.

Rousseau, David, W. J. Rea, and Jean Enwright. *Your Home, Your Health, and Well-Being.* Berkeley, Calif.: Ten Speed Press, 1988.

Stapleton, Richard M. *Lead Is a Silent Hazard.* New York: Walker, 1994.

U. S. Government Printing Office. "A Citizen's Guide to Radon." May 1992.

U.S. Government Printing Office. "Home Buyer's and Seller's Guide to Radon." March 1993.

U.S. Environmental Protection Agency. *Indoor Air Pollution: An Introduction for Health Professionals.* No date.

U.S. Environmental Protection Agency. "Drinking Water From Household Wells." September 1990.

U.S. Environmental Protection Agency. "The Inside Story: A Guide to Indoor Air Quality." April 1995.

Wald, Matthew L. "Lead Paint: New Rules, Old Questions." *New York Times,* February 12, 1995.

Wald, Matthew L. "How to Keep a Warm House from Turning Dangerous." *New York Times,* September 22, 1994.

Waldman, Steven. "Lead and Your Kids." *Newsweek,* July 15, 1991.

Winter, Ruth. *A Consumer's Dictionary of Household, Yard and Office Chemicals.* New York: Crown Publishers, 1992.

Zamm, Alfred V., with Robert Gannon. *Why Your House May Endanger Your Health.* New York: Simon & Schuster, 1980.

Chapter 10: Ventilation

Air Vent Inc. *Principles of Attic Ventilation.* 5th ed. Peoria Heights, Ill.:
    1987.

Alfano, Sal, and Clayton DeKorne. "Low-Profile Ridge Vents." *Journal of
    Light Construction,* May 1992.

Grady, Wayne. *Green Home: Planning and Building the Environmentally
    Advanced House.* Camden East, Ontario: Camden House Publish-
    ing, 1993.

Huelman, Pat. "Energy-Efficient Homes." *Minnesota Builder,* May/June
    1992.

Smith, Bill Rock. "Heat-Recovery Ventilators." *Journal of Light Construc-
    tion,* March 1994.

Vandervort, Don. "Air Exchange: Heat-Recovery Ventilation." *Home,*
    June 1994.

Chapter 11: Childproofing

Better, Nancy M. "Mother's Little Helper." *Smart Money,* June 1994.

Ferry, Ted. *Home Safety Desk Reference.* New York: Career Press, 1994.

Lansky, Vicki. *Baby Proofing Basics.* Deephaven, Minn.: Book Peddlers,
    1991.

Nissim, Laura Grossman. "Safety Awareness Doesn't Stop at the Front
    Door." *Minuteman,* April 27, 1995.

Petrowski, Elaine Martin. "Childproof All Around the House." *Home,*
    June 1994.

Vandervort Don. *Sunset's Making Your Home Child-Safe.* Menlo Park,
    Calif.: Sunset Books, 1988.

Chapter 12: Protection from Fire

Field, Frank. *Dr. Frank Field's Get Out Alive.* New York: Random House,
    1992. Included in First Alert Press Kit.

Reynolds, Julie. "Fire Escape." *Home,* October 1994.

Chapter 13: Finally Home

Bachelard, Gaston. *The Poetics of Space.* Boston: Beacon Press, 1969.

Brown, H. Jackson, Jr. *Life's Little Instruction Book,* Vol. 2. Nashville: Rutledge Hill Press, 1993.

Moore, Thomas. *The Care of the Soul.* New York: HarperCollins, 1992.

Morgan, Marlo. *Mutant Message Down Under.* New York: HarperCollins, 1995.

Owen, David. *The Walls Around Us..* New York: Vintage, 1992.

Index